DISCOVER
MONTREAL

AN ARCHITECTURAL
AND HISTORICAL GUIDE

TABLE OF CONTENTS

HOW TO USE THIS GUIDE

The preface written by Jean-Claude Marsan explains the diversity of Montreal. The introduction is a brief exposition on Montreal, its historic and economic development. A brief guide to items of interest to tourists — art galleries, houses of worship, theatres, concert halls, other attractions — is also included. The architectural styles and influences which created Montreal's built environment are summarized.

The tours are designed to begin and end at a metro station, or at a bus stop located not far from a station. Unless otherwise identified, numbers within parentheses refer to the date of construction.

The 17 tours are divided into four groups: a) Old Montreal, Downtown, Golden Square Mile, McGill; b) Chinatown, St-Denis (Quartier Latin), Saint-Louis (Montreal's Mosaic), Outremont; c) Plateau Mont-Royal, Terrasse Ontario, Maisonneuve; d) Little Burgundy, Lincoln-Tupper, Westmount. These divisions take into account historical stages or cultural links as well as geographical location.

The numbers on the maps and within the texts refer to the buildings and sites which are the most significant on each walk. Most are buildings of exceptional architectural quality, others were chosen because of their importance in the history of the area or the city. The tour proceeds from one such landmark to another, with the route indicated on the map. The chapters are supplemented by historical and biographical texts which are printed in smaller type.

An additional chapter presents seven major churches in the downtown area. Mount Royal Park and the two cemeteries on the mountain are discussed at the end of the book.

IMPORTANT DATES

1535 October 2-4: Jacques Cartier visits Hochelaga, an Iroquois village located on the island of Montreal. He names the mountain "Mount Royal".

1611 May 28: Samuel de Champlain, founder of Quebec City, explores part of the island of Montreal. His men construct a wall near the mouth of the Saint-Pierre River (now St-Pierre Street). This is the first European construction on the island.

1642 May 17: The first French colonists land on the island and found the tiny colony of Ville-Marie.

1642 October 8: Jeanne Mance establishes the Hôtel-Dieu de Montréal hospital.

1643 January 6: Paul de Chomedy de Maisonneuve, commander of Ville-Marie, erects a wood cross on Mount Royal in thanks for the colony's escape from flooding.

1645 Construction of the Hôtel-Dieu building begins.

1648 November 24: Birth of Barbe Meusnier, the first European born in Ville-Marie.

1658 April 30: Marguerite Bourgeoys begins teaching in a stable, "a stone building, 36 feet by 18 feet, located in Ville-Marie, near·Hôpi-Hôpital Saint-Joseph."

1663 The Gentlemen of Saint-Sulpice become the seigneurs of the island of Montreal.

1672 March 12: Dollier de Casson, Father Superior of the Séminaire de Montréal, lays out and names the first streets: Notre-Dame, in honor of the virgin Mary, patron of the colony; Saint-Joseph (now Saint-Sulpice); Saint-Pierre in honor of Pierre Chevrier, baron of Fancamp, one of the founders of the Compagnie de Montréal; Saint-Paul in honor of Paul de Chomedey de Maisonneuve; Saint-Jacques in honor of Jean-Jacques Olier; Saint-Charles in honor of Charles Le Moyne; Saint-Lambert in honor of Lambert Closse; Saint-Gabriel in honor of two Sulpicians — Gabriel Thubières de Levy de Queylus and Gabriel Souart.

1716 The French authorities decide to build a wall around Montreal. it would take 20 years for the town to become truly fortified.

1734 April 10: A fire, started by an escaped slave, destroys 46 houses, Hôtel-Dieu and the convent.

1760 September 8: The capitulation of New France is signed in Montreal. British troops take over the town.

1766 The town is divided into wards.

1775 May 1: The bust of George III which had been unveiled in Place d'Armes on October 7, 1773, is vandalized to denounce the Quebec Act which guaranteed use of the French language and freedom of religion. "Here is the pope of Canada and the English fool" is written on its base.
November 13: The army of the American insurgents, commanded by Richard Montgomery, enters Montreal through the Récollets Gate.

1776 April 29: Benjamin Franklin, Samuel Chase and the Jesuit Charles Caroll stay in Thomas Walker's house in Montreal. They try to convince the local populace to join the American revolutionary cause.
June 6: The American army leaves Montreal.

1778 June 3: Fleury Mesplet prints the first issue of *Gazette du Commerce et littéraire pour la ville et le district de Montréal*. Printed at Château Ramezay, this weekly later becomes *The Gazette*, the city's daily newspaper.

1792 May 27: The city is divided into two parts, east and west, with Saint-Laurent Street as dividing line.

1801 Montreal Water Works is established to provide running water to the populace.

1801-
1820 Demolition of the walls around the city.

1809 **August 17:** Construction of Nelson's Monument begins.
1809 **November 3:** *The Accommodation*, owned by the Molson family, leaves Montreal for Quebec City.
1815 **November:** Saint-Paul Street is lit at night. The following year, lamps are installed on Notre-Dame Street.
1817 **November 3:** The Bank of Montreal begins operations. It is incorporated three years later, on December 20, 1820.
1821 **March 31:** McGill College receives its Royal Charter.
1822 **May 1:** Construction of the Montreal General Hospital is completed.
1824 The Lachine Canal opens.
1824-
1829 Construction of Église Notre-Dame, designed by James O'Donnell.
1832 **April 12:** William IV gives royal assent to a law incorporating the city of Montreal.
1833 **June 5:** The first meeting of the city council. Jacques Viger is elected the first mayor of Montreal.
July 19: The city council adopts the coat-of-arms and the motto *Concordia Salus*.
1840 The city is divided into six wards.
1844 **March 14:** The city of Montreal rents Marché Sainte-Anne to the government of the united province of Canada. Montreal becomes the capital, replacing Kingston.
1849 **April 25:** Rebellion Losses Act gives compensation for property lost during 1837-38 is passed. The Parliament is burned in protest.
1851 A law is passed requiring that the mayor of Montreal be elected by popular suffrage.
1852 **July 8:** A fire destroys the Cathédrale Saint-Jacques, the bishop's palace and more than 1100 homes.
1853 **July 22:** Beginning of the construction of Victoria Bridge.
1859 **December 17:** The first train crosses Victoria Bridge.
1860 **May:** Construction of the Crystal Palace, designed by J.W. Hopkins.
November 27: Christ Church Cathedral is completed.
1861 **November 27:** Streetcars begin running.
1863 **May 1:** A telegraphic alarm system is established to warn of fires.
1865 **December 3:** First mass celebrated in Église du Gesù.
1867 **March 18:** The cornerstone of St. Patrick's Hall is laid.
1869 **December 15:** Prince Arthur opens the Montreal Curling Club.
1873 **October 14:** Opening of the Young Men's Christian Association building.
1876 Université Laval establishes a branch in Montreal, it becomes independent in 1920.
1877 F.L. Olmsted draws up plans for a park on Mont-Royal.
1878 **March 11:** Inauguration of the City Hall, later heavily damaged in an 1922 fire.
1883 Annexation of the town of Hochelaga.
1884 Annexation of the town of Saint-Jean-Baptiste.
1886 **June 28:** Canada's first transcontinental train leaves Montreal for Vancouver.
1887 Annexation of the village of Saint-Gabriel.
1892 **April 1:** It is decided to use electricity to run the streetcars.
1893 **December 2:** Lord Aberdeen, Governor General of Canada, inaugurates the Royal Victoria Hospital.
Annexation of the town of Côte-Saint-Louis.
1898 **August 22:** Completion of the new Victoria Bridge.
1899 **July 16:** First carriage crossing of Victoria Bridge.
November 21: The first automobile in the streets of Montreal.
1901 **June 24:** Parc Logan becomes Parc LaFontaine. A huge patriotic celebration is held.

1901 August 13: Opening of a new military shooting range in Pointe-aux-Trembles.
1904 July 21: Completion of a grain elevator in the port.
1905 January 28: Inauguration of the new École Polytechnique building.
July 13: Laying of the cornerstone of the Maison-Mère des Soeurs de la Congrégation, Westmount.
Annexation of the towns of Saint-Henri, Villeray and Sainte-Cunégonde.
1906 May 26: École des Hautes Études Commerciales is established.
June 8: The federal government sells Île Ste-Hélène to the city of Montreal for $200,000.
June 24: A monument to Octave Crémazie is unveiled.
August 11: First recorded fatal automobile accident in Montreal.
Part of Rosemont and part of the parish of Sault-au-Récollet are annexed.
1907 Annexation of part of the parish of Saint-Laurent.
1908 October 22: Laying of the cornerstone of the École des Hautes Études Commerciales building.
Notre-Dame-des-Neiges and additional parts of Rosemont and Sault-au-Récollet are annexed.
1909 A contractor named Pauzé begins construction of Bordeaux Jail.
October 4: Prime Minister Wilfred Laurier lays the first stone of École Technique.
October 20: Edward VII inaugurates the Tuberculoses Sanitarium by telephone.
Annexation of Saint-Louis and DeLormier, as well as part of the city of Outremont.
1910 May 28: Beginning of streetcar service between Montreal and Longueuil.
Annexation of Ahuntsic, Côte-des-Neiges, Longue-Pointe, Notre-Dame-de-Grâce, Saint-Paul, Rosemont, Tétreaultville, Ville Émard and part of the parish of Saint-Laurent.
1911 June 5: Completion of McGill University's faculty of medecine building, a gift of Lord Strathcona.
1913 March 11: The city council expropriates the land needed for Saint-Joseph Boulevard.
1914 June 10: The site of the municipal library is chosen.
October 1: Unveiling of the statue of Edward VII in Philips Square.
Annexation of part of the parish of Saint-Laurent.
1915 May 26: Île Ste-Hélène is opened to the public. It becomes the largest park in the region.
June 15: The Utilities Commission decides to begin placing electric wires underground.
1916 Annexation of the towns of Cartierville and Sault-au-Récollet.
1917 April 22: Inauguration of the Canadian Northern Railway tunnel under Mount Royal.
September 4: Official opening of the municipal library.
1918 February 6: Annexation of the town of Maisonneuve.
1921 Creation of the Metropolitan Commission.
1924 February 12: The municipal executive council accepts the construction of buildings higher than 10 storeys, under certain conditions.
December 25: The new cross erected on Mount Royal is first illuminated.
1926 February 9: Lieutenant Governor Narcisse Pérodeau inaugurates the Sun Life Building.
February 15: Official opening of the rebuilt City Hall.
November 22: Inauguration of the new Palais de Justice, designed by Ernest Cormier.
1927 January 9: A fire in the Laurier Palace Cinema kills 78 children.

1927 April 23: Sir Herbert Holt lays the cornerstone of the Royal Bank head office on Saint-Jacques Street.

1928 May 5: The opening of the Montreal Stadium is attended by 22,000 people.

1929 July 10: Completion of a new bridge across the Saint-Lawrence. It is named after Jacques Cartier in 1934.

1930 June 22: Unveiling of a monument to Vauquelin.
September 28: Unveiling of a monument to Louis-Hippolyte LaFontaine in Parc Lafontaine.
October 31: Inauguration of the Ahuntsic Bridge.

1934 July 11: The Mercier Bridge links LaSalle (on the island) to Caughnawaga.
The Montreal Symphony Orchestra is created.

1943 June 3: Official opening of the Université de Montréal building on Mount Royal.

1945 December 18: A major press campaign calling for construction of a subway system begins.

1950 July 6: Opening of the Côte-Saint-Luc railway yards.

1950 November 6: The city council approves the purchase of Viger Station to be used for municipal offices.

1951 June 16: The city takes over the streetcar company.

1952 October 27: Bus service replaces the streetcar on Saint-Laurent Boulevard.

1953 October 12: The statue to Laurier in Dominion Square is unveiled.

1954 Jean Drapeau is first elected mayor of Montreal.

1957 November 9: Inauguration of the new Hôpital Sainte-Justine building.

1959 June 26: Queen Elizabeth II and U.S. president Dwight D. Eisenhower open the Saint Lawrence Seaway.
Construction of Place Ville-Marie.

1962 May 23: Construction of the metro (subway) system begins.

1963 Place-des-Arts opens.

1967 January 11: Official opening of Château Champlain Hotel, then the tallest hotel in Canada.
March 11: Inauguration of the Louis-Hippolyte-LaFontaine bridge tunnel.
April 21: Daniel Johnson, premier of Quebec, opens the Quebec pavilion at Man and His World, site of the universal exposition.
April 27: Official opening of Expo 67.

1968 October 24: Annexation of Ville Saint-Michel.

1969 December 23: The Montreal Urban Community is created.

1970 April 25: The Mouvement Coopératif Desjardins announces construction of a five-building complex.

1972 Construction of the extension of the metro begins.

1973 Save Montreal is formed.

1976 July 17: Inauguration of the XXth Summer Olympic Games.

1983 May 27: Official opening of the Palais des Congrès.

1985 Montreal's first independent public hearings dealing with broad issues of urban planning held, on the Vieux Port.

1986 Montreal Citizen's Movement enjoys overwhelming victory in municipal election, Jean Doré becomes mayor.

1987 Federal government passes legislation making Montreal an international banking centre.

Research by Clio de neuf à cinq

MONTREAL
City of Many Faces

MONTREAL
City of Many Faces

Returning home after spending years in Europe, journalist Eve-lyne Dumas realized that she loved Montreal passionately, although she did not quite know why. The problem with this city she wrote, was, "not that Montreal lacks beauty, but rather a sense of esthetics, an accepted pattern of design which would allow us to understand the city at first glance, as we do European cities."

Paris has her boulevards, Rome her basilicas, Florence her pala-ces, and Venice her canals. What distinguishes Montreal? What is it that first comes to mind? Is it the underground city? Or the modern, multi-functional buildings such as Place Ville-Marie, Place Bonaventure and Complexe Desjardins — veritable cities within a city? What about the daring architectural innovations of Habitat 67 and the Olympic installations, known throughout the world? Or is it the more traditional features: Plateau Mont-Royal's streets lined with duplexes and triplexes, St-Louis Square, the elegant old Victorian homes, the multicultural vital-ity of Boulevard St-Laurent? It is probably none of these in partic-ular, but all of them together. Other things, too, coexist in this medium-sized city, even though its history is rather short com-pared to the thousand-year-old settlements of the Old World.

The reality of Montreal is that she is a whole and many parts at the same time: she is a paradox. She claims to be one of the most modern cities in North America, but Montreal also possesses the largest historical district on the continent, as well as the largest concentration of Victorian houses. Many complete neighbor-hoods are unchangeably traditional.

While she has a European flair which charms Americans, her carefree American attitude astonishes Europeans. While Mont-real seems to have limitless financial resources to decorate sub-way stations, dig underground passageways, create unneeded facilities such as the pavilions of Man and His World, she lacks essential services like green space and conceals pockets of pov-erty which would make a Third World leader blush. While she is the crucible of francophone Quebec's nationalism (half of the province's population lives in the metropolis) she is also the most cosmopolitan of Canadian cities. While the proportion of Mont-realers who are tenants is greater than that of any other city on the continent, they show a sense of devotion unequalled else-where.

As strange as this might seem, it is these contradictions which are at the heart of Montreal's esthetic. For there truly is a Montreal esthetic: a particular way to appreciate the city, to get the feel of it. It is rooted in the diversity of the lifestyles and in the texture of the urban landscapes.

This is the secret and the charm of Montreal, which this guide-book will help to uncover and understand. The city imposes nothing, but offers a great deal. Above all, she can be adopted: one only needs to be attentive to the opportunities which arise to satisfy one's expectations. Many tourists are at first disap-pointed by this multiplex city, as elusive as she is real. On the other hand, thousands and thousands of Montrealers are grate-ful. One thing is certain — Montreal is one of the most cherished and best loved cities of North America.

A Torontonian, interviewed during the 1979 Grey Cup game (the symbol of Canadian football supremacy) held in Montreal, was asked by a CBC journalist what he would most like to bring back to his own city. "The mountain," he answered. Wherever you are in Montreal, you can see Mount Royal. Each day, Montrealers skirt it on their way downtown and as they return home. It is a source of pleasure, identity and character.

It is somewhat sacred, as are the rocky peaks which push through the urban tissue of Rio de Janeiro, Edinburgh and Athens. Catholics, Protestants and Jews bury their dead there, as once did the native people. It is not surprising that a century ago the city fathers called upon the foremost landscape architect of the time, American Frederick Law Olmsted, to design Montreal's premier park on the summit of Mount Royal. If the life of the Venetian is not complete without regular visits to the Piazza San Marco, then that of a Montrealer would be lacking without a regular walk on the mountain, especially in springtime, when sweet winds melt the last snowdrifts.

Mount Royal sat, unshakeable, while the two major linguistic groups unfolded the city's story. With few exceptions, the French lived on one side of the mountain, the English on the other. Mount Royal became the favored scene of symbolic confrontations and conquests. Following the British magnates — McGill, Monk, McTavish — who built country estates on one slope, on the other side the French-Canadians erected Saint Joseph's Oratory, one of the most imposing sanctuaries in the world. The establishment of McGill University on the southern slope was answered by that of the Université de Montréal on the opposite side; the development of anglophone Westmount corresponded to that of francophone Outremont.

Montreal's location can best be appreciated from the lookout on Mount Royal. It is from there that the Saint Lawrence River looks its most impressive. Wide and majestic, as powerful downstream as it is above, it narrows intractably before the metropolis. The two banks are drawn together by the gigantic straps of bridges. Like Mount Royal, the river is also a symbol of Montreal: it embodies her destiny and her vast dreams in the wide breach it opens into the North American continent.

Montreal was the launching point for a number of North America's explorers, many of whom were Montrealers themselves. Louis Joliette and Jacques Marquette discovered the Mississippi River, Cavalier de Lasalle claimed all of the Louisiana territory for France's Sun King. Lemoyne founded Mobile, Alabama, and New Orleans. Lamothe Cadillac founded Detroit, while LaVerendrye explored as far as the Rocky Mountains.

They were followed by Alexander Mackenzie who reached the Arctic Ocean after exploring the river which bears his name. Simon Fraser and David Thompson climaxed these voyages of discovery by reaching the Pacific Ocean.

These names are part of daily life in Montreal. They have been used to name neighborhoods, streets, parks, schools and municipalities. It is another characteristic of the city that the most humble places evoke heroic stories and dreams of expansion.

The river enlarged Montreal's hinterland as far as the Rockies during the age of exploration and fur trading. It also favored her during the age of steam. In 1809, John Molson (the brewery owner) launched the *Accommodation*, the first paddleship on the river. The first ship to cross the Atlantic powered solely by steam was the *Royal William*, whose engine was purchased in Montreal. The first railway in the British colonies connected the villages of St-Jean and Laprairie, in order to facilitate transportation between Montreal and New York City.

In the 1880s, when the first major wave of urbanization engulfed Montreal, her port was the second largest in North America (after New York City) and the world's largest inland port. At the same time, the city became the principal terminus of the Canadian railway system, henceforth linking her with the Atlantic and Pacific coasts and the United States. All of Canada became her hinterland. She was the undisputed gateway for capital, immigrants and ideas as well as the principal industrial, financial, commercial and cultural centre of the country.

Montreal's varied urban and architectural heritage has escaped much of the blind vandalism of recent years, sometimes through a miracle and sometimes due to loud protests from the populace. It remains a testimony to her prestigious past. Thus de la Commune is a street whose homogeneity of design is rivalled only by that of Bordeaux's port street. St-Jacques Street still retains some of its Wall Street appearance, studded with temples of finance such as the Royal Bank. The patrician mansions which survive in the Golden Square Mile remind us of the affluent pretensions of the financiers and industrial magnates of the Victorian era. Construction of the Lachine Canal in the first half of the 19th century, to circumvent the Lachine Rapids, marked the birth of Canada's first industrial valley. Recently redeveloped as parkland, it offers fresh air enthusiasts unusual landscapes whose harshness is fascinating, even poetic. Windsor Station never ceased to grow, spreading arcades along Dominion Square which paralleled the expansion of its railway network accross Canada. It reminds us of the time when the train was favored as the airplane and automobile are now. The importance of these more recent vehicles can be seen in Mirabel and Dorval airports and the Decarie and Ville-Marie expressways.

The Second World War reinforced Montreal as a centre of transportation with the creation of a powerful aeronautical industry. Chosen for the headquarters of the International Civil Aviation Organization (a United Nations agency which regulates air transport) and the International Air Transport Association, Montreal became the world aviation capital. She can also lay claim to the designation of extravagant and naive capital of international events, having hosted within less than 10 years a world's fair and the Olympic Games, in 1967 and 1976, respectively.

Finally, from an urbanist point of view: with little trumpeting, Montreal developed the most extensive underground city in the world, rivalled only recently by those of much larger metropolises such as New York City, Tokyo and Philadelphia. For American architect Peter Blake, Montreal is North America's first city of the 20th century.

Nevertheless, despite her grand airs, imperial past and international pretensions, Montreal remains a place in which it is easy to live, a city respectful of individuals and groups. The dimensions of the metropolis are a great part of the reason.

It is of medium size (about 3 million inhabitants in the metropolitan area), but large enough to have abundant high quality facilities — four universities, one of the best botanical gardens in the world, an internationally acclaimed symphony orchestra. Per capita, she has the largest number of cinemas in North America and her restaurants rival New York City's claim to be the gastronomic capital of the continent. On the other hand, Montreal is neither too populous nor too large, permitting her to avoid most of the stress, congestion and anonymity which one often finds in large cities.

However, it is not just a question of size. What makes "Montreal what she is, with an atmosphere comparable to that of few other cities, a charm, vitality, at times a 'disquiet'" — as wrote sociologist Alain Médam — is that it is an agglomeration of villages. There is a kind of symbiosis between the socio-cultural reality and the spatial organization of the city. This encourages the creation of "petites patries" — more than just neighborhoods, they are almost homelands for which residents share an allegiance. They divide the city into relatively homogeneous and autonomous areas where the collective life of residents can take shape and become significant. Among large cities, only London, I believe, has a similar make-up (undoubtedly, London has more of these homelands).

This particular model can be explained in part by the way the built environment was established. Following Montreal's founding in 1642, its expansion was neither continuous nor regular. While Dollier de Casson, the first seigneur of Montreal, laid out the city's first streets (St-Paul, Notre-Dame, St-Jacques), he sent colonists to the western flank of Mount Royal, to settle Notre-Dame-des-Neiges. Two centuries were to pass before these settlements would become joined.

While the Grand Trunk Railway's shops were attracting thousands of workers and settlers to Pointe-St-Charles, the factories of rival Canadian Pacific called others to Côte de la Visitation (now known as Rosemont), a dozen kilometres further east. While the municipality of Maisonneuve took advantage of the eastward growth of the port to attract factories and become the Pittsburgh of Canada, the electrification of the streetcar meant a boom in the population of Plateau Mont-Royal to the north. While Outremont was created for the wealthy, the working class city of Verdun was born on land recently protected from river flooding.

Due to factors such a distance and physical or social barriers, these areas and many others evolved independently for a while, becoming villages or municipalities and acquiring specific characteristics and maturity before joining the urban tide.

Everywhere, a basic spatial unity was maintained in a flexible manner due to the existence of the rural divisions into *côte* and *rang*. The further subdivision of this cadastral system into city blocks and lots created the rectangular grid of Montreal, yet still preserved some of the original irregularities such as Côte Ste-Catherine and Côte Ste-Antoine roads.

A number of these districts were adopted by specific ethnic groups, creating a rare link between physical and cultural diversity. The appropriation began at the beginning of the 19th century in the inner city, where the trains and ships arrived, then extended along St-Laurent Boulevard — aptly named The Main — spreading, treelike, to the north end of the city.

Attracted by the work promised by the construction of the Lachine Canal and the Victoria Bridge, the Irish were the first ethnic group to gain a toehold in the city, creating a little Dublin around St. Patrick's Cathedral. The Chinese followed soon after, occupying a nearby district focused on de la Gauchetière street. Unlike the Irish, they are still linked to this neighborhood.

After Toronto, Montreal has the second largest Italian population in Canada (160,000 people). At first they settled on St-André and St-Timothée streets, near Dorchester Boulevard. From there they. spread northward through Mile-End, Villeray and St-Michel to the municipality of St-Léonard. The heart of little Italy is now at Jean Talon Market and Dante Park.

The Jews make up the second largest cultural community (120,000 people). After establishing the stores of St-Laurent Boulevard, they shared Outremont and Côte-des-Neiges with the francophones and now predominate in Snowdon and the municipalities of Côte-St-Luc and Hampstead. They have their own social infrastructure of hospitals, schools, community centres and synagogues.

Among the groups which settled in Montreal after the First World War, the most visible are the Portuguese and the Greeks. The latter are centred on Park Avenue and St-Laurent Boulevard, while the Portuguese occupy the area between Laval, Sherbrooke, St-Laurent and Mont-Royal. The Mediterranean colors which they use to decorate their homes are reminiscent of the Azores where most of them come from.

It would be wrong to think that only ethnic groups have these "petites patries". The two major groups also have them. For those of British heritage, Westmount and Pointe Ste-Charles are the two extremes. The francophone Québécois constitute the overwhelming majority of Montreal's population (totalling more than two million in the Greater Montreal area). Their "petites patries" are most evident in such districts as Plateau Mont-Royal and Hochelaga-Maisonneuve. It must be remembered that the great majority of Francophones have been city dwellers for only one or two generations: their parents or grandparents lived in one of the many villages which dot the Montreal plain.

In every case, ethnic or not, the flavor of each "petite patrie" or urban village comes from a lifestyle with which the residents identify. Citizens of a large city with international aspirations, Montrealers succeed in making her theirs by adopting local areas to which they feel an attachment. Sometimes the area is made up of just a few streets or even just one, which adds to the variety of the whole. For Jean-Claude Germain, a dramatist, Montreal is a "tangle of thousands of street ends" and the Montrealer lives essentially on his own street corner.

The diversity of place and lifestyle accompanies a diversity of shapes. Unlike the subway systems of most other cities, each Montreal metro station has its own character, architecture and decoration. This symbolizes the diversity in the unity of the ensemble. If there are few monuments in Montreal, and even fewer architectural masterpieces, the architecture is still rich, especially in its variety, which page after page of this guidebook will show.

Here, again, the trait is due to a particular occurrence. In the first place, Montreal, despite a relatively short history, has witnessed three well-defined periods in the art and technology of building. First was the pre-industrial period of which a number of buildings remain (Château Ramezay, the old St-Sulpice Seminary, the Calvet House in Old Montreal). The industrial period is represented by a great variety of structures, from train stations to grain elevators. Finally, Place Ville-Marie, Place Bonaventure and Complexe Desjardins are good examples of the contemporary period. In certain places, such as the d'Youville Stables, we can see at a glance the fruit of all three periods. Few other cities in North America can boast the same.

In the second place, as a result of her own history, Montreal has been the most important site of two architectural traditions, the most important Canadian city for architectural design. One tradition, which can be called "academic", was developed primarily by the British-born who wished to make of this city their cultural centre. The astonishing collection of prestigious buildings on the McGill University campus indicates the degree of excellence attained in this tradition.

The Francophones who lived for a long time in the confines of their farms in the Montreal plain, cut off from the new ideas which affected the ruling classes, developed a second popular tradition of construction which took into account the climate and the socio-economic conditions. It was used instead of fashionable architectural styles, and is demonstrated in the simple public architecture of schools, parish churches and other ecclesiastic buildings. It is seen even more clearly in the working-class neighborhoods of which some streets — Fabre in Plateau Mont-Royal, Logan in Terrasse Ontario, and Adam and Lafontaine in the Viau area of Maisonneuve — are remarkable.

Finally, let us note that aside from the 1950-1980 period which saw the expansion of the suburbs and downtown's rapid development, Montreal's major growth occurred between 1880 and 1920, at a time when eclecticism and the picturesque were emphasized in architecture. At that time, it was good form to explore as many architectural designs as possible, depending on the character of the building required. Reusing ancient styles was especially favored. This is why many diverse architectural influences are evident in Montreal. There are banks with façades taken from Greek temples and Florentine palaces, a main library and court house reflecting Roman architecture, churches with Gothic arches and Baroque volutes, convents with Byzantine cupolas, a Renaissance-style city hall, pompous homes aping Scottish manors and many other such displays.

The Montreal esthetic is there, in the diversity of lifestyles and the variety of architectural expression. This guidebook does not attempt to explore and reveal everything, it is primarily an open window onto this profusion. Following the authors in their meanders through neighborhoods and streets, you will come to have a better understanding of their enthusiasm. You will also appreciate their regret whenever some group of people were driven out of an area, or some building was demolished or altered in a destructive way. Everything which reduces this diversity, on the social or the physical plane, affects Montreal's most precious possession which makes her what she is — a city with a character and a soul.

Jean-Claude Marsan

Location

Montreal is situated on an island in the Saint Lawrence River, one of the main waterways into North America. The river leads directly to the Great Lakes, gateway to the midwest. The Richelieu, which together with the Hudson River leads to New York City, flows into the Saint Lawrence a few miles downstream from Montreal. The Ottawa River joins the Saint Lawrence just upstream from the island city and flows from the northwest.

This location was a significant advantage when waterways were the principal means of transportation for explorers and colonists. During the industrial age, the waterway became even more important. The Lachine Rapids, just upstream from Montreal, were for many years an impassable barrier for ocean-going ships. As the terminal for river transportation, the port of Montreal played a vital role in the development of the city. The city also benefits from being surrounded by the best farmland in Quebec.

Climate

Situated just south of latitude 45° north, Montreal's temperature averages -8° C (18° F) in winter and 19° C (66° F) in summer. The four seasons are clearly differentiated. Winters are harsh but the snow and ice periods are shorter and not as severe as in the rest of the province.

Size and population

The city of Montreal has a total area of 67.2 square miles (174 km²), covering 35% of the island which bears its name. The irregular shape of the city can be explained by the fact that it grew as a result of a series of annexations of surrounding villages and municipalities. The most recent was that of Pointe-aux-Trembles, at the eastern tip of the island, which was taken over by Montreal in 1982.

Montreal has about one million inhabitants. Sixty-four per cent of the residents are of French origin, 16% are Anglo-Saxon. The Italian community makes up the third largest group: 6.5% of the population. Successive waves of immigrants — Irish, Jewish, Greek, Italian, German, Ukranian, Chinese, Hungarian, Portuguese and, more recently, Haitian, Vietnamese and Cambodian — have given Montreal a heterogeneous character.

The Montreal Urban Community

The Montreal Urban Community (MUC) is a regional government covering 29 municipalities on the island of Montreal and two neighboring islands — Île Bizard and Île Dorval. The 190 square miles (493 km²) of the MUC is 76% urban, with a population of more than 1,800,000 of whom almost 59% live in Montreal. Francophones make up 58% of the population, Anglo-Saxons 24% and Italians 6%.

Created January 1, 1970, the community is administered by a Council and an Executive Committee. The Community Council is made up of the chairman of the MUC, the mayor and councillors of Montreal and the mayor or a delegate from each of the other municipalities of the community. The chairman, six representatives of Montreal and six representatives of the suburban municipalities make up the Executive Committee.

The following matters are under the jurisdiction of the Montreal Urban Community: evaluation of real estate in the constituent municipalities, establishment of a development plan, establishment of regional parks, air pollution control, sewers and water treatment, food inspection, mass transit, construction of the subway system, public safety and economic development.

The public security council has special jurisdiction over administration of the police department of the MUC. The transit commission which runs the subway and surface system is a distinct corporation which is mandated by the MUC.

In 1981, an important change was made to the MUC with the creation of permanent commissions which permit citizens to make known their views on matters such as planning, environment, fiscal evaluation and finances, public safety and mass transit.

The Montreal Urban Community is made up of the following municipalities: Anjou, Baie-d'Urfé, Beaconsfield, Côte-St-Luc, Dollard-des-Ormeaux, Dorval, Hampstead, Île Dorval, Kirkland, Lachine, LaSalle, Mont-Royal, Montréal-Est, Montréal-Nord, Montréal-Ouest, Outremont, Pierrefonds, Pointe-Claire, Roxboro, Sainte-Anne-de-Bellevue, Sainte-Geneviève, Saint-Laurent, Saint-Léonard, Saint-Pierre, Saint-Raphaël-de-l'Île-Bizard, Senneville, Verdun, Westmount and Montreal.

Montreal metropolitan region

The economic region of Montreal covers almost 1300 square miles (3300 km²) and has a population of more than 2,800,000 inhabitants. The region includes Île Jésus, the lower Laurentians and the Montreal plain which extends south from the Saint Lawrence River to the Richelieu River. The two largest municipalities are Laval and Longueuil. Laval covers the entire Île Jésus, making it the largest municipality in the province.

The province of Quebec

The British Parliament established the Dominion of Canada with the passage of the British North America Act which federated Quebec, Ontario, Nova Scotia and New Brunswick in 1867. Montreal is the most important city of the province of Quebec, which is the largest province and, after Ontario, the most industrialized, urbanized province. It also has the second largest population (6,438,403). It is the only majority francophone state in North America.

With an area of 594,860 square miles (1,540,509 km²), Quebec is about three times larger than France or the state of Texas. Quebec has a parliamentary system of government based on the British model. It is subdivided into 122 electoral ridings and nine administrative regions.

Its economy is based primarily on natural resources (mines and forests). State-owned Hydro-Québec is a world leader in hydroelectric power production.

Industrialization

Since Montreal was the transportation hub of British North America, it began to industrialize. Grain mills, sugar refineries and clothing factories were established. As the financial and industrial focus of the new Dominion in the late 1800s, Montreal was in its gilded age. Its buildings reflected this economic splendor. Transportation mushroomed, especially after the Second World War, and there was rapid urbanization. The population began to leave the city and settle in the new suburbs.

The commercial downtown developed outside of Old Montreal. The migration began up Beaver Hall Hill, then along Ste-Catherine. It started because merchants wanted to be closer to their affluent customers who had left the narrow streets of the oldest part of the city for the slopes of Mount Royal in what came to be known as the Golden Square Mile. During the 1960s and 70s, large multi-functional buildings concentrated commercial and business development — Place Ville-Marie, Alexis-Nihon Plaza, Complexe Desjardins.

The population residing in the downtown core declined and some areas deteriorated. Montreal was following the sorry lead of many American cities. But compared to them, the decline of the central city never went as far. Now the trend is to revitalize the central business district, the heart of the city. Montreal, having always maintained its downtown, has perhaps a shorter hill to climb.

The Port

Located 1000 miles (1600 km) from the Atlantic Ocean, Montreal is one of the world's major inland ports. Situated at the entrance to the St-Lawrence Seaway which permits ocean-going ships to proceed an additional 1100 miles (1700 km) into the continent, Montreal is also a gateway to the great producing and consuming areas of central and western Canada and to the American midwest.

More than 70 companies and agencies connect Montreal with 275 other port cities around the world. A substantial river fleet transports cargo between Montreal and the Great Lakes ports. Almost 5,000 ships, more than half of them ocean-going, dock in Montreal each year. More than 20 million tonnes of cargo were shipped through the port of Montreal in 1982. Recently, the development of six terminals and other ultramodern equipment has made Montreal the largest container port in Canada and the fourth largest port on the Atlantic coast of North America.

The port has been open year-round since 1962. During the winter, icebreakers work day and night, if necessary, to maintain a route through the river. Harbor booms, artifical islands and other anti-ice apparatus help keep the channel open, permitting access to the port.

Port installations stretch for 15 miles (24 km) and can handle all kinds of ships. Its 117 mooring births, 36 transit sheds, four grain elevators with a total capacity of 550,000 tonnes and six container terminals can take care of all kinds of cargo.

Other features include a refrigerated shed for imported fruit, and an automatic floating crane capable of lifting 250 tonnes.

Economy

As an international centre of finance, Montreal was for many years the stage for the transfer of capital necessary for the development of Canada. Four of the six largest Canadian banks (the

Royal Bank of Canada, the Bank of Montreal, Banque Nationale du Canada and the Mercantile Bank of Canada) have their head offices and a great deal of their other facilities here. Five large trust companies (Trust Général du Canada, Montreal Trust Company, Société Nationale de Fiducie, Fiducie du Québec and Crédit Foncier) and many of the large insurance companies also have their head office in Montreal. Another important member of the city's financial community is the Caisse de dépôt et de placement which manages Quebec Pension Plan funds and is the largest single Canadian shareholder.

The ninth most populous city in North America, Montreal is one of the most important manufacturing centres in northeastern North America. In addition to the traditional manufacturing sector, which includes the production of clothes and textiles, a broad spectrum of industrial production is carried out in the Montreal area.

Half of Canada's aeronautical industry is located in Montreal. Other important components in Montreal's economy are the manufacture of transportation equipment (locomotives, rapid trains, subway cars), electrical appliances and parts, the transformation of asbestos, primary metals, petroleum, chemicals and pharmaceuticals. In addition, there are more than 50 Montreal companies which specialize in information processing and computers.

University and research centre

Bilingual Montreal has two francophone universities (Université de Montréal and Université du Québec à Montréal) and two anglophone (McGill University and Concordia University). McGill University and Université de Montréal are traditional institutes of higher learning which have made Montreal the premier Canadian centre of medical research. Concordia University and Université du Québec à Montréal are celebrated for their flexible approach to schooling of the part-time and mature student.

With 40,000 students, Université de Montréal is the city's largest. Its international stature comes from researchers such as Hans Seyle (famous for his studies on stress), Gustave Gingras (rehabilitation), Lionel Groulx (history). Among affiliated institutions is the École Polytechnique; its nine different engineering programs rank it one of the best in the country. The École des Hautes Études Commerciales is the oldest management school in Canada. The work of the Centre de Recherche des Mathématiques Appliquées is known throughout the world.

McGill University is the oldest of Montreal's universities and one of the leading research institutions in North America. Its 22 faculties and professional schools, its many centres, institutes share a world-wide reputation for excellence in teaching and research. McGill's downtown campus forms an integral part of the fabric of the city. Other facilities include 16,000-acre (6,500 ha.) Macdonald College campus on the western tip of the island. McGill's strength is multi-disciplinary and is reflected in such names as Wilder Penfield (neurology), Frank R. Scott (law), Claude Champagne (music), Kelvin Ogilvie (biotechnology) and Phil Gold (cancer research).

Université du Québec à Montréal (UQAM) is part of the state network of universities which are distributed throughout the province. The offspring of the fusion of the Ste-Marie classical college and other private schools, UQAM was created in 1969 partially as a response to the growing need for part-time studies. There are now about 36,000 students. The disciplines offered are divided into six branches: management sciences, literature, sciences, graduate studies, social sciences and fine arts. UQAM has the second largest linguistics department in North America.

Born of the union of Sir George Williams University and Loyola College, Concordia is Montreal's newest university. About 13,000 of its 26,000 students attend classes on a part-time basis. There are four faculties: arts and science, commerce and administration, engineering and computer science, and fine arts. Within arts and science are *colleges* which provide an interdisciplinary approach to subjects such as community and public affairs or women's studies. Its commerce and administration faculty is the largest in Canada. The Centre for Building Studies is involved with problems such as sound-proofing, heat conservation and the design of new building techniques. Fine arts is recognized as the finest faculty in Canada and is one of the few which have been successful in uniting visual and performing arts. Concordia's Conservatory of Cinematographic Arts is playing an increasing role in the community.

The dynamism of the university world has stimulated an expanding sector of research and development in private and government corporations. In addition, three of the 10 largest engineering consultant firms are located in Montreal. About 40% of their work is for foreign projects. Electrical transmission, aeronautics, communications are the most dynamic fields of research.

Hydro-Québec's research arm, I.R.E.Q., has gained an international reputation. In communications, the Canadian Broadcasting Corporation, Northern Telecom, Bell Canada, Teleglobe Canada and CNCP Telecommunications maintain extensive research facilities in the city.

ARCHITECTURE

Architecture under the French régime in Quebec (1608-1763) was based on the Norman and Breton house. It was a wide and shallow building face with stuccoed stone and topped with a steeply-sloping roof pierced by dormer windows. Over the years, the local inhabitants adapted this style to the climate: the roof became less steep, the house acquired a basement and the eaves extended beyond the walls. During this period, there were two types of churches: *à la recollette* (without transept; evident in the square apse of the Ursuline's Chapel in Quebec) and with a transept (such as the original Notre-Dame church).

After 1763, when the British took control of Quebec, Montreal architecture returned to ancient styles, as was also the case in Europe and the United States. Successively the Gothic, Greek, Classic and Baroque styles were revived. Like most North American cities, Montreal buildings were also influenced by the French Second Empire style which was used for many public buildings such as the City Hall.

The most important architects working in Montreal were John S. Archibald, Victor Bourgeau, George Browne, Ernest Cormier, Harold Featherstonhaugh, Robert Findlay, William Footner, Henri Labelle, J. Omer Marchand, Edward and William Maxwell, Percy Erskine Nobbs, James O'Donnell, John Ostell, Maurice Perrault, Bruce Price, Charles J. Saxe, William Thomas, Joseph Venne and John Wells.

Archibald, John Smith (1872-1934) was born in Inverness, Scotland and came to Montreal in 1893. He apprenticed with Edward Maxwell. In 1897 he formed a partnership with Charles Jewett Saxe, another junior architect in the Maxwell office. The partnership lasted until 1915.

Archibald's approach to classicism is evident in the Masonic Temple (Lincoln-Tupper tour). On the other hand, he used a Moorish motif in the picturesque design of de Sola's house (Golden Square Mile). Other Archibald buildings on the tours: Bishop Court Apartments, 1907 (Downtown); École Technique (with Maurice Perreault), 1909 (St-Louis); La Sauvegarde, 1915 (Old Montreal B).

Marchand, J. Omer (1873-1936) was born in Montreal and spent five years studying at the École des Beaux-Arts de Paris where he acquired a deep knowledge of antique architectural styles. He designed the Canadian pavilion at the 1898 Paris Universal exposition. Among his most prestigious Montreal works are Église Ste-Cunégonde (Little Burgundy), the Chapel of the Grand Séminaire (Lincoln-Tupper) and the Maison-Mère des soeurs de la congrégation de Notre-Dame (Westmount A).

Maxwell, Edward (1867-1923) and **Maxwell, William** (1874-1952). The Maxwell brothers designed a number of mansions for affluent Montrealers. They were also adept in the design of public and commercial buildings.

Edward did his apprenticeship in Boston and opened a studio in Montreal in 1892. His early work, for example Meredith House, 1892-93 (Golden Square Mile), illustrates the blend of Romanesque and Renaissance which he developed during his training in Boston. He is best known for the train station/hotels which he designed for the Canadian Pacific Railway Company.

William, his younger brother, became his partner in 1902. Together they designed buildings in the Classical Revival style. The house built for James Ross, 1908 (Golden Square Mile) reveals the Beaux-Arts training of William Maxwell.

Other Montreal buildings designed by Edward Maxwell are the residence of H.V. Meredith, 1893 (Golden Square Mile); of H.A. Allan, 1894, (Golden Square Mile); of R.A.E. Greenshields, 1895 (Golden Square Mile) as well as the Merchant's Bank of Halifax, 1896 (Little Burgundy); London and Lancashire Life Building, 1898 (located near Place d'Armes) and Hosmer House, 1900 (Golden Square Mile).

Both brothers worked on the Unitarian Church of the Messiah, 1907-10 (church tour), the High School of Montreal, 1913 (McGill and its Ghetto), Maxwellton Apartments, 1915 (across from the Roddick Gates, McGill tour).

Nobbs, Percy Erskine (1875-1964) was born in Haddington, Scotland and spent a large portion of his early years in Saint Petersburg, Russia. A graduate of the University of Edinburgh, he studied with Robert Lormier, one of the masters of the Arts and Crafts movement. Like Lormier, Nobbs believed that a building should appear to have sprung forth from its local environment. Therefore he championed the use of local materials, traditions and craftsmanship. In 1901 he began to work for the London City Council under Owen Fleming and Charles Winmill, two disciples of Philip Webb who had been the close friend and partner of William Morris, the founder of the Arts and Crafts Movement. Nobbs' Canadian work displays Webb's style.

In 1903 Nobbs came to McGill University to accept the Macdonald chair of architecture. He tried to instill a respect for local traditional architecture in his students. His buildings harmonize perfectly with their surroundings, in both shape and size (a telling example is the Pathological Institute, McGill tour). In addition to designing a plan for the university campus, he was the architect of a number of its buildings, including the McGill Student Union (1904), now the McCord Museum, and the Macdonald Engineering Building (1907). The houses located on Clarke Avenue and Grove Park, on the Westmount tour, and the Drummond Medical Building, 1929 (Downtown tour) are other examples of his fine work. Always concerned with low-cost housing and sanitary conditions in working-class neighborhoods, he became president of the Town Planning Institute of Canada in 1928, vice-president of the Montreal City Improvement League in 1930 and a member of the London Royal Society of Arts in 1939.

Ostell, John (1813-1892). Ostell was one of the most important architects in 19th-century Montreal. He was born in London and came to Montreal in 1835. His architecture was part of the English Classical Revival, with Palladian tendencies. He was responsible for the towers of Notre-Dame Church (Old Montreal C), the Grand Séminaire (Lincoln-Tupper), some of the buildings of McGill University as well as its overall plan, the Customs House in Place Royale (Old Montreal C) and the first Palais de Justice (Old Montreal B).

Price, Bruce (1845-1903) was born in Cumberland, Maryland and opened an office in New York City in 1877. His most important Canadian works are the Château Frontenac in Quebec City, Windsor Station (Downtown) and the Viger train station and hotel (St-Denis Street). He also constructed a number of homes. His architecture, known as the Château style, is best known for its free interpretation of medieval styles; it owes a great deal to Henry Hobson Richardson.

The influence of Sullivan and the Chicago School was also felt (e.g., Unity Building in the Chinatown tour; Coronation Building, Downtown tour). Circa 1930, a new style inspired by Le Corbusier and the Bauhaus School came to Montreal. Marcel Parizeau and Ernest I. Barott were the principal followers of this style. Among the important foreign architects who have designed buildings in Montreal are McKim, Mead and White (Bank of Montreal, Old Montreal C), York and Sawyer (Royal Bank, Old Montreal C), I.M. Pei (Place Ville-Marie, Downtown), Ludvig Mies Van der Rohe (Westmount Square), Pier Luigi Nervi (Tour de la Bourse on Place Victoria).

Montreal architects of international stature include Ray Affleck, Moshe Safdie and Dimitri Dimakopoulos.

Ludvig Mies van der Rohe (1886-1969) was one of the fathers of the International Style. His architecture is characterized by the simplicity of its shapes. Neither ornamentation nor curve interrupts the perpendicularity of the lines. The harmony of volumes, the careful choice of materials, the detailing and the refinement of the lay-out has caused his architecture to be imitated but never equalled. His work includes the German Pavilion at the Barcelona International Exposition (1929), the Seagram Building (New York City) and Westmount Square (Westmount A tour).

Pier Luigi Nervi was born in Italy in 1891. An engineer, he specialized in concrete design and his work displays a total mastery of this material. Nervi is as esthetically sensitive an architect as he is an inventive and resourceful technician. His works include the Salle des Conférences of the UNESCO building in Paris (1957), the Pallazzetto dello Sport and the Pallazzo dello Sport in Rome (1957, with Vittellozzi and Piancentini). When completed in 1966, The Tour de la Bourse (Old Montreal C) was the tallest building with reinforced concrete structure in the world.

Architectural influences

American Beaux-Arts (circa 1898-1914) Beaux-Arts Classicism is characterized by imposing designs ornamented with a plethora of details. Frequently a building will display stones finished in a variety of styles. The style can be identified from its use of projecting pavilions with imposing columns which are often paired, and by strongly emphasized cornices displaying statues. Windows are surrounded by balustrades and by columns capped by simple pediments. The buildings are frequently crowned by a large parapet or a balustrade, and sometimes by a dome. An example is the Maison Mère des Soeurs de la Congrégation de Notre-Dame (Westmount tour).

Arts and Crafts (circa 1885-1914) An offshoot of the Gothic Revival, the Arts and Crafts Movement represented a humanist reaction to the devastating effects of industralization during the 19th century. The adherents of this movement sought to purify and improve architecture and design by returning to the essential. They preached a return to the tried and true methods of ancient builders and artisans. They hoped to create a practical and modern design; the most progressive Arts and Crafts architects attained a pre-modernist functionalism which was in harmony with the environment.

Chicago School: After the Great Chicago Fire in 1871, Chicago builders were attracted to the possibilities of cast iron and steel. The use of the metal structure with a brick skin permitted construction of the first skyscrapers. Decorative elements were simplified and a new esthetic, harmonizing with the industrial age, was born. This original American architecture was primarily created by Adler and Sullivan. All modern architecture sprang from the Chicago School.

Classical Revival was characterized by allusions to previous styles, primarily Greek and Roman architecture. This movement began during the 18th century and was used primarily for public buildings in North America. A brief renewal of the style occurred in the 20th century.

The International Style was a result of the new belief in the virtue of industrialization which was popular in the decade after the First World War. Its promoters believed profoundly in the industrial revolution of the 20th century and championed a moral and esthetic cult of the machine. The cubical form, the rejection of ornamentation, and a predilection for right angles are characteristics of this style. Westmount Square (Westmount tour A) is a late example of the International Style.

Italian Renaissance (circa 1860-1875): Generally, buildings whose design was influenced by the Italian Renaissance display symmetric façades crowned by large cornices. Façades show a

great deal of articulation and windows are always arched. Sculptures, superposed orders, varied motifs and a combination of these elements create an attractive play of light and shadows. Buildings on Ste-Hélène Street (Old Montreal A) display this style.

Neo-Baroque: Although at its inception the International Style was revolutionary in its scorn for adornment and its emphasis on straight lines, it had become the norm by 1930. An analogy can be made with the Baroque style of the 17th century which introduced the use of curves and elaborate ornamentation as a reaction to the restrained classical style. The Neo-Baroque used unusual shapes such as the ellipse, parabola, diamond and broken lines. Concrete, which can be worked into unexpected, spectacular shapes and has the advantage of encompassing large areas without interior support, was favored.

The Neo-Baroque skyscraper displays lines as pure as its International brother, but it can just as easily take the shape of a pyramid or present concave or convex curves. Two examples are the office tower, 1980 Sherbrooke West (Lincoln-Tupper) and the Saint-Jean-Baptiste-de-la-Salle Church (Maisonneuve).

Andrea Palladio (1508-1580) was an architect and amateur archeologist who was entranced by antiquity. He used columns, pilasters, arcades and pediments in a unadorned style.

Second Empire Style head was popular circa 1870-1890. Mansard roofs and dormer windows characterize the Second Empire Style. Chimneys were important elements in this style and were designed in a classical manner. Large buildings are made up of pavilions, with the roof of each given a particular treatment. This highlighted articulation accentuates the three-dimensionality of the design. Another feature of this style is the superposition of the different classical orders.

Louis Henry Sullivan (1856-1924) was born in Boston and became the dominant force in the Chicago school of architecture. He and his partner Dankmar Adler used a cast iron structure to build the first modern skyscrapers such as the 1891 Wainwright Building in St-Louis and the 1895 Guaranty Trust in Buffalo. Sullivan's buildings are simple in design, with all lines based on right angles (an exception was made for the top floor which often displayed rounded windows). Ornamentation which extends from the ground floor (often geometric or floral designs) to the highest floor (a decorative frieze) characterize Sullivan's works. His buildings followed the concept of a column with a definite base, shaft and capital.

Henry Hobson Richardson (1838-1886) is considered to be a fore-runner of modern architecture and was one of the first American architects to progress beyond European influences. This is not to say that European tradition was eliminated. Richardsonian Romanesque was an interpretation of the Romanesque which emphasized rusticated stone surrounding arches. An entire generation of architects imitated him. His most important works include Trinity Church in Boston (1877), Austin Hall at Harvard University (1883) and numerous train stations such as that at North Easton, Mass.

Save Montreal is a citizen's group concerned with the quality of life in the inner city and the preservation of Montreal's architectural heritage. It promotes the planned development of the city, based on the needs of Montrealers.

During past years, Save Montreal has been successful in preventing the demolition of such buildings as Windsor Station, the Soeurs Grises complex on Dorchester Boulevard, Prison des Patriotes, Monument National and Shaughnessy House.

In 1983, Save Montreal revived the *Prix Orange* and *Prix Citron* awards (initiated by the Montreal Society of Architecture) to buildings of good and poor design.

ACCESS AND TRANSPORTATION

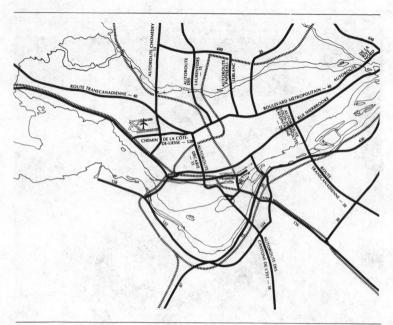

Road

From the United States, **Interstate 87** joins **autoroute 15** which is connected to Montreal by the Champlain (toll) and Mercier bridges. Interstate 91 joins autoroute 10 (toll road) which also leads to these two bridges.

From Ontario, the Trans-Canada Highway (**autoroute 20 or 40**) crosses îles aux Tourtes after Vaudreuil and continues to the city where it becomes Metropolitan Boulevard. The Decarie exit leads to the west of the city and downtown (centre-ville), the St-Denis and St-Hubert exits lead to the eastern part of the city.

Coming from Quebec City along the north shore of the St-Lawrence River, stay on **autoroute 40** until the Metropolitan Boulevard. There are a number of possible exits.

From the east along the **Trans-Canada Highway**, the Louis-Hippolyte Lafontaine tunnel/bridge leads to the city (follow the signs marked Centre-ville) as do the Jacques-Cartier, Victoria and Champlain bridges.

From north of Montreal, the **autoroute des Laurentides #15** ends at Metropolitan Boulevard. To go downtown from there, take Cremazie Boulevard east until St-Denis Street, go right (south) on St-Denis.

Note also that many of Montreal's streets are one way. Vehicles on Ste-Catherine, the main commercial artery of downtown Montreal, proceed from west to east.

Railway

Due to its history and its geographical location, Montreal is the centre of a vast railway network, the hub of the main lines in eastern and western Canada. It is also connected to those of the eastern United States.

Canadian National and **Canadian Pacific** railways have their head

offices in Montreal. They span the continent and are connected
via American railroads to New York, New England and the Great
Lakes.

VIA Rail (intercity passenger service)
871-1331
CN: Central Station,
935 de la Gauchetière West

CPR: Windsor Station,
Peel and de la Gauchetière
Amtrak 1-800-436-8725
935 de la Gauchetière West

Air travel

Montreal has two international airports, Dorval and Mirabel,
which are respectively the second and ninth busiest in Canada.
With a capacity of 60 million passengers per year, Mirabel is an
airport of the 21st century, one of the most modern in the world.
It is also the only airport in North American which is accessible to
cargo 24 hours a day. With a 400,000-tonne annual capacity,
Mirabel could become the largest cargo centre in Canada. The
federal government has plans to make it a duty-free zone, the
first in Canada.

Mirabel International Airport
(overseas flights). Access by autoroute
15, 4 miles (6 km) from exit 35, and
by 148. Tél.: 476-3010

Dorval International Airport
(Domestic flights and flights
to the United States) Access by
autoroute 15 and Côte-de-Liesse, or
autoroute 40. Tel.: 636-5921

Mass transit

Montreal's subway system, the metro, opened in 1966. Its total
length is more than 30 miles (50 km) and there are more than 50
stations. The pneumatic tires of its cars made it the first truly
silent and comfortable system in North America. Once completed, it will have 98 stations and extend for about 80 miles (125
km). It is planned to integrate the metro with the existing com-
muter service offered on CN and CP railway lines and construct a
surface metro joining the eastern and western extremities in the
northern portion of the island.

The bus and subway (metro) form a unified system throughout
the metropolitan area. A single fare gives free transferring privileges from bus to metro and vice versa. The Montreal Urban
Community Transit Commission has a fleet of 2000 vehicles,
making it one of the largest in North America. Most buses which
run of the main traffic arteries go to a metro station. For information, telephone AUT-OBUS.

Tickets can be purchased in booklets, and monthly C-A-M pass
is available which gives unlimited use of the transit system at a
reduced cost. For individual rides, exact change is required for
the bus, while change for small bills are available at the metro
station. Children under five years of age can ride free of charge
when accompanied by an adult. Senior citizens and students pay
a reduced rate upon presentation of a transit commission identity card.

Inter-city bus service
The Voyageur terminal is at 505
de Maisonneuve east
(Berri-DeMontigny metro station). For
schedules and other information,
telephone 842-2281.

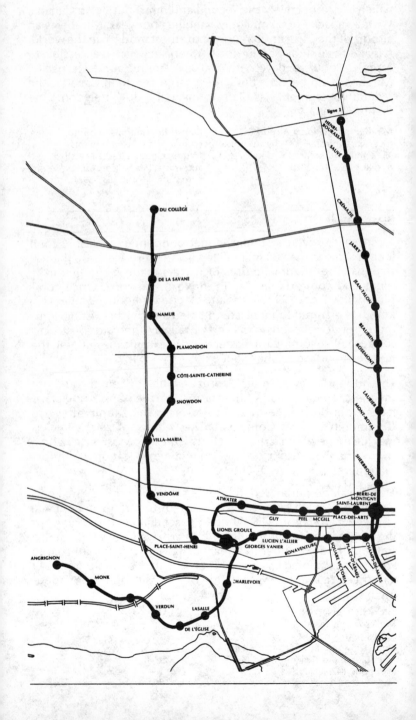

- Metro stations

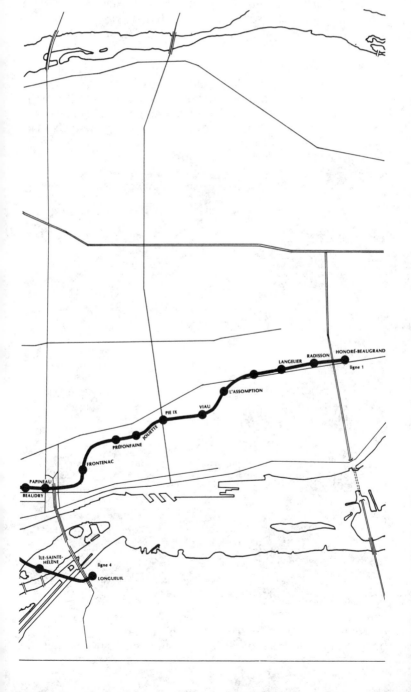

Urban issues

As with a number of North-American cities, Montreal has no official overall development plan. Consequently, the piecemeal approach to integrating certain projects too often has led to corrective measures which create even greater problems. Here, as elsewhere, the automobile has absorbed a large part of the urban tissue, through the widening of some streets and the construction of a system of highways (still incomplete). The proliferation of parking lots has damaged the downtown area and aggravated traffic problems.

The disappearance of much of Montreal's rich architectural heritage has helped depersonalize the city. It is too easy in Montreal to demolish without needing to show that new construction will be built.

During the 1970s, when some other cities had acquired a sense of the importance of preserving their architectural heritage, many of Montreal's most distinctive buildings were lost. The Van Horne Mansion (Sherbrooke Street) was the most glaring example; there were many more. Many fine homes, many substantial examples of Victorian and pre-war industrial and commercial buildings were lost to the demolition ball.

During the last 15 years, many buildings in the central area between Dorchester, Sherbrooke, University and Atwater have been demolished, although it was estimated in the mid-1970s that there were already enough vacant lots in the central city area to allow for the construction of all buildings Montreal would require until the end of this century. Lots on Bishop, de Maisonneuve and other streets lay empty for many years.

In the last five years, Montreal has seen a marked increase in interest in the renovation and reuse of old buildings. Old neighborhoods such as Plateau Mont-Royal and Maisonneuve are becoming quite popular with homeowners who are buying vintage houses and renovating them. (Not surprisingly, this has meant a stiff increase in housing costs). The idea that urban design and planning merit close attention and input from experts and citizens is accepted in the Montreal of 1987. The recently-elected administration plans a development plan for the downtown (first in the city's history) and has mandated a committee to recommend districts which merit municipal protection as "heritage sites".

Montreal Underground

During the last 20 years, the city has been a veritable laboratory of urban experimentation. Construction of Place Ville-Marie in 1960 initiated a new phase of building which transformed the physical appearance of the downtown core. For the first time such a large project took into account the principals of segregation of different types of circulation (vehicular, service and pedestrian) and the effect on the surrounding area. A direct result was the underground city which Montreal enjoys today.

Together with the metro network, to which it is connected, underground Montreal provides climate-controlled access to a thousand stores and boutiques, a number of department stores, two railway stations, almost a dozen hotels, more than 25 bank

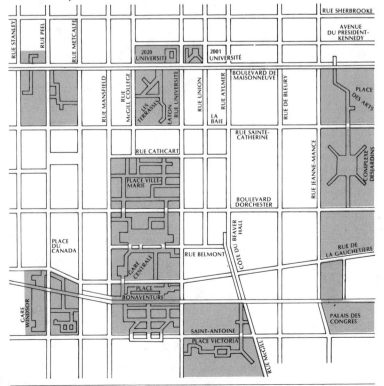

branches, nearly 10 000 parking spaces, a hundred restaurants and bars, more than 20 cinemas, three theatres and a concert hall, art galleries and many commercial buildings.

The extensive network of commercial malls makes all the services of a large city accessible without going outside. Thus someone could live in Westmount Square, work in Place Ville-Marie, shop at Plaza Alexis-Nihon, hear a symphony at Place-des-Arts, dine at Complexe Desjardins, end his evening at a bar in the Bonaventure Hilton Hotel, without ever having to brave the rigors of a Montreal winter.

A bilateral city

Saint-Laurent Boulevard, which bisects the city, divides the streets into east and west, with numbering of addresses beginning at the boulevard. Strictly speaking, the streets do not run due east and west. Infact, in Montreal the sun appears to rise in the south. This is because the streets were laid out in reference to the Saint Lawrence River which was defined as flowing due east; in fact it flows to the northeast.

ACTIVITIES

Music

As the city of churches, Montreal is a major centre of organ music, perhaps the most important in North America. The organ of Saint Joseph's Oratory, constructed by Von Beckerath, is the largest on the continent. Among the noteworthy organists are Gaston Arel, Hélène Dugal, Kenneth Gilbert, Bernard and Mireille Lagacé and Réjean Poirier.

Salle Wilfrid-Pelletier of Place des Arts offers classical music and opera by the Orchestre Symphonique de Montréal and the Opéra du Québec.

Chamber music is provided by the Société Pro Musica in Salle Maisonneuve and by McGill University's Chamber Music Orchestra which performs at Pollack Hall and Christ Church Cathedral.

The Société de Musique Contemporaine du Québec plays contemporary music in many concert halls.

Principal performers: Pierrette Alarie, Maureen Forrester, Louis Quilicot and Leopold Simoneau.

Place des Arts is Montreal's cultural centre for the performing arts. It offers music, opera, theatre, classical and modern dance. A number of companies use it for their regular season including the Orchestre Symphonique de Montreal, McGill Chamber Music Orchestra, the Société Pro Musica, the Ladies' Morning Musical Club, les Grands Ballets Canadiens and the Compagnie de Théâtre Jean-Duceppe. The complex has three halls: Salle Wilfrid-Pelletier (3 000 seats), Théâtre Maisonneuve (1 700 seats, Théâtre Port-Royal (800 seats). Place des Arts is directly connected to the metro station which bears its name.

Place des Arts, 175 Sainte-Catherine West, 285-2112; box office/ reservations: 842-2112.

Concert Halls

Atelier Continu
1200 Laurier East 270-1175

Bibliothèque nationale
1700 Saint-Denis 873-4553

Cathedral Christ Church
Northeast corner of University and
Sainte-Catherine 288-6421

Concerts Début 878-9680

Concerts d'Orgue de Montréal
524-4021

**Conservatoire de Musique du Québec
à Montréal**
100 Notre-Dame East 873-4031

St. Paul Anglican Church
379, 44th Avenue, Lachine 634-1965

Église Notre-Dame
116 Notre-Dame West 849-1070

Church of St. Andrew and St. Paul
3415 Redpath 842-3431

Église Saint-Jean-Baptiste
at the corner of Rachel and Henri-
Julien streets 842-9811

Événements du Neuf 343-6479

Faculté de Musique de McGill
392-8224

Forum
2313 Sainte-Catherine West
932-6131

**Ladies' Morning Musical Club
(L.M.M.C.)** 932-6796

Musica Camerats 482-4629

Opéra de Montréal 285-4290

Pro Musica 845-0532

Salle Claude-Champagne
200 Vincent-d'Indy, Outremont
272-4261

Salle Le Plateau
3710 Calixa-Lavallée

Salle Marie-Gérin-Lajoie, U.Q.A.M.
Pavillon Judith-Jasmin,
405 Sainte-Catherine West 282-3000

Salle Pollack
555 Sherbrooke West 392-8224

Salle Redpath
3459 McTavish

Salle Ukrainienne
5213 Hutchison

Salle Wilfrid-Pelletier
Place des Arts 842-2112

Théâtre F.A.C.E.
3449 University

Théâtre Maisonneuve
Place des Arts 842-2112

Théâtre Saint-Denis
1594 Saint-Denis 849-4211

Theatre

Dozens of Montreal theatres put on plays in French. The **Centaur Theatre** (453 St-François-Xavier, 288-1229) is Montreal's premier English playhouse which is open throughout most of the year. The **Saidye Bronfman Centre** (5170 Cote-Ste-Catherine Road, 739-7944) also puts on plays. In addition, there are dinner-theatre performances and groups such as the **Black Theater Workshop** (1968 de Maisonneuve W., 932-1104) and the **Playwright's Workshop** (4001 Berri, 843-3685).

Theatres and cafe-theatres

Café de la Licorne
2975 Saint-Laurent Blvd., 843-4166

Compagnie Jean-Duceppe, Place des
Arts 842-8194

L'Eskabel
1235 Sanguinet St., 849-7164

Espace Libre
1945 Fullum St., 521-4199

Théâtre de Quat'Sous
100 des Pins Ave., 845-7277

Théâtre Denise Pelletier
4353 Ste-Catherine E., 253-8974

Théâtre du Nouveau Monde
84 Sainte-Catherine W., 861-0563

Théâtre du Rideau Vert
4664 St-Denis St., 844-1793

Théâtre expérimental des Femmes
5066 Clark, 271-5381

Théâtre populaire du Québec
500 Sauvé W., 387-6219

Sports

Montreal has three professional sports teams, the most famous of which is the Canadiens hockey team. Since it was founded in 1910 it has won the Stanley Cup, emblem of North American hockey supremacy, 23 times. The Canadiens play at the Forum. The season begins in October and continues till March.

In 1967 Montreal was the first city outside of the United States to be awarded a National Baseball League franchise. In 1981 the Montreal Expos won first place in the eastern division of the league. Home games are played at the Olympic Stadium, the season is from mid-April to October.

The Montreal Alouettes of the Canadian Football League also use the Olympic Stadium, 4445 Pierre-de-Coubertin Avenue. Information: Hockey — 932-6131; Baseball — 253-3434; Football — 252-1052.

Among the other international sport competitions is the Canadian Grand Prix of car racing which is held on the Gilles Villeneuve track on île Notre-Dame. The race track is named after Gilles Villeneuve who was on the Ferrari team until his death in 1982.

The Montreal International Marathon has welcomed the world's finest runners since 1979. About 10,000 runners partipate each year.

USEFUL ADDRESSES

Tourist information

Maison du Tourisme
Government of Quebec
2, Place Ville-Marie 873-2015

Office des Congrès et du Tourisme du Grand-Montréal
(P.O. Box 889), Floor F, suite 1
Frontenac, Place Bonaventure,
Montreal, H5A 1E6

Palais des Congrès
201 Viger Avenue West 871-8122

One of the most versatile and modern convention and exhibition centres in North America. It includes 31 meetings rooms which are designed to be used with audio-visual equipment and interpreting services. From 80 to 6,000 people can be accommodated. The convention centre is connected to Montreal's underground network and to the metro (Place-d'Armes station). A number of artworks are on display in the centre.

Airlines

Air Canada 931-4411
Air France 284-2825
British Airways 287-9133
Delta Airlines 335-5520
Eastern Airlines 483-6363
Pan Am 288-4204

For bus and metro information
telephone AUT-OBUS (288-6287)

Lost and found
(in the bus and metro):
Berri-DeMontigny metro station
877-6006

Taxis

Coop 725-9885
Diamond 273-6331
LaSalle 277-2552
Veterans 273-6351

Weather forecast:
636-3026

Consulates

France, Place Bonaventure, 878-4381

Great Britain,
635 Dorchester Boulevard West,
866-5863

United States, Place Desjardins,
281-1886

Telegrams:

CNCP Telecommunications
861-7311
Canada Post 283-4185

Tickets:

Ticketron (288-3651) Tickets for major concerts, shows, sports events, etc. may be purchased at Ticketron outlets and at all The Bay and Sears stores.

Observatories

Mont Royal Look-out
Camillien Houde Road
on Mount Royal
Westmount Look-out (Westmount B)
Saint Lawrence Seaway
Lachine Canal
Miss Olympia, **which cruises the Saint Lawrence River**

Accomodations

High season is between May 1 and October 31. Many hotels are located downtown. Arrival time is generally 1 p.m. and reservations are honored until 6 p.m. Many hotels do not charge a supplement for children staying in their parents' room. There are single, double and triple rates. Prices in Canadian dollars range between $55 and $300 per day for a single and $70-300 for two people. Tourist homes and Bed & Breakfasts offer lodgings at lower cost, $20-50 for a single room and $25-60 for a double during high season.

For further information, consult the Guide de l'hébergement touristique, available by writing the Office des Congrès et du tourisme, P.O. Box 889, Montreal, Quebec, Canada H5A 1E6. Telephone number for Canada: (514) 873-2015.

THREE USEFUL ADDRESSES

International Youth Hostel
3541 Aylmer, Montreal, Quebec
H2X 2B9. telephone 843-3317. $8 for members, $10.00 for non-members.

Y.M.C.A. 1450 Stanley, Montreal, Quebec H3Q 2W6.
telephone 849-8393. $28-45 single, $34-50, double.

Y.W.C.A., 1355 Dorchester W, Montreal, Quebec H3G 1T3
telephone 866-9941, $24-36 single $33-50 double

Campgrounds

There are a number of campgrounds in the area around Montreal. Some of those with full facilities are located in Pierrefonds, and Pointe-aux-Trembles on the island itself; south of the island there are campgrounds in Brossard, Beloeil, Sainte-Catherine and Saint-

Philippe; to the west on île Perrot, in Vaudreuil, Pointe-des-Cascades and Repentigny.

Emergencies

Both the **Police and the Fire** departments can be reached by dialing 911

Poison-Control
Montreal Children's Hospital
934-4456
Ste-Justine Hospital 345-4931

24 Hour Pharmacy 527-8827

Distress Centres
Tel Aide 935-1101
Suicide-Action 522-5777
Alcoholics Anonymous 376-9230

Health Emergencies 911
Ambulance 911
Hospitals:
Hôtel Dieu 844-0161
Jewish General 340-8222
Montreal Children's 934-4400
Montreal General 937-6011
Royal Victoria 842-1231

Information for the handicapped

A pamphlet which gives information on accommodations, access to concerts, museums, parks, churches and other public places, in addition to sports and outdoor activities for the physically handicapped is available from:

Office des Congrès et du Tourisme du Grand-Montréal, Place Bonaventure, C.P. 889, Montreal H5A 1E6.

Organized tours

Bus

Tours leave from major hotels and Dominion Square
Gray Line/MUCTC,
1241 Peel
866-4641
Murray Hill
937-5311

Boat (from May 15 to September 30)

Montreal Harbor Cruises 842-3871
Departure is from Victoria Pier, at the foot of Berri Street.

Horse-drawn calèche (from May 1 to November 30)

Departure from Notre-Dame Street, between Bonsecours and Gosford streets, Dominion Square and Mount Royal.

Taxi

Departure from Dominion Square.

Walking tours

Save Montreal gives "mobile workshops" during the summer (282-2069)

Parks

LaFontaine Park
(North of Sherbrooke Street East, between Christophe-Colomb and Papineau)

This 100-acre park (40 ha) includes playgrounds, tennis courts, a small zoo (see Activities). There are two man-made lakes, one with an illuminated fountain which is one of the most beautiful in North America. Canoes and paddle-boats can be rented near the snack for use in the lower pool.

Mont-Royal Park
Bus #11 goes from Mont-Royal metro station to Beaver Lake. Car access is by Remembrance Road (to the west) and Camillien Houde (to the east). There are also paths from Pine Ave. at Peel, and Park Ave. opposite Duluth St., and a stairway at Cote-des-Neiges Road and The Boulevard.

The park has an area of almost 500 acres (200 ha). An impressive view of the central city, the Saint Lawrence River and the Monteregian mountains can be seen from the look-out. At the summit is a 100-foot (30 m) cross which is illuminated at night. The Beaver Lake portion of the park offers an art gallery and a fast-food restaurant. There is often folk dancing on summer evenings. During the winter there are facilities for skating and tobogganing. Parking is available.

Angrignon Park
3400 des Trinitaires, Angrignon metro station, 872-2815.
This 266 acre (107 ha) woods is the winter home of the Jardins des Merveilles Zoo.

Lachine Canal, 283-6054
Guided bicycle tours leaving from McGill and de la Commune streets are offered on summer afternoons. Groups can phone the above number to make reservations for the tours or for historical presentations.. Parks Canada manages the area around this historic canal, which was constructed in 1825. A 7.5 mile (12 km) bicycle path (used for crosscountry skiing in the winter) and four boat ramps are among its attractions.

Île Notre-Dame, 872-6222
This artificial island was created for

Expo 67. Now it is a municipal park. It is used for Les Floralies an international flower exhibit, all summer long and for the Grand Prix du Canada automobile race. It sits alongside the Saint Lawrence Seaway entrance and offers a unique view of the river and Montreal.

Île Sainte-Hélène
(île-Ste-Hélène metro station)
This island has a number of tourist attractions such as Man and His World, the Alcan Aquarium, La Ronde amusement park and the Old Fort and Museum. The Fraser Highlanders and the Compagnie Franche de la Marine put on 17th-century military parades at the fort. Most activities are held between the St-Jean-Baptiste Day (Quebec's official holiday, June 24) and Labor Day (the first Monday in September).

Botanical Gardens
4101 Sherbrooke East 272-1171
H: grounds: all day until sunset; greenhouses: 9 am — 6 pm. The third largest botanical garden in the world. There are 30 outdoor gardens, nine display greenhouses exhibiting 25 000 different species, including unique collections of orchids and bonsai trees. Guided tours are available for groups, telephone 252-8865. A snack bar is located on the grounds.

Public Markets

Public Markets are open from 7 a.m. to 6 p.m. Monday through Wednesday and on Saturday; 7 a.m. to 9 p.m. on Thursday and Friday.

Atwater Market
Atwater Street, south of Notre-Dame Boulevard (Lionel-Groulx metro station) 872-2009
At its liveliest on Saturday. Local farm produce is offered from outside stalls. Inside, meats, cheeses, fish, natural foods and imported fruits and vegetables are on sale. It is located a few blocks away from the many antique stores on Notre-Dame, between Guy and Atwater streets.

Jean-Talon Market
7075 Casgrain, near the Jean-Talon metro station 842-4620
An open-air market with an international flavor. In addition to local produce, there are butchers, specialty meat, fish and cheese stores. This is where Montreal's Italian community shops.

Maisonneuve Market
4375 Ontario East 256-4974
Open from April 1 to December 1. It offers Quebec agricultural products from outdoor stalls; there are also some food stores.

Houses of Worship

Anglican
Christ Church Cathedral
Ste-Catherine at Union streets, 879-1996
Remarkable architecture (see Church tour). Organ recitals are given at noon on some weekdays.

Buddhist
Montreal Buddhist Church
5250 St-Urbain 273-7921

Greek Orthodox
Église Orthodoxe roumaine
de Montréal, 1840 Masson 522-3314

Greek Catholic
St. George Greek Orthodox Cathedral
2444 Côte Ste-Catherine Road 739-5517

Hindu
Hindu Mission of Canada (Quebec)
Inc. 955 Bellechasse 270-5557

Jewish
Spanish and Portuguese Synagogue (Orthodox), 4894 Ste-Kevin 737-3695

Shaar Hashomayim (Conservative), 450 Kensington 937-9471

Temple Emmanu-El (Reform), 4100 Sherbrooke West 937-3575

Moslem
Islamic Centre of Quebec, 2520 Laval, Saint-Laurent 331-1770

Presbyterian
Church of Saint Andrew and Saint Paul
3415 Redpath, 843-3431

Roman Catholic
Chapelle Notre-Dame-de-Bonsecours
400 Saint-Paul East 845-9991
(The Sailors' Church, see Old Montreal tour) H: 9 to 11:15 a.m., 1 to 4:15 p.m., closed Monday

Saint Patrick's Church
460 Dorchester Blvd. W., 866-7379

**Église de la Visitation
du Sault-au-Récollet**
1841 Gouin Street East 388-4050
*The church was built between 1749
and 1752. Originally, the dimensions
of the building were 100 feet by 45 feet
(30 m by 13.5 m) with no transept and
terminated by a square apse. Additions of a new façade were undertaken
by John Ostell in 1850. He added two
bays to the nave and an imposing
Gothic Revival façade. The bell towers
were completed in 1870. The interior
was decorated by David Fleury-David
between 1816 and 1828.*

Église Notre-Dame
Place d'Armes 849-1070

*H: 7:45 a.m. to 6 p.m.
Rich in history, this church is also of
interest because of its architecture and
its interior decoration (see Old Montreal tour).*

Mary Queen of the World
Dorchester and Cathedral Street
866-1661
*H: 7 a.m. to 8 p.m. The Roman Catholic
cathedral is a replica of Saint-Peter's in
Rome (see Downtown tour).*

Unitarian

Church of the Messiah
3415 Simpson 935-1522

Universities

Guided tours by appointment

Concordia University
1455 de Maisonneuve West
848-4970

McGill University
845 Sherbrooke Street West
398-3770

Université de Montréal
2900 Édouard-Montpetit 343-6030

Université du Québec à Montréal
1187 Bleury Street 282-3268

Museums

Museum of Decorative Art
Château Dufresne
2929 Jeanne d'Arc Street
(Pie IX metro station) 259-2575
*H: noon to 5 p.m., Thursday through
Sunday only
Affluent residence of the turn of the
century. Bimonthly exhibitions. The
library is accessible by appointment.*

Château Ramezay
280 Notre-Dame East 861-3708
*H: 10 a.m. to 4:30 p.m., closed Monday
Erected in 1705, residence of the gov-
ernors of Montreal. Period furniture,
paintings and clothes of the 18th century. Seasonal exhibitions.*

Marc-Aurèle Fortin Museum
118 St-Pierre 845-6108
*H: 11 a.m. to 5:00 p.m., Tuesday
through Sunday;
Canadian landscape watercolours*

Maison Saint-Gabriel
2146 Favard 935-8136
*H: 1:30 p.m. to 4:30 p.m., closed Mon-
day
This house was built at the end of the
17th century. It was used by Marguerite Bourgeoys to welcome the "Filles
du Roy" who were sent from France as
wives for the settlers. Furniture and
other artifacts from the era are on
view.*

McCord Museum
6980 Sherbrooke West 392-4778
(see McGill Tour)

Montreal Museum of Fine Arts
1379 Sherbrooke Street West 285-1600
*H: 11 a.m. to 5 p.m., closed Monday.
Representative Western paintings and
sculptures ranging from ancient to
contemporary times. Oriental sculpture and pottery. Pre-Columbian art,
Amerindian sculpture and artifacts.
Also seasonal exhibits and events.*

Montreal History Centre
335 Saint-Pierrre Street, 845-4236
*H: 10 a.m. to 4:30 p.m., closed Mon-
day.
Exhibits and audio-visual presentations of Montreal's history from 1642
to the present.*

Musée d'Art Contemporain
Cité du Havre 873-2878
*H: 9 a.m. to 6 p.m. Tuesday, through
Sunday, closed on Monday.
Contemporary international and
Québécois artists, various events.*

Lachine Canal Interpretive Centre
7th Avenue and Saint-Joseph Blvd.
*H: Wednesday through Sunday,
10 a.m. to noon, 1 p.m. to 5 p.m.*

Musée Historique Canadien
3715 Queen Mary Road 738-5959
*H: 9 a.m. to 5 p.m.
Wax museum, the exhibits are primarily religious.*

David M. Steward Museum
Fort Sainte-Hélène 861-6701
H: 10 a.m. to 5 p.m.

Closed Monday from September to May
Models, engravings, uniforms, weapons and other artifacts of New France's military history.

Musée Marguerite-d'Youville
1185 Saint-Mathieu 932-7724
H: 9 a.m. to 11:30 p.m.; 1:30 p.m. to 6 p.m.
Dedicated to the founder of the Grey Nuns order, guided tour.

Bank of Montreal Museum
129 St-Jacques

Musée du Cinéma
Cinémathèque Québécoise
335 de Maisonneuve East

Musée Marguerite-Bourgeoys
Église Notre-Dame-de-Bonsecours
400 Saint-Paul
H: 9 a.m. to 11:15 a.m.; 1 p.m. to 4:15 p.m.

Museums in the area

Canadian Railway Museum
122-A Saint Pierre Street,
Saint-Constant 1-632-2410; 1-638-1522
H: 9 a.m. to 5 p.m., open every day from May to September, weekends only, during the other months.
Large collection of railway material. Steam locomotives, all kinds of railway cars and streetcars. On Sunday, a train and a streetcar are in operation and accessible to the public.

Musée d'Art de Saint-Laurent
615 Sainte-Croix, Saint-Laurent
747-7367
H: 11 a.m. to 5 p.m., closed Saturday and Monday
The permanent collection contains Amerindian art and traditional Quebec handicrafts. Changing exhibits of

Quebec artists and artisans.

Musée historique de l'Électricité
440 Chambly Road, Longueuil
677-5733
H: 10 a.m. to 5 p.m., Sunday through Thursday
The collection covers three different sectors: domestic appliances, communications and industrial equipment. There are also changing exhibits.

Musée Regional de Vaudreuil
431 Roche, Vaudreuil 1-455-2902
H: 11 a.m. to 5 p.m., closed Monday, except for groups who have reserved. Permanent collection of objects used in traditional Quebec daily life. Changing thematic exhibits.

Art Galleries

Montreal has so many art galleries that this is not an exhaustive list.

Alliance
680 Sherbrooke St. W. 284-3768

Amrad Art Africain
1522 Sherbrooke St. W. 934-4550

Art 45
1460 Sherbrooke St. W. 843-5024

Art Sélect
6810 St-Denis St. 273-7088

Articule
4060 St-Laurent Blvd. 842-9686

Artlenders
318 Victoria Avenue 484-4691

Atelier J. Lukacs
1504 Sherbrooke St. W. 933-9877

Aubes
3935 St-Denis St. 845-5078

Bellefeuille
1212 Greene Ave. 933-4406

Bernard Desroches
1444 Sherbrooke St. W. 842-8648

Claude Lafitte
1446 Sherbrooke St. W. 288-7718

Concordia
1455 de Maisonneuve Blvd. W.
848-4751

Contemporary Art
2165 Crescent St. 844-6711

Continental
1450 Drummond St. 842-1072

Cultart
360 Roy St. E. 843-3596

Daniel
2159 Mackay St. 844-4344

Dare-Dare
1320 Laurier St. E. 526-6765

Dazibao
4060 St-Laurent Blvd. 845-0063

Dominion
1438 Sherbrooke St. W. 845-7471

Don Stewart
2148 Mackay St. 932-2852

Du Cygne
1451 Sherbrooke St. W. 935-6971

Elca London
1616 Sherbrooke St. W. 931-3646

Eskimo Art
1434 Sherbrooke St. W. 844-4080

Espace Ovo
307 Ste-Catherine W. 849-6253

Graff
963 Rachel St E. 526-2616

Impression
4826 St-Denis St. 843-4491

John A. Schweitzer
42 Pine Avenue W. 289-9262

Klinkhoff
1200 Sherbrooke St. W. 288-5972

Ko-Zen
532 Duluth E. 842-0342

La Guilde Graphique
9 St-Paul St. W. 844-3438

La Magie de l'Art
1235 Guy St.

L'Art Français
1434 Sherbrooke St. W. 277-2179

Lippel
1324 Sherbrooke St. W. 842-6369

Ludovic
1390 Sherbrooke St. W. 844-9788

Martal
1460 Sherbrooke St. W. 842-0151

Michel-Ange
430 Bonsecours St. 875-8281

Mihalis
1500 Sherbrooke St. W. 932-4554

Morency
1564 St-Denis St. 845-6442

Nouvel Âge
350 Sherbrooke St. E. 286-0331

Optica
3981 St-Laurent Blvd. 287-1574

Pierre Savoie
4840 St-Denis St. 849-7409

Pink
1456 Notre-Dame W. 935-9851

Powerhouse
3738 St-Dominique St. 844-3489

Serge Lacroix
4593 Rivard St. 843-4535

Skol
3981 St-Laurent Blvd. 842-4021

Studio Altaire
2021 St-Laurent Blvd. 270-4465

Tapestry
3964 St-Laurent Blvd. 288-3467

Treize
4015 Drolet St. 288-5903

Verre d'Art
1518 Sherbrooke St. W. 932-3896

Waddington et Gorce
1504 Sherbrooke St. W. 934-0413

Watson
1434 Sherbrooke St. W. 849-9389

Festivals

The Montreal Film Festival *is held in the late summer.*
The Festival de Jazz de Montréal *is held in July.*

Celebrations are held to mark.
March 17, **Saint Patrick's Day** *(a parade on Ste-Catherine Street),*
June 24, **Saint-Jean-Baptiste Day** *(in all parts of the city)*
In early October, **the Autumn Moon** *(in Chinatown).*

At the foot of Place Jacques-Cartier, south of de la Commune Street, the **Festival du Vieux Port** *is held all summer long (844-3301). Stage performances, films, children's activities, artisan workshops and boutiques, and sports events are offered most evenings.*

Salons

A number of Salons are held in Place Bonaventure's exhibition hall.

Salon des Métiers d'Art *Artisanry*

Salon de l'Automobile *Automobiles*

Salon Nautique *Boats*

Salon du Livre de Montréal *Book*

Salon du Camping *Camping*

**Salon de l'Agriculture
et de l'Alimentation**
Food and farming

Salon de l'Habitation *Housing*

Salon des sciences et de la technologie
Science and technology

Salon du Ski *Skiing*

Salon de la Femme *Women*

Salon de la Jeunesse *Youth*

For further information, contact the Director, **Hall d'Exposition**, Place Bonaventure, P.O. Box 1000, Montreal, H5A 1G1 397-2222

Additional information on other shows are available from the **Office des Congrès et du Tourisme du Grand Montréal**, Place Bonaventure, 1 Frontenac, Floor F. P.O. Box 889, Montreal, H5A 1E6

Other attractions

Alcan Aquarium
La Ronde, île Ste-Hélène 872-4656
H: From May 1 to June 19: week-ends, 10 a.m. to 10 p.m.; during the week: 10 a.m. to 5 p.m. From June 19 to August 29: 10 a.m. to 10 p.m. every day.

Bourse de Montréal
800 Place Victoria, third floor, 871-2424.
Montreal Stock Exchange visitors' gallery (10 a.m. to 4 p.m. weekdays); guided tours.

Blue Bonnets Race Track,
7440 Decarie Boulevard 739-2741
H: from 7:45 p.m., Monday and Wednesday through Saturday, Sunday from 1:30 p.m. Harness horseracing.

Dow Planetarium
1000 St-Jacques W. 872-4530
Performances are given every afternoon except Monday, also some evening. Hour-long astronomical talks presented on a hemispheric dome screen. The program is changed approximately once every two months.

Guilde Canadienne des Métiers d'Art,
2025 Peel Street 849-6091
H: Monday through Friday, 9 a.m. to 5:30 p.m., Saturday 10 a.m. to 5 p.m.. Store and exhibition of Quebec craftmanship.

Jardins des Merveilles
4000 Calixa-Lavallée 872-2815,
mid-May to the end of September
H: 10 a.m. until sunset. Fairy tales are the theme of this small zoo. Sea lion performances are prsented throughout the day.

La Ronde
île Ste-Hélène 872-6222
H: Weekends during May, daily from June until Labor Day, 12 p.m. to 2:30 a.m. Amusement park with rides, performances, restaurants and bars.

Lachine Rapids Tours
105 de la Commune St., 284-9607
Jet boat through the Lachine Rapids. Mid-May to September, between 10 a.m. and 6 p.m. Also rubber rafting during the summer months.

Man and His World
Île Ste-Hélène 872-6222
From the end of June to the end of August.
H: site, 8 a.m. to midnight; activities and pavilions, 10:30 a.m. to 7:30 p.m.. National and international exhibitions, playgrounds and picnic tables, boats for rent, theatre and other live performances.

Olympic Park
45435 Pierre-de-Coubertin Avenue
H: 9 a.m. to 5 p.m. in summer, 11 a.m. to 2:45 p.m. in the winter. Guided tours of the Olympic Stadium, Velodrome and swimming installations. Home of the Expos baseball team, Concordes football team and the Manic soccer team.

The Post Office house,
640 Ste-Catherine Street W 283-4603
H: 8 a.m. to 5:45 p.m., Monday through Friday, 8 a.m. to 4:45 p.m. on Saturday. Philatelic centre selling Canadian stamps. Guides visit by reservation only.

Regional attractions

Abbaye cistercienne
de Notre-Dame-du-Lac,
1600 Chemin Oka, Oka 1-479-8361
The Trappist monks of Oka are famous for their cheese. The abbey is located near the Paul-Sauvé provincial park and the Calvaire d'Oka, sculpted out of wood by François Guernon in 1775.

Caughnawaga see Kahnawake

Centre d'Interpretation de la Pomme
488 Principale Street, Rougemont
1-469-4747
H: May 1 to October 1, 10 a.m. to 5

p.m., Tuesday through Saturday, 10 a.m. to 6 p.m. on Sunday. Audio-visual presentations on apples and apple growing, in an old refrigerator warehouse.

Fort Chamblay,
2 Richelieu Street, Chambly
1-658-1585
National historic park which dates from 1709. Guided tours of the restored part of the fort, the site and St. Stephen's Chapel.

Fort Lennox,
Saint-Paul de l'île-aux-Noix
1-291-5700
H: 10 a.m. to 5:30 p.m., daily from mid-May till Labor Day, weekends during the rest of the year. This 1819 British fort is a national historic park. Arms and artifacts from the 18th century are on display. The fort is accessible by ferry.

Île des Moulins,
Terrebonne, route 344 1-471-2122
H: 10 a.m. to 6 p.m., May 1 to September 30. Historical interpretation centre, a provincial park which contains five buildings which date (in part or in whole) from the first half of the 19th century. There is a flour mill, a sawmil, the seigneurial office, the bakery and a newer flour mill. Animation.

Kahnawake (Caughnawaga),
1-632-6030
H: 10 a.m. to 12 p.m., 1 p.m. to 5 p.m. Museum and Fort St-Louis, Iroquois Amerindian reserve. The main mission buildings from 1717 and 1745 still stand. Relics of the Blessed Kateri Tekakwith. Mass celebrated in Iroquois Sundays at 10:30 a.m.

Moulin Legaré,
Saint-Eustache 1-472-9529
H: 9 a.m. to 12 p.m., 1 p.m. to 5 p.m. Constructed in 1783, this water mill still works. It is used to grind corn and buckwheat grown on local farms.

Park Safari,
Hemmingford 1-454-3668
H: early May to early September, 10 a.m. to 4 p.m. A zoo without cages where people remain in their cars to drive by the animals. Mammals from North America, Eurasia and Africa. Games and rides, magic shows and an international circus during the summer.

Saint Lawrence Seaway,
Saint-Lambert (access is near the Victoria Bridge) 672-4110
The observation deck is open from May 1 to the end of October from 8:30 a.m. to sundown.
The 8-mile (13 km) bicycle path is open on weekends (8:30 a.m. to 6 p.m.) from mid-May to mid-June and from mid-September. During the summer it is open from 8:30 a.m. to 8 p.m. daily. Montreal is at the heart of this ship passage way which extends 1000 miles (1600 km) to the east and 1300 miles (2100 km) to the west.
The Saint-Lambert Lock is the entryway to the Seaway itself. Here, the water level changes by 15 feet (4.5 m). The observation deck has a scale model of the Seaway.

Sanctuaire du Sacré-Coeur (de la Réparation)
3650 de la Rousselière 642-5391
This pilgrimage centre is under the direction of the Capuchin Friars. The Byzantine style chapel dates from 1910.

Wilfrid Laurier House,
Ville des Laurentides (Saint-Lin)
1-439-3702
H: weekends in April and September, daily from 10 a.m. to 4 p.m. from mid-May till early September. During the winter by appointment only.
The 1840 home of the first francophone Prime Minister of Canada is a national historic monument. The personnel are dressed in period costume.

44

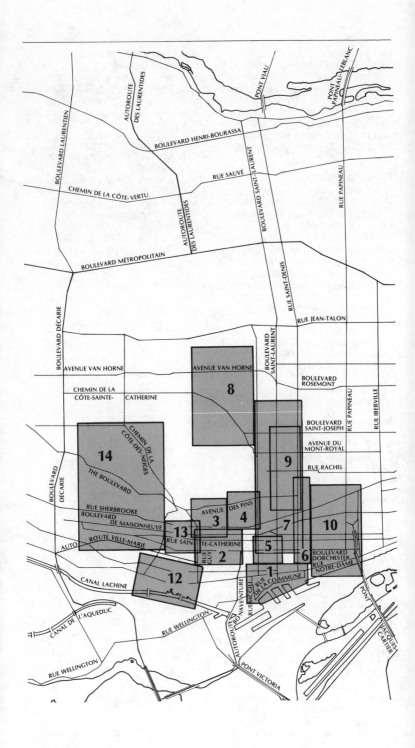

GENERAL MAP
OF THE WALKING TOURS

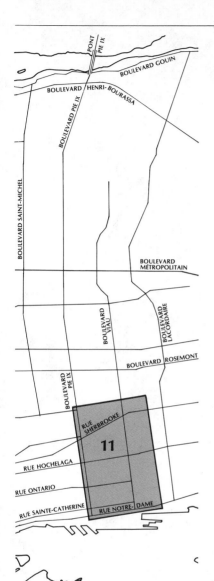

OLD MONTREAL

The walk through the area where Montreal took root and flourished is about three miles (5 km) long and includes buildings and monuments which merit lengthy study. As a result, the itinerary has been divided into three parts, each beginning and ending near a metro entrance. Each walk takes about an hour and a half, but the lure of the many interesting boutiques and art galleries coupled with the historic beauty of the buildings and public places may cajole one into spending a good two or three hours on any one walk. It is easy enough to plan a lunch stop in one of the many picturesque restaurants on the way.

History

Old Montreal was surrounded by fortifications until the beginning of the 19th century. The rough stone wall which was 18 feet high (5.4 m), four feet wide (1.2 m) at the base and three feet wide (0.90m) at the top was supplemented by an exterior slope and a deep trench.

There were four main gates into the walled city: to the west, the Récollet Gate at Notre-Dame Street; to the north, the St-Laurent Gate; St. Martin's Gate (or Quebec Gate) on St-Paul Street; the Port Gate opening directly to Place du Marché, now called Place Royale.

A mid-1800's photograph, looking east, of the port of Montreal.

Because of the hilly topography of the area, many of the buildings in the town were taller than the walls and thus unprotected from attack by land or by river. The defensive importance of the walls was also lessened by their flimsiness which would have made them difficult to maintain if attacked.

In any case, the citizens of Montreal were not convinced of the need for these mediocre ramparts, especially since they were the ones required to assume the cost of the walls. They felt that Montreal was becoming a commercial rather than a military city and the walls presented an obstacle to its economic growth.

In 1801 Royal assent was received for the demolition of the walls. Three commissioners (one of whom was James McGill, founder of McGill University) were appointed to oversee the task. Demolition was completed in 1821 but the area outside of the walls had already been settled.

The old faubourg des Récollets. To the west of the historic quarter, its devastation hidden by old buildings on St-Antoine and McGill streets, is the former Récollets suburb. The area between St-Antoine, McGill, de la Commune streets and the Bonaventure autoroute consists, primarily, of parking lots tempered here and there by some early buildings which have miraculously survived the years.

Le Petit Séminaire was constructed there in the early 19th century, using stone most likely taken from the recently-levelled fortification walls. Unfortunately, all that was left of the building —one of Montreal's oldest — disappeared in 1980. Some interesting buildings do remain, notably those at the intersection of William and King streets.

The old faubourg des Récollets, Montreal's first suburb, was made up of the area west of the wall between St. Martin's Stream and the little Saint Peter River. These two waterways flowed approximately where St-Antoine and St-Paul streets are now located, meeting at Montfort and Notre-Dame streets, the present location of Dow Breweries.

While the area now seems to be hardly more than an empty shell, its history and convenient location could well generate a thriving community. Access by metro, bus and private transportation is as easy as downtown. With the redevelopment of the zones on its periphery, now is an opportune time to diversify the area's activity.

Faubourg des Récollets could become a link between the modern downtown, the old city and the river. It is not difficult to imagine a dynamic rebirth of this neighborhood which would offer historic landmarks, old buildings renovated for housing, new commercial construction and green space established on the empty land. The much promised "window on the river" which is to provide a lush linear park along the St. Lawrence, would be a dramatic backdrop.

Jacques Viger Commission. On August 16, 1962 the City of Montreal instituted the Jacques Viger Commission to oversee the restoration of Old Montréal. The Viger Commission was established to deal with all aspects of conservation including both the interior and exterior of buildings.

The by-law established the limits of the sector for restoration as Berri Street to the east, Commissioners Street (de la Commune) to the south, McGill Street to the west and Craig Street (St-Antoine) to the north. Three years later the city reduced the sector by changing the north boundary to Notre-Dame. This permitted the construction of the Banque Canadienne Nationale building on Place d'Armes and the Palais de Justice on St-Jacques.

In April 1981, the city extended the boundaries of Old Montreal for subsidy purposes to include the area between St-Antoine, de la Commune, des Soeurs Grises (one block west of McGill Street) and the extension of St-Hubert.

Unfortunately, a number of historic sites within the old quarter have disappeared, leaving nothing but a commemorative plaque. But on the walking tours, we will see some 19th-century

English and French architecture, as well as a few rare examples of the French style of the 18th and even 17th century.

On practically every street you will perceive the results of the trend to conservation and restoration of old buildings. The old girl is exchanging corset and parasol for designer jeans and make-up. It is a refreshing change, but one which can cause some difficulties. Sometimes make-up is garish and the result is false.

Stone Skeleton Architecture. At its best, this architecture is characterized by a simple system of beams and pillars with a stone skeleton façade separated by expanses of glass. The open floor plan offers a minimum of obstruction and a maximum of flexibility with immense bay windows which let in as much natural light as possible.

These buildings were constructed at a time when architecture was still hampered by the need for supporting walls and still under the influence of historic styles. Yet they are a logical, economical and apparently spontaneous answer to commercial and industrial needs of a new era. The architectural treatment and the structural design evoke architectural functionalism which was perfected by Sullivan and, later, adopted by Le Courbusier and his disciples to become the basis for the modern International architectural movement of the 20th Century. As such it is the forerunner of our modern office building.

Unfortunately, there is little information about this type of architecture which made no claim to be an architectural style. It first appeared in the cities of the American East Coast during the 1820s, but the Montreal version was probably influenced by the Royal Engineers' pragmatic and direct way of designing buildings.

Aside from the technological innovation involved, these buildings testify to an architectural quest for composition, proportion, articulation and scale. In general, these façades are articulated vertically, and the height of each successive storey diminishes. When the building is capped by a mansard roof, strongly projecting dormer windows attract the attention of the passerby. Flat roofed buildings were terminated with a cornice.

Also evident is the attempt to fit these constructions into the built environment already present. The Grey Nuns's warehouses on St-Pierre and the buildings across the street show the same arcades and the same rhythm in the façades. In addition, the strong horizontal lines assure unity on the block. In other cases, vertical lines predominate; and there are façades in which neither vertical nor horizontal lines dominate. What is apparent is a well proportioned rectangle or square of stone (e.g., 374-384 St-Paul West; 367-373 Place d'Youville).

While stone skeleton façades preceded cast-iron façade architecture, the two kinds of construction have such an affinity that they often apparent in the same building. In Montreal, stone framework buildings are more common than in the United States, where cast iron frames predominated from 1850 to 1880.

OLD MONTREAL
Tour A

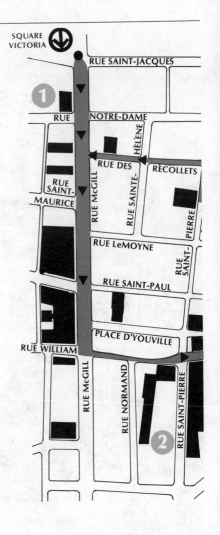

1 The Wilson Chambers Building
2 Hôpital général des Soeurs Grises
3 Caserne centrale des pompiers
4 Place Royale

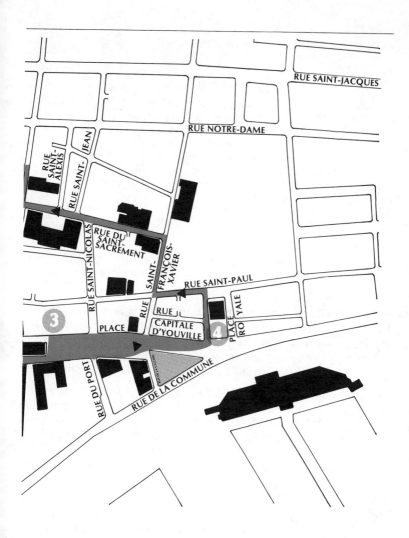

RUE SAINT-JACQUES

RUE NOTRE-DAME

RUE SAINT-ALEXIS

RUE SAINT-JEAN

RUE DU SAINT-SACREMENT

RUE SAINT-NICOLAS

RUE SAINT-FRANÇOIS-XAVIER

RUE SAINT-PAUL

PLACE ROYALE

PLACE

RUE CAPITALE D'YOUVILLE

RUE DU PORT

RUE DE LA COMMUNE

Access: Place-Victoria metro station.

1 The Wilson Chambers Building

The Wilson Chambers Building (502-510 McGill) is a rare example of the lovely commercial Gothic architecture of its time (1869) and recalls the original Parliament Buildings in Ottawa. Charles Wilson was the first owner. Wilson, an Irish Catholic, had been mayor of Montreal during the Gavazzi riot of 1853 which pitted Catholics against Protestants. Wilson was blamed for the riot, although there is no evidence of his guilt. At the time this building was constructed, Wilson was a member of Canada's first Senate.

The stone structure and glass in-fill design of the **474 McGill** building was quite advanced for the time (early 1860s). The buildings on this block, as well as those on the south side of St-Maurice Street, are similar to the buildings which once surrounded Victoria Square.

At **460 McGill** is a late 1880s building, with a recently-cleaned façade. Its rich decoration and large bay windows can be appreciated despite modifications made to the ground floor. Most McGill Street buildings were originally quite impressive but some have deteriorated with the street's decline in the past few years.

The Dominion Block at 400-408 McGill Street is a trio of buildings with distinguished sculpted façade. Unfortunately, the original mansard roofs of these 1860s buildings have been removed. As is the case with many early 19th-century buildings, the Dominion Block façade was designed to look like a series of European villas, one above the other. The corner is especially well-executed. The fire in the early 1980s gutted 408 McGill. The city has purchased the property and intends to rebuild.

The Petit Séminaire once stood a block to the west of McGill Street, at 708 St-Paul. However the historic ruins of one of Montreal's first schools were demolished in 1980. They could have been the focal point for a park, as is often done in Europe.

The headquarters of the Grand Trunk Railway were once at **360 McGill**. With its plethora of architectural decoration, the building seems more suitable for a hotel than an office building. The lobby boasts a marble staircase with cast iron balustrade. The little Saint Peter River still runs under this building.

Further down, the 100 McGill building was once used as the main office of the Hudson's Bay fur trading Company. Once upon a time, nearby 600 d'Youville Street was a train station; it was recently converted into a restaurant and an antique shop.

The area between de La Commune, Place d'Youville and des Soeurs Grises streets is **Pointe-à-Callière**, the birthplace of Montreal. Samuel de Champlain landed there in 1611 and that's where **Paul Chomedey de Maisonneuve** brought the first colonists in 1642.

Paul de Chomedey, sieur de Maisonneuve (1612-1676) founder of Montreal, was born in Neuville-sur-France. He founded Ville-Marie and was the first governor of the island of Montreal. He gave land to those willing to clear it and knew how to brighten the life of the colonists while prudently administering his land. He returned to France when the island was transferred to the French crown and given to the Sulpicians in 1663.

The Harbor Commission building during one of the many floods of the late 1800s.

The Third Customs House (400 Place de la Commune) dates from 1912-1916, although the north side was added 20 years later. Faced in buff sandstone and granite, it is a late example of Beaux-Arts classicism. (The second Customs House no longer stands).

The modular pyramid building in the distance is **Habitat**, designed by Moshe Safdie for Expo '67, as an experiment in residential architecture.

The Allan Building at the southwest corner of St-Pierre and de la Commune streets, is well-designed for its site's shape. As befits the head office of the Montreal Ocean Steamships Company, this 1858 Italianate style building squarely faces the port. Undoubtedly, the owner, Sir Hugh Allan, used the octogonal tower to observe port activity and the arrival of his ships. Allan was also a promoter of railway transport in the mid-1800s.

Beside the door, one can see a marker of the flood of 1886. Canada Mortgage and Housing Corporation (CMHC) plans to sell this building to an enterprise which will respect its importance in Montreal port history.

As you walk, take a look at the many turrets and towers of Old Montreal which dot the skyline.

2 Hôpital général des Soeurs Grises

The recently restored Grey Nuns General Hospital is on Normand Street. D'Youville Street was named for the founder of this religious order, Marguerite d'Youville. The origin of the name «Soeurs Grises» is obscure.

Initially called Soeurs de la Charité (Sisters of Charity) they were renamed Soeurs *Grises*, meaning "tipsy", by those who persecuted and ridiculed them. Were the Nuns intoxicated? Or did they sell alcohol to the Amerindians?

According to documents of the period, neither was true.

The central part of the hospital is the most ancient section, its stone foundations were built by the Charron Brothers in 1693. The walls were erected in 1765, while the two wings were added between 1847 and 1851.

Discouraged by the lack of fresh air and the frequent floodings in this area, the nuns moved to a new building on Dorchester Street in 1871. To obtain funds for their facilities for the sick and destitute, the newest pavilion of the old hospital was demolished that year and the lot sold to the city for the extension of St-Pierre Street.

The last vestiges of the chapel and of the hospital's west wing can be seen on St-Pierre Street. The warehouses were built on the east side of this new part of the street between 1871 and 1874. During the 1960s, the nuns wanted to demolish these fine examples of industrial architecture to rebuild the hospital. The plan was fortunately discarded.

The magnificent stone skeleton façades reveal advanced architectural treatment for the time. The ground floor is unified by vigorous arcades, and triplets of windows on the upper floors are separated by powerful masonry pillars. Here is a distillation of the architectonic principles of the Chicago School of the late 1800s —light, space, ventilation and solidity. CMHC has renovated these buildings for use as luxury housing and office space.

3 Caserne centrale des pompiers

The Fire station was built in 1915 in the style of Norman Shaw. His work — popular in late 19th-century England — was a charming, sensitive and imaginative mixture of 17th-century Dutch style and the English styles of Queen Anne and William and Mary. The gables are particularly lovely.

The fire station was renovated after an agreement was signed between the Quebec Minister of Cultural Affairs and the City of Montreal at the end of the 1970s and is now open to the public. This accord resulted in a number of real estate improvements in Old Montreal: the structure of the fire station was restored, part of the General Hospital was renovated by the Grey Nuns, archaeological digs were undertaken. The façades of some buildings are being cleaned by their owners, while others are being recycled.

In the area which is now known as Place d'Youville there was once a building which housed the colonial legislature. This parliament was created as a result of the 1837 Rebellion which had called for responsible government in Canada. There sat representatives from Canada-East (Quebec) and Canada-West (Ontario).

In 1849, rioters set fire to the Parliament building to protest the Rebellion Losses Act. Lord Elgin had given royal assent to this bill which compensated losses caused by both the rebels and the British soldiers. The Tories (the conservative group) believed this money would go to those who had revolted. They marched to the legislative building while Parliament was in session, set it afire and prevented firemen from extinguishing the flames. Parliament met at Bonsecours Market before being moved to Kingston, then to Quebec City, and finally to Ottawa.

The Centre d'Histoire de Montréal museum is housed in the fire station. It offers an interesting presentation of the city's development.

The Saint-Peter River was later covered over between McGill Street and the fire station, and the square was created.

St.Anne's Market in 1869

The d'Youville Stables reopened in the autumn of 1968 after extensive renovation by a group of Montreal businessmen, who were among the first people to see the investment potential of Old Montreal. The Norman-style interior courtyard is quite charming and worth a look. If the truth is to be told, the stables were not located here. They were in a more remote part of the property.

Originally, the land was owned by the Frères Hospitaliers, then by the Soeurs Grises. The westernmost building was erected in the 1700s and city files record it as being a potash or lye warehouse. The east building was built by the Soeurs Grises between 1825 and 1865. Its most interesting use was that of the warehouse of a grain merchant who supplied the Confederate Army during the U.S. Civil War.

The building at **317 Place d'Youville** is quite attractive, so is 224 Place d'Youville which was designed by Hutchison and Steele, for use as a warehouse by W.W. Ogilvie.

The handsome 1895 building at 204 is embellished by a terra-cotta band. We can be thankful that the upper floor addition, added 50 years later, is hardly noticeable. Facing it, at 201-203 Place d'Youville is a fine building of the 1870s, recently renovated.

Pointe-à-Callière was initially a fort surrounded by a wooden palisade. According to the plans of Jean Bourdon, drawn circa 1646, this was the exact spot which Samuel de Champlain baptized "Place Royale" upon his visit in 1611.

At the corner of de Callière and de la Commune was one of the most fabled establishments of Victorian Montreal. **Joe Beef's** Tavern thrived c. 1860-1984. Before laws against cruelty to animals were in force, Charlie McKiernan entertained his customers with two bears, a buffalo and other living animals in a basement menagerie. It is said that no one was ever refused food, drink or shelter by the irrepressible "Joe Beef" as McKiernan was called.

The **statue**, Pointe-à-Callière's only ornament, is of the Honorable John Young, first chairman of the Montreal Harbor Commission. He was instrumental in making Montreal the second largest port in North America, despite the fact that it was closed for five months of the year because of the ice.

4 Place Royale

It was in March 1644, at Place Royale that de Maisonneuve shot at close range the Iroquois chieftain who had almost killed him. Later, the market was set up here during the French régime. As the principal public place in the settlement, this was the scene of the reading of proclamations, the exchange of news and gossip. Here also malefactors were placed in pillories to suffer the jeers and taunts of the crowd.

The Obelisk commemorates the foundation of Ville-Marie and bears the names of the first colonists, members of the Société de Notre-Dame de Montréal who were organized by Jérôme Le Royer de la Dauversière, the king's tax collector. De Maisonneuve, a career soldier from the age of 13, was the colonists' com-

mander. Jeanne Mance, founder of Hôtel-Dieu, and Père Vimont were among the group of 24 French people who landed in this area on May 18, 1642.

In less than two centuries, Montreal became a major port for foreign ships. The Customs House (designed by John Ostell) was built on Place Royale in 1836 and the building is now occupied by Agriculture Canada.

The Gazette, Montreal's daily English newspaper, was established one block west of Place Royale by Fleury de Mesplet in 1778. It was Montreal's first newspaper. Benjamin Franklin had sent Mesplet to Montreal during the American occupation of British North America, in order to drum up support for the Revolutionary cause.

Along St-Paul stand notable buildings with stone skeleton superstructure. Vertical lines predominate at 215 and 221-231.

(A few blocks to the west, at 374 and 400-402 are other fine examples of stone skeleton architecture).

The Centaur Theatre (453 St-François-Xavier Street) is housed in a 1903 Beaux-Arts style building which was the home of the Montreal Stock Exchange until 1965. Montreal's oldest professional English playhouse received an award for recycling this building.

The building at the southwest corner of St-François-Xavier and St-Sacrement was built in 1874 for the Montreal Telegraph Company. This company inaugurated a telegraph line between Quebec City and Toronto in 1847. Later, the Great Northwestern Telegraph Company acquired the building.

Le Devoir, one of Montreal's most respected newspapers, is situated in the stately building at 211 St-Sacrement. The Montreal Stock Exchange moved here in the 1860s from their first home which was in the Exchange Coffee Shop on St-Paul Street. They left St-Sacrement and moved to what is now the Centaur in 1903. Founded in the early 1830s, the Montreal Stock Exchange is the oldest in Canada.

The plaque at 221 St-Sacrement records the fact that this was once the home of the Marquis de Lotbinière, royal engineer of New France during the 1750s. Further on, at 300 St-Sacrement is the original home of the Montreal Board of Trade which dates from the beginning of this century. This building was erected directly on the foundations of one which had burnt down; you can see that the first layer of stone above ground remains from the earlier building. The Montreal Board of Trade was founded in 1822 and is now located on Beaver Hall Hill.

There are a number of stone skeleton buildings along other streets in this part of Old Montreal. Two well-designed impressive cornices can be seen at 434 St-Pierre and 430 Ste-Hélène. Pretensiousness has spoiled 445-449 St-Pierre: prestige was the overriding concern.

The fire escape at 417 des Récollets only slightly diminishes the charm of this most interesting example of stone skeleton sculpture. We are struck by its grand proportions and powerful capping. The building is modulated vertically, with each successive floor diminishing in height.

Take McGill Street north to the Victoria Square metro entrance, or go on to Tour B *by walking east on St-Jacques to Place d'Armes.*

OLD MONTREAL
Tour B

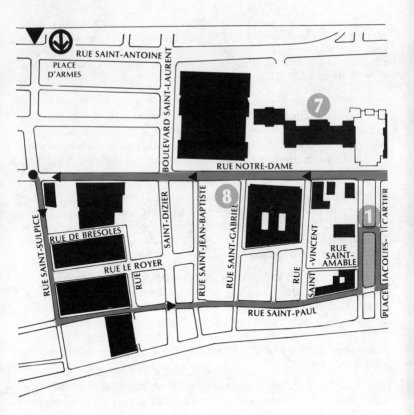

1 Place Jacques-Cartier
2 Marché Bonsecours
3 Notre-Dame-de-
   Bonsecours
4 Maison Papineau
5 Château Ramezay
6 Hôtel de Ville
7 L'ancien Palais de Justice
8 Nouveau Palais de Justice

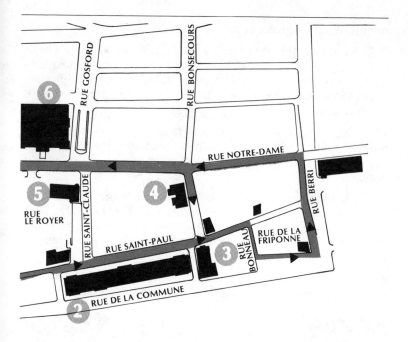

Access: Place-d'Armes metro station

Tour B covers the best known part of Old Montreal. Throughout the 20th century this area has attracted tourists who come especially to see Bonsecours Market and Notre-Dame-de-Bonsecours Church, probably the most historic buildings in the entire old quarter.

This tour also shows some examples of buildings which have been converted into homes. As in many other cities, living in the most historic part of Montréal has acquired a certain *cachet* and appeal.

At the southeast corner of Notre-Dame and St-Sulpice stood at one time the residence of the famous explorer Daniel Du Lhut who founded the city of Duluth, Minnesota. This was also the site of the first lay school in Montréal, opened in 1683 by the Sieur de la Prairie.

Antoine Laumet de Lamothe-Cadillac, founder of Detroit and later a governor of Louisiana, lived on the other side of Notre-Dame.

In 1862, the construction of a series of warehouses began in the blocks between the streets of St-Sulpice, St-Dizier, de Brésoles and St-Paul, on the site of Jeanne Mance's Hôtel-Dieu. The warehouses were recently recyled for housing and renamed **Les Cours LeRoyer**. It was an inspired move, for their open stone skeleton façades — unusual in their era — provide plenty of light for the new homes.

At the northwest corner of St-Paul and St-Sulpice streets, across from Les Cours Le Royer, was the home of one of the most illustrious Canadian families, the Le Moynes. Charles Le Moyne raised ten sons here. One of them, Pierre, born in 1662 became the **Sieur d'Iberville**.

Pierre Le Moyne, sieur d'Iberville (1661-1706), born in Quebec was the most celebrated military officer of the Franch regime. Most of his exploits were against the English on Hudson's Bay and he captured a number of forts, including Mosipi, Rupert and Albany. He destroyed English settlements on the west coast of Newfoundland and captured Fort Nelson in 1697. Recalled to France after the treaty of Ryswick, he was sent to establish a French colony at the mounth of the Mississippi. He arrived in 1699 and established Fort Maurepas at the site where now stands Biloxi, Mississippi. He was named Chevalier de Saint Louis and became governor of the French colony of Louisiana in 1700.

Look eastward to admire the pleasing curve of St-Paul Street, formed by the harmonious ensemble of greystone façades on the south side. Behind the stepped roofs rises the majestic dome of Bonsecours Market.

Note the distinctive ornamentation at 50 St-Paul West. Huge Grain Elevator No. 1 once loomed behind. The complexities of grain handling required an architecture made up of a series of geometric forms, such as gigantic rectangles and long cylinders. These utilitarian masses were visually out of scale with the neighboring buildings and cut off the view of the river. However, they were significant examples of functionalist architecture. Le Corbusier was the first to appreciate the design potential of these austere structures. He included photographs of Montreal grain elevators in his book *Towards a Modern Architecture*.

The North West Fur Company had its main warehouse in the rear of the building at 161-163 St-Paul East. This company was founded by a group of Montrealers directed by Simon McTavish and the Frobisher brothers. The company merged with the rival Hudson's Bay Company in 1821.

La Maison du Patriote at 169 St-Paul East was part of the substantial Viger property. It was built around 1775 and was spared by the fire of 1803.

Denis-Benjamin Viger published *Le Spectateur* and other newspapers, in the early 1800s, at 177-181 St-Paul East.

1 Place Jacques-Cartier

Place Jacques-Cartier, circa 1890.

The public square located between Notre-Dame and St-Paul streets was officially named in 1847. With its summertime mall, formal flower beds, 19th-century style street lamps and cobblestones, Place Jacques-Cartier has regained an air of yesteryear. Tourists and Montrealers alike enjoy sitting in its outdoor cafés, absorbing the atmosphere and pausing to enjoy the street entertainment.

The residence of the Marquis of Vaudreuil, governor of New France, was erected in 1723 in the southern part of the square, with gardens extending to Notre-Dame Street. It succumbed to flames 80 years later. That year the land was purchased by Périnault and Durocher who divided the

area into lots and ceded the central portion (the present public
space) to the city. The Marché
Neuf was established at the end of
the 18th century, and used until

the completion of the Marché
Bonsecours.
At the north end of the square is
Nelson's Monument, erected in
1809.

Viger House at the southwest corner of St-Amable and Place
Jacques-Cartier (410 Place Jacques-Cartier) was probably constructed by Jacques Viger in the early 19th century, father of the
first mayor of Montreal and uncle of **Denis-Benjamin Viger** who
lived there later.

Before its restoration, the stone walls of Viger House were hidden under thick layers of plaster, while the façade was marred by
an anachronistic store window. Two surviving windows from the
original design served as models for the others which have been
restored to their original appearance.

Denis-Benjamin Viger (1974-1861) was a radical lawyer and politician who went
to Westminster in 1828 with John Nelson and Augustin Cuvillier to air French-
Canadian grievances before the British Parliament. He returned to England three
years later in order to support accusations made against Stuart, the colonial attor-
ney general.

As a partisan of his cousin Louis-Joseph Papineau, Denis-Benjamin was imprisoned after the 1837 Rebellion and released 18 months later. In addition to *Le
Spectateur*, Viger sponsored *La Minerve*, and *L'Aurore*.

Del Vecchio House, at 404 Place Jacques-Cartier, was built circa
1807 on land which was once part of Governor Vaudreuil's
garden. This house was built by Pierre del Vecchio and was
owned by his family until 1946. It was restored by C.I.L. Limited
during Canada's centennial in 1967.

At 438-442 Place Jacques-Cartier is another stone-skeleton
building with each successive storey diminishing in height. East
of the square, St-Paul Street takes on a completely different
aspect. The buildings are shorter, classical and more restrained.
This sector underwent less transformation in the late 1800s since
the wealthy families who had their homes here were less
inclined to sell their property.

Rasco's Hotel (295 St-Paul Street) was built in 1836 and soon
gained a reputation as one of the finest hotels in North America.
While this building was originally designed in the Classic Revival
style, it has lost all architectural details, including the original
arched windows. The city, owner of the structure, restored it in
1982.

Francisco Rasco was an Italian who came to Canada at the beginning of the 1800s to manage the British and American Hotel for
the Molson family. He and his brothers operated a retail establishment located in Maison Del Vecchio.

In addition to a lavishly decorated restaurant which attracted the
"beau monde" of the city, Rasco's Hotel had a number of salons,
a concert hall and a ballroom. Among the regular patrons were
Louis-Hippolyte La Fontaine, Robert Baldwin and Georges-
Étienne Cartier. In 1842 Charles Dickens and his wife stayed here
and a small street is named in his honor.

2 Marché Bonsecours

Bonsecours Market (1845) is a long, imposing building whose most attractive façade faces the river side. The architect, William Footner, kept in mind that most people came to Montreal by river. Therefore he designed the building so that they would view its best side when they had their first glimpse of the city. John Browne was responsible for the decorations. The magnificent cast iron doric columns were imported from England.

The Renaissance-style dome above Bonsecours was the first erected in Montreal (1864). It was rebuilt after fires claimed it in the late 1940s, but destroyed again in a 1979 conflagration. Fireproof materials were used for the most recent reconstruction.

When the market first opened, it was located in the basement and along the exterior. The Bonse-cours building was used as Montreal's City Hall from 1852 to 1878. Like many American city halls, the building also housed a reception room, council chambers, municipal offices, and the police headquarters. After the burning of the Parliament Buildings in the square in 1849, the legislature sat in the unfinished Bonsecours Market. In 1964 the City renovated the interior for use as municipal offices.

The first Canadian exhibition was held in the upper floors of Bonsecours Market in 1850. Prize-winning products were exhibited at the London's International Exhibition the following year.

3 Notre-Dame-de-Bonsecours

It was Marguerite Bourgeoys who first conceived the idea of constructing a chapel to the Virgin Mary outside of Ville-Marie's palisade. Marguerite Bourgeoys came to Ville-Marie with de Maisonneuve and founded the first Canadian religious order, Congrégation Notre-Dame. Construction of Notre-Dame-de-Bonsecours began in 1657, but work was interrupted shortly after for about 20 years. In 1672 Mother Bourgeoys returned from France with a small wood statue of the Virgin Mary containing a relic of Saint Blaise which was unveiled at the chapel's inauguration in 1675.

While poor reconstruction undertaken between 1885 and 1890 has altered the original design of the church, several features characteristic of Québécois building style can still be seen — the arched door, the wood belfry and the "oeil-de-boeuf" (small round window in the gable).

The sanctuary quickly became a place of pilgrimage; it still is today. Sailors come to give thanks for being saved from shipwrecks and other dangers. The sailors' devotion to this church is apparent from their donated carvings on display. The statue of Mary was not harmed by the fire that damaged the building in 1754 and is now kept at the Maison Mère de la Congrégation Notre-Dame, on Sherbrooke Street West. Inside the church is a museum dedicated to the life of Marguerite Bourgeoys, recently raised to sainthood by Pope John Paul II.

Maison du Calvet on the northeast corner of Bonsecours Street, is a typical early Quebec house, built in 1770. It now houses a museum of early Quebec furniture. Note its fieldstone walls, steeply-pitched roof (to prevent snow from accumulating) and small, asymmetric windows. Originally, ox blood was used to stain the frames of the windows.

This house was restored by the Ogilvy department store in celebration of their 100th anniversary. It was originally part of an estate left by **Pierre du Calvet**, a French Protestant who was sympathetic to the American independence movement.

Pierre du Calvet, was born in France of Huguenot parents. He came to Quebec in 1758 to be a fur trader. In 1775, Calvet declared his support for American independence from England. He was imprisoned for having given information and supplies to the American general Montgomery. Since he gave supplies to George Washington, he was accused of treason and banished. In 1784, he went to England where he tried to explain his reasoning in a work he published the next year. The English translation was published under the title *An appeal to justice* by Peter du Calvet. He died in 1786 when the vessel which was taking him to his homeland was shipwrecked.

The recent infill structure at 435 St-Paul is well integrated with the rest of the block: note the archway which echoes the building next door. The buildings at 445 and 447 St-Paul have both been restored; a portion of the latter dates from 1710.

Bonneau Street was originally known as **Rue de la Friponne**. The royal stores of the French régime were located here. *Friponne* means rogue in French and legend has it that the name comes from **Intendant Bigot's** shameful practice of swindling the settlers and fur traders.

François Bigot, (1703-1777), lawyer and civil servant, born in Bordeaux, was intendant of New France. As commissioner of Louisbourg, his embezzlement was the cause of the fall of that fort in 1744. He established stores in Quebec City and Montreal in 1748 and began to sell supplies from France at exhorbitant prices. He and his friends were enriched through bribes, theft and corruption. During his tenure, New France was lost to the English. When Bigot returned to France, his property was seized and he was exiled in 1761.

The building (with anachronistic atrium roof) at 417 Berri was part of Dalhousie Station, setting for the departure for Vancouver of Canada's first transcontinental train on June 28, 1886.

The Quebec Gate of the fortifications was located here at a time when this part of St-Paul Street was called St-Martin's Street, hence its other name of St-Martin Gate.

Parks Canada has reconstructed George-Étienne Cartier's House (458 Notre-Dame East) in an unconvincing attempt to re-create its appearance in the mid-1800s. The museum exhibits are more authentic than the building itself.

4 Maison Papineau

Dollier de Casson, Father Superior of the Sulpicians, signed the deed which gave this land to Pierre Renaux in 1692. Papineau House (440 Bonsecours Street) dates from 1785 and was purchased in 1847 by Louis-Joseph in the Legislative Assembly and leader of the 1837 Rebellion in Lower Canada). Remarkably, the house remained in the Papineau family until 1920, having housed six generations.

Eric McLean, music critic and member of the Viger Commission, restored the greatly deteriorated building when he moved in during the early 1960s. He was the first person to move into Old Montreal and begin the renewal of the historic quarter. To restore the house, two brick storeys were eliminated and the dormer windows replaced, while, inside, 19 layers of wallpaper were removed. The walls are four feet (1 m) thick and the current façade is made of wood which has been painted and cut to look like stone. The restoration of this house was based on information gleaned from engravings found in the Château Ramezay collection.

5 Château Ramezay

The Château Ramezay was built in 1705 for Claude de Ramezay, the eleventh governor of Montreal (1703-1724). The façade is of rubble stone, with cut-stone trim. The iron S-shaped bars which you can see on many buildings in Old Montreal are the ends of rods which extend through the beams to anchor them in place.

After de Ramezay's death in 1755, his family sold the building to the Compagnie des Indes which then renovated and enlarged it to its present size. During the 1775 occupation, American Army headquarters were located here. Generals Richard Montgomery and Benedict Arnold stayed here, as did Benjamin Franklin and other members of the continental congress. Later it became successively a court house, the headquarters of the provincial department of instruction, and a school.

Under the union of Canada East and Canada West (1840-67), Château Ramezay served as the seat of government.

Now it is owned by the city of Montreal. Its present occupants, the Antiquarian and Numismatic Society, have made it a museum which houses early Canadian and Amerindian artifacts.

Claude de Ramezay (1659-1724), statesman, born in Lagesse, France came to New France in 1685 and was named governor of Trois-Rivières five years later. He was commander of the colonial troops (1699), governor of Montreal (1704), seigneur of Monnoir (1708) and of Ramezay (1711).

6 Hôtel de Ville

The municipal council decided to construct a city hall worthy of the growing city in the late 1860s and they purchased land on the northwest corner of Notre-Dame and Gosford streets. Architects Alex Hutchison and H.M. Perrault constructed a Second Empire style building which was inaugurated by mayor Jean-Louis Beaudry in March 1878.

In 1922 a fire left only the exterior walls standing; they were preserved, and an independent metal framework was erected inside to support an additional floor. Although reconstruction was not completely finished in February 1926, the new City Hall was officially opened at that time by Mayor Charles Duquette. Unfortunately, the addition of an extra storey altered the elegant proportions of the original structure.

Montreal's flag flies from the City Hall. The city's first coat of arms and flag were adopted in 1939 during the visit of King George VI and Queen Elizabeth. The design commemorates the four original founding people: French, English, Scottish and Irish. The municipal administration adopted a more stylized symbol in the 1980s.

On the southwest corner of the building is a plaque which honors Jacques Viger, Montréal's first mayor. It was he who created the city's motto: *Concordia Salus* (Salvation in concord).

Montreal City Hall before the fire of 1922.

Jean Drapeau was mayor of Montreal for 29 years. He was first elected in 1954 at the age of 38. Although defeated in re-election in 1957, he enjoyed an overwhelming victory in 1960, together with the Civic Party which he created. "Disciplined democracy", as he termed it, was admired by his many voters who re-elected him eight times. During Drapeau's terms in office Montreal became an internationally renowned city with the metro system, Expo 67 and the 1976 summer Olympic Games. Although a provincial investigation into the Olympics' cost overruns concluded he had mismanaged the project, he was re-elected in 1982, albeit by a reduced margin.

Jean Doré was elected mayor of the city in 1986, after Drapeau's retirement. His Montreal Citizen' Movement dominated council has begun to institute procedures for public consultation, city planning and urban design.

Nelson's Column, rising over Place Jacques-Cartier, dates from 1809 and is the oldest remaining memorial in Montreal. Surprisingly, Nelson faces away from the river. This is said to be the first monument to Napoléon's vanquisher. The statue portrays Lord Nelson in full uniform, holding a piece of mast surrounded by a ship's rigging. The original statue was of artificial stone imported from England. This material was less expensive and was thought to be more durable than stone or bronze. However, the statue deteriorated because of the elements and it was replaced in 1981.

If you are wondering why Nelson's victory should have been commemorated in Canada, Eric McLean has reported that news of Nelson's victory at Trafalgar was announced during a New Year's Eve celebration at Montréal's Exchange Coffee House. A number of people immediately decided to raise a monument. A number of well-known French Canadian families contributed, as did the Sulpician Fathers.

North of Notre-Dame Street is **Place Vauquelin**, which is the site of a monument to Jean Vauquelin (1728-1772), commander of the French fleet in New France and defender of Quebec City. The statue is the work of French sculptor Eugène Benèt.

The Silver Dollar Saloon was located at 174 Notre Dame. Its proprietor is said to have encrusted silver dollars in the floor. The building houses the municipal tourist office.

The Maison des Arts de la Sauvegarde (152 Notre-Dame East) was built between 1795 and 1805 and carefully restored by la Compagnie d'Assurance Vie la Sauvegarde when they purchased it in 1912. Originally, the lower floor of this house was probably used for living and sleeping, and the upstairs for storage. Other buildings had offices on the ground floor and living quarters above. This house is built of stone with a fire-wall rising above the line of the roof to prevent the spread of fire from one building to another. Since, in those days, space was limited, the custom was to build a broad house near the sidewalk and provide a garden in the rear. Houses were covered with whitewashed wood as protection from the elements. Notice the rough stone walls, shutter hooks, the tin roof and the small windows.

As you walk along Notre-Dame, you will see the three Palais de Justice, or Court Houses, each in a different architectural style.

7 L'ancien Palais de Justice

The Court House of 1856 was designed by John Ostell and Maurice Perrault, winners of an 1849 government competition. Ostell also designed the Customs House in Place Royale and the original McGill University Arts Building. This building is located on the site of an earlier court house which was built in 1800. It exemplifies the classical revival style, popular at that time, as indicated by the Ionic columns. The dome and third storey were added in 1890 at a cost twice that of the original construction. The wings of this rusticated greystone building are recessed to break the monotony. Many English and American court houses of the same vintage are very similar in style.

Civil Code cases were heard here. Unlike the other provinces which follow English common law, Quebec (as well as the state of Louisiana) adopted the Napoleonic Code. Originally, the court house was also used for official receptions such as the one which welcomed the Prince of Wales in 1860, when he inaugurated the Victoria Bridge. It is owned by the city administration, and houses the Commission d'Initiative et de Développement Économique de Montréal as well as a tourist office.

8 Nouveau Palais de Justice

Across the street, at 100 Notre-Dame, is the second court house which was used for criminal cases. It was designed by the Montréal architects L.A. Amos, C.J. Saxe and Ernest Cormier and completed in 1926. Cormier designed the bronze doors of this building, as well as those of the United Nations building (New York City) and of the Université de Montréal. The doors of the Palais de Justice are decorated with six bas-reliefs which illustrate the history of criminal law. The suspension of these heavy doors was so well executed by Edgar Barndt that only one man is needed to maneuver them. The Latin inscription on the cornice reads: "He who transgresses the law shall seek the help of the law in vain." The building now houses offices of the ministry of cultural affairs.

It is located on what was once part of Lambert Closse's land. He was awarded this fief in recognition of his bravery in fighting the Amerindians.

Place de la Justice is the dark glass building just east of St-Laurent. It was completed in 1971 and was designed by the architects David, Barett and Boulva, the firm which designed the Banque Canadienne Nationale building on Place d'Armes.

In Montreal's early days, St-Paul Street was the commercial centre. Originally, offices and stores were located on the ground floor with the upper storeys used for housing. As the city grew, more office space was required and by the 1850s new buildings were constructed on this street. They are not very tall because the elevator was not commonly used before the 1870s. Also, fire fighting facilities were inadequate for the protection of multistorey buildings.

The façades of these buildings are interestingly eclectic, with details varying between floors in a manner truly Victorian. As mentioned in the introduction, these stone skeleton buildings are remarkably modern in their use of glass and stone. In fact, some of them have glass-to-stone proportions superior to recent commercial buildings such as Place Ville-Marie.

At the time they were built, architects were beginning to take into account the needs of a technological society. Although they were unable to completely cast off classical vocabulary (in fact, they created cast iron capitals and Roman arches) their work does display some of the new principles postulated by Sullivan and Adler.

The commercial buildings between 38 and 60 are decorated in a mix of different styles.

Place-d'Armes metro station is nearby.

OLD MONTREAL
Tour C

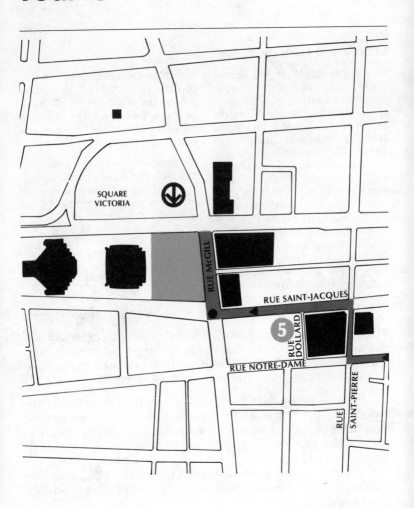

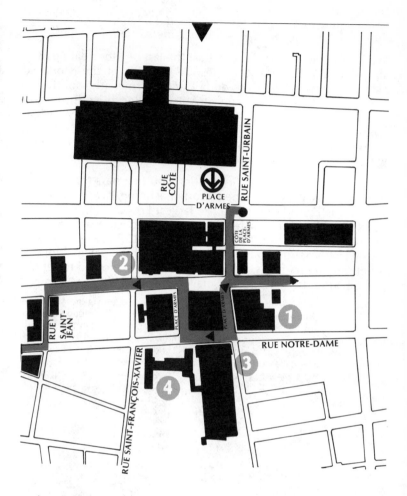

1 The New York Insurance
  Company
2 The Bank of Montreal
3 Église Notre-Dame
4 Vieux Séminaire
5 The Royal Bank

Tour C begins at the Place-d'Armes metro station.

Walk along St-Antoine Street, past the last of Montreal's pawn-shops. You will see a Romanesque building of the **Montreal Street Railway** at 102 Côte de la Place d'Armes (the southwest corner of St-Urbain Street and St-Antoine). Beside it is the façade of the McKim, Mead & White annex of the Bank of Montreal whose main building will be seen later on this walk. On the northwest corner of St-Antoine and St-Laurent stands a building with unusual, almost hieroglyphic, decorations.

Walking up the slope at St-Laurent, you first pass the modern building of **La Presse** and then its original home. *La Presse*, at 7 St-Jacques, is considered to be the largest French-language daily newspaper in all of North America. **Wolfred Nelson** once lived on this site. As one of the leaders of the 1837 Rebellion, he was exiled in perpetuity to Bermuda. With the principal goals of the rebels attained a few years later, Nelson was allowed to return and became the first elected mayor of Montreal.

Wolfred Nelson (1792-1863), born in Montreal, was surgeon general for the militia in 1812. Representative for Sorel from 1827 to 1830, he joined Papineau and called for armed resistence at the assembly at Saint-Charles in 1837. He led the Patriotes at Saint-Denis-sur-le-Richelieu and was captured and exiled to Bermuda in 1838. He returned to Montreal in 1842 and represented Richelieu in the legislature between 1844 and 1851. He was mayor of Montreal in 1854.

La Banque du Peuple, at 55 St-Jacques, was greatly damaged in a fire in 1980. This Italianate bank building (designed in 1873 by Perrault, Ménard and Venne) fits in well with the rest of the buildings on Place d'Armes and is another link in the chain of Montreal's history. The Banque du Peuple was the first French-Canadian bank in Montreal. In 1835 it opened its first office on the corner of St-François-Xavier and St-Sacrement.

Banque du Peuple was chartered in Montreal in 1844 by a private group created in 1835. At the time of Confederation it was one of the six largest banks in the country. Its prosperity lasted another 50 years but in the end one-third of the $5.3 million capital was lost.

Across the street, at 54 St-Jacques, is a house built in 1729. A restaurant has occupied the ground floor since the beginning of this century.

Place d'Armes, although not the oldest square in the city, is perhaps the most interesting historically because all the forces which shaped Montreal's history are represented in the buildings around it. To simplify the itinerary, the tour is not set out in chronological order, but follows instead the most direct route. For the sake of those who would rather approach the buildings in a chronological fashion, they were built in the following order: Vieux Séminaire 1680-83; Notre-Dame Church 1829; Bank of Montreal 1845; New York Insurance Company 1889; Aldred Building 1928; Banque Canadienne Nationale 1966.

1 The New York Insurance Company

The New York Insurance Company was completed in 1889 and was the first skyscraper in Montreal. It was designed by the American firm of Babb, Cook and Willard who chose Scotch firebrick and sandstone for the walls. The sculptures on the façade are by Henry Beaumont. This is one of the first major Montreal buildings that was not built in local greystone. It now houses the Société de Fiducie du Québec. Perfection of safe elevators in the United States during the 1850s enabled the construction of buildings more than six storeys high. Although this building was designed after the Chicago School had devised an architectural treatment for cast-iron skyscrapers, the New York Insurance Company building is very conservative in its design. While steel was used for the floors and the roof, masonry walls still support the structure on each floor. In this respect, the use of stone skeletons (as in buildings on the other Old Montreal tours) demonstrates a more advanced technique.

An example of Henry Beaumont's artistry.

The Aldred Building (507 Place-d'Armes) was built circa 1928, at about the time the last addition to the Sun Life Assurance building was made (see downtown tour), yet its architectural treatment was more modern than that of the Sun Life addition. The multiple set-backs might be more pleasing on a building three times its height. Art Deco lovers should visit the lobby to admire the richly decorated ceiling and elevator doors, and the delightful frieze featuring birds on telephone wires.

Place d'Armes' history begins in 1654 when the square served as a cemetery for the Hôtel-Dieu hospital located a block south of here. The area became a public space upon the opening of the first Notre-Dame Church in 1678, and a public square slowly took shape. A bust of George III was erected in its centre in 1773.

This was the first monument erected in the city. During the American occupation on the night of May 1, 1775, vandals removed the statue's head and scribbled "Here is the pope of Canada and the English sot" on the base. The head turned up years later in the old Place d'Armes' well and is now part of the McCord Museum collection.

During the 1832 electoral campaign, a riot erupted between the Patriotes, with **Jos Montferrand** at their head, and the Tories. At the beginning of the 1837 Rebellion, the site was again the scene of a battle when the Doric Club attacked the Sons of Liberty.

The city had acquired the site from the Sulpicians in 1836, and in 1848 the square was converted into a fenced-in park with an attractive fountain where the statue of de Maisonneuve is now situated. Undoubtedly, one of the reasons this was done was to prevent the public square from being used for political confrontations.

Joseph Favre (Jos Monferrand) was a legendary strongman. Born in Montreal (1802-1864) to a family known for is physical strength. Tall (six feet, four inches, 1.96 m), muscular yet slim and agile, he was said to be able to make a mark with his heel in the ceiling. He won his first boxing match at the age of 17 when he responded to the challenge of an English boxer who had been proclaimed champion of Canada after a match at Champ-de-Mars. Monferrand knocked him out with one punch.

Paul de Chomedey de Maisonneuve, the founder of Montreal, is honored by a **statue**, sculpted by Philippe Hébert. It was unveiled in 1895 by Sir Adolphe Chapleau, the lieutenant-governor of the province. The statue shows de Maisonneuve holding the banner of France; around him are other Montreal pioneers: Jeanne Mance, one of several women who helped found the city in 1642 and who was the first secular nurse in North America — she established Montreal's first hospital, Hôtel-Dieu; Louis Hébert, portrayed with scythe in hand, was the first farmer in New France; Lambert Closse, the other European, was town major and defended the fort from 1647 to 1651. The Amerindian is one of the Iroquois who frequently attacked the French usurpers of their land. (The Amerindian threat lasted from the founding of the city until 1660, when a truce was signed.) The dog is Pilote, said to have had an uncanny knack of sniffing out the presence of the hostile Iroquois.

Bas-reliefs at the base of the statue indicate the founding of the Congrégation de Notre-Dame de Montréal; the first mass celebrated at Pointe-à-Callière in 1642; Maisonneuve shooting the Iroquois chief in 1644 at Place d'Armes; the Massacre of Dollard des Ormeaux's men at Long Sault in 1660.

2 The Bank of Montreal

The Bank of Montreal in 1891.

The Bank of Montreal was the first bank in Lower Canada (Quebec). It was founded in 1817, at a time when British, Dutch, Spanish, French and Portuguese coins were all accepted as legal tender in the colony. Its original office was at 32 St-Paul Street. In 1819 a building was constructed on St-Jacques, just west of the present building. This Palladian building dates from 1845-48 and was designed by John Wells. The original dome was eliminated in 1859 and then replaced 44 years later. The New York firm of McKim, Mead & White remodelled the building in 1905, constructing an immense, awe-inspiring basilica-shaped main hall graced with Corinthian columns of dark green syenite. The American architects extended the building to St-Antoine and added a fine façade on that street. Inside the building is a fascinating Museum of Numismatics open during regular banking hours.

The façade on Place d'Armes has Corinthian columns and pediment sculptures designed by the Scottish sculptor John Steele. In addition to a sailor and a colonist, music and literature are depicted, as is the coat-of-arms of the bank. The latter is flanked by two Amerindians — one being the "noble savage," while the other is portrayed as rejecting the products of European civilization.

3 Église Notre-Dame

The church of Notre-Dame has a history as old as the city. The first chapel was a simple bark-covered structure built within the fort in 1642. Seventeen years later the congregation moved to a new chapel near the Hôtel-Dieu Hospital. It had a stone foundation and was made of wood. In 1678, the Baroque Revival church of Notre-Dame was begun on Notre-Dame Street, following the European style of planting the church right in the centre of the main street. It was demolished in 1830.

The current structure, one of the first Gothic Revival style churches in Canada, was inaugurated in 1829. It was designed by an Irish-American architect, James O'Donnell, who had already completed two Gothic-style churches in the United States. He outdid himself for Notre-Dame. His contemporaries considered this church the most magnificent in North America, and Gothic Revival became the predominant style for Catholic churches in Quebec for the next 75 years. O'Donnell was influenced by the Gothic Revival as expressed in England. Notre-Dame has been compared to London's Saint Martin's-in-the-fields. O'Donnell converted to Catholicism and his body is buried in a crypt in the basement of the church.

Lack of funds delayed the construction of the 227-feet (69 m) high twin towers until the early 1840s when they were finished by John Ostell who followed O'Donnell's plans. They, too, have an English flavor and resemble Westminster more than they do Notre-Dame de Paris. The main bell, (known as Jean-Baptiste or le Gros Bourdon) is still one of the largest in the world, weighing about 12 tons. While, originally, a dozen men were required to ring it, today it is powered by electricity. It is used only on special occasions. The three statues on the façade were executed by Baccirini in 1864, in artificial stone. They represent Saint Joseph, Saint John the Baptist and the Virgin Mary.

Place d'Armes in 1873.

Not until 1876 were there sufficient funds to complete the majestic interior which was designed by Victor Bourgeau. His use of the Gothic style was modified by incorporation of Canadian techniques such as wood carving and carpentry. Eleven stained-glass windows were unveiled in 1929, the church's centenary. Their subjects were sketched by art historian J.B. Lagacé and executed in Limoges, Belgium. Notre-Dame Church is a veritable treasure house of Quebec religious art, for all of her most important artists collaborated in its construction and decoration. For many years, this church dominated Montreal's skyline. It is one of the few 19th-century buildings still used for the original function.

4 Vieux Séminaire

The Seminary is the oldest building in Montréal. The Société de St-Sulpice was founded by Jean-Jacques Olier. The Sulpicians came to New France in 1657 and constructed a residence in the gardens, south of the present building. Their first building was replaced in 1680 by the one still standing. In 1663, The Associates for the Conversion of the Savages of New France in the Island of Montreal had passed on to the Gentlemen of St-Sulpice the debts and privileges of their society. Thus the Sulpicians became seigneurs of the island of Montreal and nearly every piece of property on the island can be traced back to a deed, or lease, issued by the Sulpicians during the last 300 years.

As Father Superior, Gabriel de Queylus played a crucial role in the organization and establishment of Ville-Marie. The Sulpicians recruited and equipped the colonists with money, tools and arms. They had a great deal of authority and influence during the first part of the history of Montreal. Dollier de Casson, a later superior of the Sulpicians, was Montreal's first historian and was also responsible for the laying of the city's first streets.

The architect's original sketch for the Seminary has been preserved. It shows a large symmetrical building with cellar windows, three storeys and an attic. At each end of the building was a small square tower. This is a plan similar to that of some monasteries in France. Although the courtyard wall is not shown on the original plans, it is reported to have been in place in 1712. The entire east wing was pulled down in 1850 to make room for a new administration building. All that remains is a trace of the fireplace which can be seen in the courtyard wall.

The Seminary clock, the work of Paul Labrosse, is said to have been installed before 1701. For a long time it was the only public clock in Montreal. It was repaired in 1751 and modified, so that the hours would chime inside the seminary as well as outside. A new set of works was installed in 1821, which was replaced by an electric movement in 1966.

Banque Canadienne Nationale, the black glass skyscraper at 500 Place d'Armes, was until 1975 the head office of one of the two Canadian banks directed by French-Canadians. It later merged with Banque Provinciale to form the **Banque Nationale du Canada.**

St-Jacques Street, circa 1887.

Until the 1860s, **St-Jacques** was a street lined with three storey buildings, with shops on the ground floor and living quarters above. Then merchants left the street and moved to Victoria Square, while banks and other investment institutions opened offices in the five-storey commercial buildings which were constructed during that decade. At that time Montreal was Canada's financial centre and many an audacious enterprise was planned from these offices during the next century. St. James Street — as this street has always been referred to by the anglophone establishment — remained Canada's Wall Street until around 1970.

The Royal Bank's 1907 head office, at 221 St-Jacques, was used by the Banque Provinciale for a number of years before it merged with the Banque Canadienne Nationale. Howard C. Stone was the architect. The monumental statues represent four of Canada's most important natural resources.

Tattersall, at 244 St-Jacques, was once the main office of Max Aitken (later **Lord Beaverbrook**). He controlled the Steel Company of Canada, Canada Cement and the Eastern Power Company from behind this superbly-adorned façade. Edward Maxwell designed this 1889 building.

William Maxwell Aitken (Lord Beaverbrook), press magnate and statesman, was born in Maple, Ontario (1879-1964). He was one of the most important Canadian industrialists and later became a major newspaper publisher in England. He was elected to the House of Commons at Westminster in 1911 and became a baron in 1917.

The Montreal Star, once Montreal's largest English daily paper, was located at 245 St-Jacques until it ceased publication in 1979. Francis Dunlop designed this building in 1899 with reinforced floors to support the heavy printing presses.

One portion of the **City and District Savings Bank** at 262 St-Jacques, dates from 1870. You can see that Michel Laurent was successful in designing an opulent façade without making it seem overbearing.

(Turn left on St-Jean to reach Notre-Dame Street) The former head office of Sun Life Assurance Company is at 266 Notre-Dame. While a fire heavily damaged it in 1979, all four of its attractive façades are still intact. A journalist at *La Presse* recently described the façade as having as many architectural and sculpted details as an insurance policy has restrictive clauses.

The St-Jean Street side was built in 1883 for Samuel Waddell, a railway supplier. Sun Life bought the adjoining lot in 1889 and commissioned Robert Findlay to construct 266 Notre-Dame. Henry Beaumont also did the sculptures on the façade of this building. Sun Life bought Waddell's building in 1897. An architectural firm purchased the buildings after the fire, renovated them to lease to stores and offices. (Return to St-Jacques via St-Pierre Street).

Molson's Bank at 288 St-Jacques is in the Second Empire style, popular when it was constructed in 1866. Its architect, George Browne, was one of Montreal's most prolific. The doors of the manager's office and the boardroom are magnificent. Above the entrance is a bust, said to be that of John Molson. Not only did Mr. Molson have his own bank in which to deposit the profits from his brewery, he also printed his own money. Some of these banknotes are on display in the Bank of Montreal Museum.

The stucco and wrought iron decorations in the lobby and along the staircase of the building directly opposite (275 St-Jacques) are very well executed. Sculpted above the entrance are representations of peace and industry.

Bas-relief sculpture at 275 St-Jacques.

A 1907 city by-law allowed commercial buildings to be built as high as ten storeys. This greatly changed the appearance of the street. Two decades later an amendment set a limit of 110 feet (33 m), above which set backs were required in an effort to prevent monolithic towers. The Royal Bank Building is a good example of the effect of this by-law.

5 The Royal Bank

The former head office of the Royal Bank (360 St-Jacques) was built in 1928 by the New York architects York & Sawyer under the supervision of S.G. Davenport, the bank's chief architect. This was the first building in Montreal which was taller than the spires of Notre-Dame Church. When it was built, the Royal Bank was the tallest edifice in all of the British Empire.

The building is made up of distinct parts: a massive pedestal, a tower with two setbacks and a lantern dome crowning the apex of the roof. The details of the windows and the portal of the main façade are reminiscent of Michelozzo's Medici Palace in Florence. However the composition of the pedestal takes elements from the San Carlo Theatre in Naples. The pedestal displays channel-coursed masonry, with the stone projecting in an attractive manner. Above are a row of columns in the Tuscan order which are terminated by double pilasters framing the coasts of arms of various provinces. A cornice completes the parapet.

The corners of the tower portion of the building are accentuated by a change in the texture of the stone which gives an impression of stability to the edifice. A colonnade and horizontal bands highlight the tower. The three attic storeys of the tower are terminated in a pyramid roof and capped by a lantern to give the building a distinctive profile.

The interior can be described in one word: ostentation. The doors of the main entrance are framed in a series of oversized bronze replicas of Canadian coins. The lobby has a heavily coffered ceiling whose modelled relief ornaments are in dull rose, blue and gold.

To the right and left are arched openings to vaulted halls of lesser height. A short, broad flight of marble steps opens onto the main hall, creating a majestic impression from the street level below. The arches and the walls of the entire interior are in dressed limestone with Brianhill sandstone, ranging in color from reddish buff to cool grey. Plinths of dark grey marble heighten the effect. The walls of the main banking room are decorated by a succession of sculpted circles bearing the coats of arms of Canada's provinces, and the cities of Montreal and Halifax. The arches over the openings on the exterior are repeated inside. Above is a dentilled string with a fairly deep frieze of opposed chimeras and urns in relief. The heavily coffered ceiling shows patterns of chimeras interspersed with rosettes. The tellers' counters are in Levanto marble and the screens are in bronze. The floors are of travertine inlaid with a broad running border in mosaic tile. A bronze inlay in the centre bears Canada's royal coat of arms.

In other parts of the building, the square coffered, barrel-vaulted ceilings rest on rectangular pillars. Sculpture and goldleaf decorate these vaulted ceilings which are inspired by the Classical Roman era.

The Nesbitt Thomson Company building, at 355 St-Jacques, was three-storeys tall when initially built for the Merchant's Bank of Canada in 1871-72. The five storeys added 30 years later were in the same style; it is fortunate that the additional brick storey is set back from the façade and, hence, almost invisible. The ground floor lobby is one of the finest in the district, especially now that its original splendor has been restored.

The building at 363 St-Jacques Street was originally Nordheimer's Hall where lectures, concerts and receptions were held. The large bay windows and vigorous stone façade are suprisingly modern, given its 1888 construction date.

Haymarket Square, in the early 1800s. Saint Patrick's Church (to the right) is still standing. At that time the buildings around the square were mainly residential.

Victoria Square at the turn of the century. By this time residences had given way to commercial buildings.

After the city walls were demolished in 1801, what is now **Victoria Square** became known as Commissioners' Square. After the 1835 installation of a sewer system and wood sidewalks, the name was changed to Haymarket Square. Montreal entered a period of rapid growth during the 1850s which was also a decade of serious fires, some of which damaged buildings on Victoria Square.

The residential buildings around Victoria Square gave way to commercial establishments. Prominence came to the square with the construction of the first Morgan's Store in 1845.

In 1860, the square received its present name, to mark the opening of the Victoria Bridge by the Prince of Wales. An 1866 photograph shows churches and elegant homes to the north, gardens in the south and, to one side Saint Patrick's Hall, a social centre for the Irish community. The hall succumbed to flames in 1872. The **statue** of Queen Victoria is by Marshall Wood and was unveiled in 1873.

During the 1880s, Victoria Square attained the height of its importance as Montreal's central business district. Many merchants and manufacturers left St. James street to move to the Square. So did department stores and a number of furniture and shoe factories, but most banks and other financial institutions remained on St. James. The first YMCA was built on Victoria Square in 1873.

When Morgan's moved away from the commercial district to Ste-Catherine Street in 1892, people scoffed. However, Morgan's quickly attracted the affluent English clientèle of the Golden Square Mile. This move ushered in the decline of Victoria Square's commercial importance, with other department stores quickly following Morgan's up Beaver Hall Hill. Morgan's is still there, now known as The Bay. The YMCA moved away from the square in 1890. The original building was destroyed by fire 30 years later.

By 1910 the square was on its way to becoming a vacuous, undefined and uncherished public left-over. Street re-routing and other changes during the construction of the metro largely destroyed any remaining sense of coherence. The statue of Queen Victoria was moved to its present remote location during the construction of the metro, destroying the focus of the square. Landscaping, completed in 1979, has made some improvement and the Square is certainly crowded with nature-starved office workers from the nearby buildings, during sunny lunch hours. Nevertheless, this open area is a far cry from the attractive green space of Victorian times.

The federal government office building north of St-Antoine (circa 1950) stands in the place of a very handsome group of furniture factories built 75 years earlier. Today, the northwest view is blocked by a mass of 20th century architecture, including the 1983 Complexe Bell/Banque Nationale. But last century's four- and six-storey buildings still stand to the northeast; behind them you can see the steeple of St.Patrick's Church.

The distinctive Metro Entrance (St-Antoine, corner McGill Avenue) was a gift from the City of Paris to mark the 1966 opening of Montreal's subway system. Hector Guimard's many metro entrances in Paris are well-known examples of Art Nouveau. Examine the sinuous forms of the light-posts; this 1890s style was noted for its use of plant-like designs. Would Queen Victoria have appreciated such French art in her square?

On the site of Saint Patrick's Hall, at 759 McGill, is **Canada Steamships Lines**. It was originally built for Greenshields Wholesale Dry Goods in 1903, while the small addition at 751 was built two years later. The construction of a retail store on the square was then a very shortsighted business decision and the store was soon forced to move to follow its clients. The building was extensively renovated by its present occupants when they moved in, as can be inferred from the 1930s style lobby.

At Fortifications Lane is a historic plaque which commemorates the old fortified walls of the city which ran along what is now McGill Street.

The Bank of Nova Scotia building at 715 McGill was once the Eastern Townships Bank. However all that remains of the 1909 building is the lower floor façades on McGill and St-Jacques streets.

The Place Victoria building, known as the **Tour de la Bourse**, was erected in 1966 as the fourth home of the Montreal Stock Exchange. This is a 47-storey building which contains a two-level shopping arcade connected to a metro station. The building was designed by architect Luigi Moretti and engineer Pier Luigi Nervi who created a powerful-looking tower supported by four well-proportioned trusses, faced in pre-cast concrete. The building is curtained in aluminum and divided into three equal units which are separated by mechanical floors providing air-conditioning and other services.

In 1986 the green space of Victoria Square was extensively redesigned. The result, at least for the area south of St-Antoine, is not a great improvement as a great deal of concrete has been added and the sunniest area — much appreciated by lunching office workers — now has no seating.

(Although our tours of Old Montreal have included the most important buildings, a number of attractive and historic edifices have unavoidably been left out. We hope we have provided sufficient material about the development of architecture in Montreal to allow you to strike out on your own and discover other points of beauty)

The Square Victoria metro station has two entrances, one at McGill and St-Jacques, and the afore-mentioned one at St-Antoine.

DOWNTOWN

DOWNTOWN MONTREAL

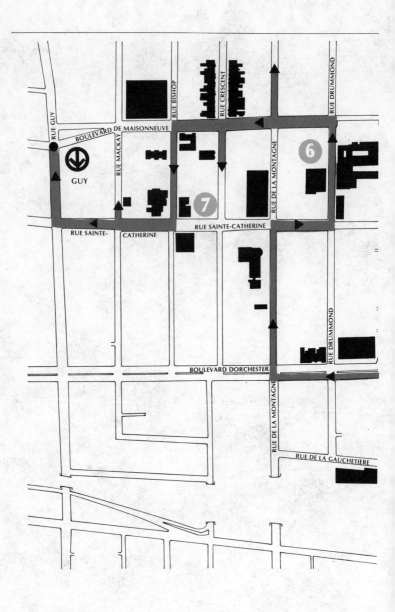

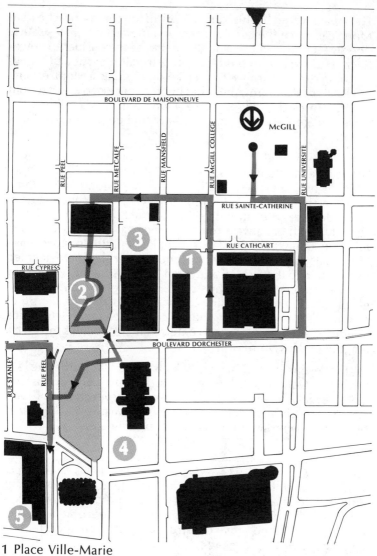

1 Place Ville-Marie
2 Dominion Square
3 Sun Life Building
4 Cathédrale Marie-Reine-
  du-Monde
5 Windsor Station
6 Drummond Medical
  Building
7 The Coronation Building

The area covered by this tour comprises the commercial heart of Montreal. Since the late 19th century, the section of Ste-Catherine Street between Guy and Bleury has been considered downtown. However, with the recent construction of such buildings as Complexe Desjardins, Université du Québec à Montréal and the Palais des Congrès, there has been a concerted effort to shift the centre of the city eastward. Gone are the days when the corner of Ste-Catherine and Peel was dubbed the focal point of Montreal.

It may not have the grandeur of New York's Fifth Avenue or Paris's Grands Boulevards, but Ste-Catherine is still the street which Montrealers (especially anglophone Montrealers) think of when they speak of downtown. Unlike many an American city, Montreal's central business district never declined in importance. It has always remained the heart of the city, pulsating every moment of the day. The major department stores have their flagships on Ste-Catherine, and smaller shops are deemed to have joined the fashion and retail "establishment" when they open an outlet either on the street or in one of the shopping levels of the adjoining buildings. Downtown is also the centre of Montreal's famed underground city which connects office buildings, shopping areas and entertainment facilities through a lengthy pedestrian network.

In the evening, the streets which cross Ste-Catherine are thronged with people going to restaurants, bars, discos and clubs. Even after-hours (liquor licenses prevent alcohol sales after 3 a.m.), some discos and restaurants remain open. By day or by night, downtown Montreal is an exciting area.

Itinerary

McGill metro station, where this 2-hour tour begins, is a perfect introduction to downtown. Linked via underground pedestrian walkways to Sherbrooke and Ste-Catherine streets, this station serves as the hub of downtown today. It has become a magnet for commercial and office construction with each new building

McGill College Street south of Sherbrooke, 1869. Note the stone fence.

provided with direct access to the subway system through this station. It connects directly with three separate shopping complexes, two department stores and two office buildings.

Art Deco aficionados may be interested in visiting the ninth floor of Eaton Department Store which is connected to the metro station. Here is a restaurant designed by Jacques Carlu in 1931, inspired by the dining room of the luxury liner *Île-de-France*. The restaurant consists of a lofty chamber flanked by horizontal windows and supported by a range of pink and soft grey marble columns. A 35-foot (11 m) high ceiling, two pre-Raphaelite murals and brightly decorated frescoes with a culinary theme complete the effect. Le 9ᵉ is one of Montreal's finest Art Deco interiors.

This part of Montreal's central business district is undergoing profound transformation. Once all the office tower/shopping complexes are completed, there will be many times more retail space linked through underground passageway than exists on Ste-Catherine, hitherto the most important shopping artery. The underground network used to be primarily north-south and as such complementary to the east-west commercial street.

Now shoppers will be able to walk in a climate-controlled environment from The Bay and the Promenades de la Cathédrale shopping mall to Eaton, and the shops of 2020 and 2001 University, Centre Eaton, Place Montréal Trust and then to Simpson and Le Cours Mont-Royal five blocks away. Up until now, Montreal's underground network was divided into two separate parts, with no link made below Ste-Catherine Street. New tunnels below Ste-Catherine Street will link this "super-mall" to the shops and offices of Place Ville Marie, Central Station and Place Bonaventure.

It may seem like an ideal solution for shopping in Montreal's harsh climate. However, there are profound differences between the public street and the semi-private areas of enclosed shopping complexes. The owner of each building can choose whom he wishes to allow inside or to exclude, and what activities are permissible.

Is the market large enough to support all these stores? Will anyone choose to shop outdoors? Unfortunately, no studies have been carried out to analyze the economic and social impact of these new projects. A number of the clothing and shoe stores on Ste-Catherine have already given way to fast-food restaurants, video arcade stores and other less appealing uses.

Should Ste-Catherine Street continue to decline we may lose not just a shopping street, but also Montreal's Ramblas, a place for people to promenade, to look at storefronts, yes, but also to look at other people. Montrealers take pride in this street which has a 3 a.m. rush-hour, both of cars and pedestrians. Will this continue?

(Walk down McGill College Avenue, turn left on Cathcart and then right on University to appreciate the entire form of Place Ville-Marie)

1 Place Ville-Marie

The collection of office buildings known as Place Ville-Marie have the cruciform Royal Bank Building as focal point. It was built above the Canadian National railway tunnel which leads to the suburbs north of the mountain. Although when it was erected in 1959, downtown was beginning to shift eastward along just-widened Dorchester Boulevard, this distinctive addition to Montreal's built environment kept the focus on this part of the city. Place Ville-Marie was the first building in Montreal to combine office, retail, hotel and leisure functions. It is not just the cross shape — a response to the need for natural light in an edifice with so much floor space — which distinguishes Place Ville-Marie. The shopping promenade underneath was the very first such area protected from Montreal's harsh winter climate.

Although its uniform grid plan might appear pedestrian compared to Les Terrasses, the promenade is always crowded. Fifteen thousand people work in the buildings, while more than 75,000 pass throught it each day. Place Ville-Marie symbolizes Montreal. Aside from the fountain with an expressionistic reclining woman, and the noon-time lunch crowd, the plaza of Place-Ville-Marie has virtually nothing of interest. It was initially designed simply to set off the cruciform building as was the style in the early 1960s. The roofing over of the stairways is not really much of an improvement. Its pavement is frequently in shadow and buffetted by high winds which are caused by the narrow distance between the tall buildings and also by the cruciform shape; a flaw which is apparent in a number of downtown streets.

The Capitol Theatre.

The Strand Theatre.

The Capitol Theatre.

Loews during renovations.

Guardian Trust is located at Mansfield, at what used to be the "west end" branch of the Bank of Montreal. When this building was constructed in 1889 this was almost the outskirts of the city. The building was carefully renovated and the exterior cleaned after the bank vacated the premises in 1982.

At one time a number of fine movie theatres were located on this part of Ste-Catherine Street. Few survive and those that do have been greatly changed. The Palace has been completely transformed; the Capitol and the Strand are gone, replaced in 1973 by a smoked-glass building which retains the Capitol's name, but nothing else.

During the era of the silent movie, the Strand was the home of pianist William Eckstein, one of the world's greatest motion picture interpreters. The Capitol, designed by Thomas Lamb and opened in 1921, was the finest of Montreal's cinemas. The interior of these theatres, along with the Loew's, were designed in the eclectic manner which combined the style of a grand 19th-century opera house with the exotica of the movies themselves. The Loew's (1917) was subdivided into five theatres in 1976. Although most of the original plasterwork remains, its beauty has been diminished by the renovations.

On the south side of Ste-Catherine, between Metcalfe and Peel streets, is the **Dominion Square Building**, built in 1927 in the Florentine style. Ross and MacDonald were the architects. Construction of a major tourist information facility and underground parking garage began in 1986.

Above, the square in 1914. Note the YMCA building which was later replaced by the Sun Life Building (what you can see next page).

2 Dominion Square

"Like Trafalgar Square in London, it is surrounded by an impressive array of public buildings of various styles; here, however, they are at least related to each other by the green space which they face. Reflecting the taste of those days, it appears like an endearing city-size 'bric-à-brac'. Around this square is found the largest concentration of notable public, religious, and commercial buildings that Victorian architecture ever produced in Montreal... Saint-James (Mary Queen of the World) Cathedral, for instance, is a chrystallization of the neo-Baroque trend introduced by Bishop Bourget... Windsor Station is unquestionably the most interesting monument in the square and is also the one in Canada which best reflects the architectural vision of Henry Hobson Richardson. The very beautiful Saint George's Church is one of the finest examples of neo-Gothic structures in Montreal or in Canada. The initial Windsor Hotel reflected the cosmopolitanism of Paris in the days of the Second Empire... Today, Dominion Square has lost some of its glamor: the original part of the Windsor Hotel has been demolished and the neighboring skyscrapers have not only considerably disparaged the cathedral's pride and dwarfed Windsor Station's scale, but also disrupted the feeling of spatial unity around the square. In spite of this change (and a somewhat constrictive landscaping) the square remains the landmark it has been for a century. As a centre of attraction for pedestrian and vehicular traffic it is a place that generates activities and is one of the most authentic, magnetic and magnificent environments in Montreal." (Jean-Claude Marsan, *Montréal en évolution*)

Dominion Square became a Roman Catholic cemetery in 1799. St-Antoine cemetery was used to bury many of the victims of the 1832 cholera epidemic. At that time, the cemetery extended west as far as Stanley Street, and south to where the cathedral now stands. By the 1850s, residential buildings began to appear around the square and, as the population expanded, the city outgrew this burial place. It was decided to establish a larger cemetery on the mountain in 1855.

As the city spread out, the English population began to gradually build houses in the area to the northwest of the city. The old cemetery was subdivided and the tombstones and coffins which were exhumed were moved to the new cemetery, off Côte-des-Neiges Road.

While the land was being cleared, a controversy arose over the exhumation of the graves. Some people were outraged at the sacriligious way of removing the bones. Others feared that a new outbreak of cholera would result from the digging up of the remains of those who had died from the disease. The Sanitary Association of Montreal recommended that the city make the area into a park. An 1869 petition convinced the municipal authorities to adopt this plan, and Dominion Square became a public park soon after. The remaining graves were left untouched and some were discovered years later. One was found near the main entrance of the Windsor Hotel during construction of the Canadian Imperial Bank of Commerce Building in the early 1960s.

3 Sun Life Building

Across Mansfield Street from Dominion Square is the immense grey granite "temple" of the Sun Life Building, which replaced the YMCA in 1914. The insurance company was originally located in a building just off St-Jacques Street when that street served the functions that Ste-Catherine does today. Sun Life decided to move here when Dominion Square became the new downtown. The 1914 building is to the southwest. Two wings (one 26-storey, and one 10-storey) were added on the north and east sides in the 1920s. At that time this was the largest building in Canada.

In the centre of the square is a monument to the fallen soldiers of the Boer War in South Africa. It was designed in 1907 by the architect brothers Edward and William Maxwell and sculpted by George W. Hill.

Across the square, the **statue** of the Scottish poet Robert Burns (1759-96) watches the remnant of Windsor Hotel. The hotel (1170 Peel Street), Montreal's grandest in its time, was designed by American archictects Hardenbergh and Gilbert. It included an Egyptian and a Turkish Room as well as a French Empire dining room. All that remains of the hotel today is the addition built in 1906. Originally, the hotel extended to Dorchester Boulevard but the main part was demolished after a series of small fires, giving way to the 45-storey Canadian Imperial Bank of Commerce in 1962. The Windsor has been converted into office space, and an atrium added. Note the Henry Moore sculpture near the corner.

Before crossing Dorchester Boulevard to go the cathedral southwest of the square, take a look at the statue (facing south) of Sir Wilfred Laurier, prime minister of Canada between 1896 and 1911. It was conceived by Émile Brunet. The Sun Life fountain of 1897, commemorating Queen Victoria's diamond jubilee, was also sculpted by George W. Hill. Findlay was the architect.

The rotunda of Windsor Hotel, 1880.

4 Cathédrale Marie-Reine-du-Monde

Mary, Queen of the World Cathedral was originally named in honor of Saint James (Cathédrale Saint-Jacques). It was built between 1875 and 1894 under the direction of the church architect, Victor Bourgeau, as a replacement for the cathedral on St-Denis Street which burnt down in 1852. It is a reduced-scale reproduction of Saint Peter's in the Vatican City. Monseigneur Bourget, second bishop of Montreal, decided to place the new Roman Catholic cathedral in the western part of the city, challenging the Protestant churches in their fief on Dominion Square.

Bourgeau was vehemently opposed to the idea of copying Saint Peter's. As an architect, he considered such a replication, especially on a smaller scale, to be a travesty. Despite his principles, he was obliged to come to the aid of Father Michaud, the amateur who was placed in charge of the project. Inside, the canopy under the dome is exquisite. It was executed by Victor Vincent in 1900, and is a copy of Bernini's baldachino in Saint Peter's.

The cathedral is overshadowed by Place Ville-Marie.

In front of the cathedral is the **statue** of Bishop Ignace Bourget (1799-1885) sculpted in 1903 by Louis-Philippe Hébert. Hébert was a well-known sculptor of the time, responsible for many Montreal monuments such as the one of Paul de Maisonneuve, Place d'Armes. Monumental sculpture was an important component of architectural design in the late 1800s.

(Walk to the part of the square which is south of Dorchester Boulevard)

The **statue** of Sir John A. MacDonald, Canada's first Prime Minister, was placed in the south part of the square, now officially called Place du Canada, in 1894. It is the work of English sculptor George Wade. A tomb, complete with headstone, was disinterred near the statue in 1931. Found were the remains of one John Henry of Galway, Ireland, buried 80 years before. He was reburied in the same place.

From the southwest corner of Dominion Square (at the intersection of de la Gauchetière and Peel), you can see the Château Champlain Hotel, resembling an immense cheese grater.

A bit to the east of it is **Place Bonaventure**, a massive beige concrete building which combines exposition hall, hotel, roof-top garden, shopping promenade and showrooms. The network of pedestrian passageways is complex. It is patterned on the paths of those who use it, and the architect has highlighted certain focal points of activity which serve to punctuate the pattern.

Bonaventure metro station was designed as an extension of the urban stage. Architect Victor Prus used materials common to the street to bring the city-dweller through a series of familiar experiences. It is one of the most important metro stations in Montreal, since it is connected by an underground network to Windsor and Central stations, Place Ville-Marie, Place du Canada. "It is a veritable urban cross-roads in a bewitching spatial volume modelled on a succession of groined vaults," remarked an article in *The Canadian Architect*.

5 Windsor Station

Windsor Station was the first commercial building on the square. Before it, only churches and houses lined these streets. Montreal's first train station was in Dalhousie Square, near the old Quebec Gate in the eastern part of Old Montreal. The Canadian Pacific Railway Company (CPR) decided to establish its offices and operations further west and chose Dominion Square as the new site.

After the construction of the transcontinental railway, the CPR chose well-known New York architect, **Bruce Price**, to design the station and head office. This building is of great historical and architectural importance. Price used the Richardsonian style characterized by reinforced openings, rusticated stone and arched windows. The building displays strength and power. Price's original building extends to the third bay window along de la Gauchetière and to the third window beyond the square turret of the façade on Peel Street.

As the railroad company grew, so did its offices. In 1900, Edward Maxwell designed the wing along de la Gauchetière. By maintaining the use of arcades, his and later additions are in keeping with the original building. Maxwell was also responsible for a number of CPR hotels and many residences in the Golden Square Mile. In 1906 a brick extension along de la Gauchetière was added and six years later the wing on Peel Street was extended all the way to St-Antoine. Other additions were made in the early 1950s.

Windsor Station's concourse was completed in 1913 and its glass roof makes it worth a visit. The bronze statue was a donation of the MacCarthy Foundation. It was installed in 1921 to honor those who constructed the transcontinental railroad.

Windsor Station is one of the few 19th-century buildings still remaining on Dominion Square. It has been the scene of important events in the history of the people of Canada. Many soldiers left Montreal from this station to go off to battle. Many immigrants fleeing the poverty of Europe arrived here, some to remain in Montreal, many more to continue on to the Prairies. A building like this is a witness to history.

Thus, when Canadian Pacific announced in the early 1970s that

it planned to demolish Windsor Station, many people were appalled. A number of groups, including the Jacques Viger Commission and Friends of Windsor Station, were successful in lobbying to save this architectural and historic monument.

Glasswork in the Windsor Station concourse.

The station was a precursor to buildings in the same style which soon appeared across Canada. **Price** was one of the most influential American architects working in Canada. It was he who launched the Château style in this country. His first Canadian work was the Château Frontenac (Quebec City). He also designed the Banff Springs Hotel, Viger Station and Royal Victoria College.

Saint George's Anglican Church was built in 1870 in the Gothic Revival style by William Thomas (also the architect of the Mount Stephen Club). The spires on the tower were added 20 years later. The first Saint George's had been built in 1842 on Notre-Dame Street. When the anglophone population moved west, the congregation also moved. The main pulpit was taken from the original church. Wood sculptures on the sanctuary, choir and the baptismal fonts were executed in England, while the transept screens and the chapel sculptures are the work of the Casavants in Ste-Hyacinthe, Quebec. It is interesting to note that the tapestry and the pulpit in the chapel were donated by Westminster Abbey and were used during Queen Elizabeth's coronation in 1952.

By 1879, the area around Dominion Square included a number of places of worship: the Methodist Church of Canada (corner of Peel and Dorchester), Cathédrale Saint-Jacques, (Mary, Queen of the World), the Knox Presbyterian (corner of Mansfield and Dorchester), Saint Paul's Church (site of the Queen Elizabeth Hotel); Erskine Presbyterian (site of the Dominion Square Building); the American Presbyterian (corner Dorchester and Drummond).

It is not suprising, then, that at a dinner given in his honor at the Windsor Hotel in 1881, noted humorist Mark Twain said: "This is the first time I ever was in a city where you couldn't throw a brick without breaking a church window."

The Hotel Laurentien was located between Dorchester Boulevard and Saint George's Church. This was the first large commercial building in Montreal to be faced with aluminium. Its reasonably priced rooms and downtown location attracted a regular clientèle. Nine years after the hotel was demolished in 1977, an office tower was built on the site. It is only a co-incidence that it bears a similar name, since its principal tenant is an insurance company with no links to the hotel.

Centre Sheraton is on Dorchester Street, one block to the west. Promoters had already spent $30 million on this 900-room hotel when construction was interrupted in the late 1970s. The original investors were unwilling to risk more money after a series of poor tourist seasons in Montreal. The hotel finally opened in 1982 after the Sheraton chain took it over. A number of important works of art, including paintings by local contemporary artist Lucie Laporte, are displayed in the hotel.

Until 1985 there was a small row of greystone houses on the north side of Dorchester a block west of here. After the street was widened, it lost its elegance — originally rivalling Sherbrooke Street — and the homes were converted to restaurants and rooming houses.

Mountain Street is flanked by parking lots. It is on the edge of a neighborhood made up of just seven short streets. This small district is bounded by Sherbrooke, Peel, Dorchester and Mackay which combine the varied intimacy of New York's Greenwich Village with the contrived elegance of Toronto's Yorkville. Fine 19th-century homes have been converted to every possible use. The area's restaurants, bars and discos are favorite haunts of singles and students, while art galleries and designer shops attract the wealthier browser. At first glance, one sees a vibrant, active sector. But the glamor and activity of Crescent Street on a warm summer night mask the forces of deterioration at work in this neighborhood. Due to its position just west of the central business district, this area became the target of redevelopment pressures in the 1960s and early 1970s.

The charm of a few blocks of Crescent, Bishop and Mountain cannot change the problems of the area. To revitalize the Bishop-Crescent area, most outdoor parking lots should be eliminated, green space created and conversion from housing to office space stopped.

There are two explanations for the name Mountain Street. One is that it was named after the Anglican bishop of Montreal, Jacob Mountain. The more likely explanation — since the street seems to have had this name before 1793 when Bishop Mountain was in Montreal — is that it follows an Indian trail up the mountain.

Mountain Street presents a few houses dating from the end of the 19th century. At 1194 is the 1889 home of John Murphy, the decorator responsible for the interior of Windsor Station. Sir Joseph Hickson, general manager of the Grand Trunk Railway, lived at 1214 Mountain. This 1865 house is now occupied by the Office Franco-Québécois pour la Jeunesse which offers young people study trips in Quebec and France.

At 1220-30 is the former Académie Bourget, built in 1914. For a number of years, Concordia University's Visual Arts Department studios took advantage of the ample natural light provided by these large windows.

Twelve thirty-four was built in 1859 for David R. Wood who sold it to Sir Alexander Galt seven years later. Galt was a Father of Confederation and a railway promoter. Joseph G. Wray and his brothers purchased the house in 1902 to transform it into a funeral parlor. They added the large bay window and entrance in the front in the late 1920s. In 1978, this building welcomed livelier occupants when it re-opened as a smart disco. The chapel, including the organ, was preserved but other walls were knocked down to make the interior more spacious.

On the northeast corner of Ste-Catherine is the original granite stone building of **James Ogilvy and Sons**, of 1895. Now Ogilvy's is located in the 1910 building, also in granite, which is on the west side of Mountain. The two buildings were designed by David

Sir Alexander Galt's house, 1899.

Ogilvy, a member of the owner's family. General Lumis, contractor for the later building, went bankrupt during its construction, because he failed to take into account the added expense of building on unstable soil. It was necessary to dig quite deep to reach solid rock which could support the foundations.

As you walk to the east (right) along Ste-Catherine, you will see that the storefronts on the ground floor mask the true age of many of the buildings. In an effort to spruce up downtown, in 1981-82 the city of Montreal widened the sidewalks of Ste-Catherine Street, adding inlaid brick and also installed the spiralling lamp-posts.

Drummond Street and environs were ceded to the city by John Redpath (owner of the Redpath sugar refinery) in 1842. The street was named in honor of his wife, Jane Drummond.

The Bank of Montreal, at 1205 Ste-Catherine, was built in 1921 as a branch of the Merchant's Bank of Halifax. The section to the north, added in the mid-1950s, was so well-integrated with the original that it is virtually indistinguishable. The interior was renovated in 1979 by the architectural firm of Stahl and Nicolaidis after it was gutted by a fire. This fine example of re-utilization of space was awarded a prize by the Ordre des architectes du Québec.

6 Drummond Medical Building

Walking north, the Drummond Medical Building, at 1414, was built in 1929 of brick and Indiana limestone. Percy Nobbs was the architect. Nobbs was noted for his work at McGill University (see the tour which covers McGill). The façade of the building in front of you is decorated with multi-colored glazed tiles. The iron canopy over the entrance is the original one. The north side (to the right) with bisected windows, is an elegant treatment of rationalist composition.

The lobby still has the original decorations which were also designed by Nobbs who was adept in the design of everything from furniture to stained glass. The stencilling on the lobby ceiling shows late Victorian influence, but the light fixtures are Roaring Twenties.

A decoration by Percy Nobbs, typical of his use of natural motifs.

The **Young Men's Christian Association** left Dominion Square and moved to this site (1441 Drummond) in 1913. Along with physical fitness, the YMCA has always offered high school and business courses to allow men to further their education after work. In 1926 the academic division became co-educational and received the name of Sir George Williams College, in honor of the British founder of the YMCA. It became a university, the fifth in Quebec, in 1948.

With increased enrollment in the 1950s, a new building was needed for the university. It was decided that despite the expense of downtown land, the institution would stay in the area to best serve its traditional evening school clientèle. The Kenneth Norris Building, named after the college's first principal, was inaugurated in 1956. A sixth floor was added in 1960 to house the library. In 1966, the university's main edifice, the Hall Building, was completed. You will see it later on the tour. (The Mount

Stephen Club across the street from the Norris Building is discussed in the Golden Square Mile tour).

Turn left on de Maisonneuve, then right on Mountain to see a few affluent homes of the late 1800s. Note especially 2115 Mountain, built by Robert Findlay for Daniel Stroud, coffee and tea merchant. Henry Beaumont was responsible for the sculpture on the façade.

(Walk along de Maisonneuve Boulevard one block west to Crescent Street.) Crescent Street, and Bishop one block further west, were once part of the Montreal Lacrosse and Cricket Grounds. The land was donated by printer and stationer Charles Phillips in 1864. Row houses were first built here in the 1870s. Phillips, the largest land owner in the area, had an estate which extended from Mackay to Mountain and from Sherbrooke to the CPR tracks. His house was on Dorchester, near Mackay.

Row housing was built on Crescent Street between de Maisonneuve and Sherbrooke from 1890 to 1914. A variety of materials such as brick, local greystone, limestone, buff and red sandstone were used. Now these homes are fashionable shops and offices. The view to the north along Crescent Street is pleasantly capped by the Erskine and American Church.

On the east side, at 2015, is the former house of David R. Brown, architect. Medieval details — such as the stone monks which support the windows — are characteristic of the Tudor style, popular when it was built in 1905. The building was renovated and the interior completely redesigned in 1982.

Crescent Street south of de Maisonneuve attracts a frenetic crowd. This block is spiced with bars and restaurants. For more than a decade, Winston Churchill Pub and Thursday's have been popular with those who enjoy stylish crowd scenes.

The Britannia Apartments, at 1454-62 Crescent, were constructed in 1905 with a greystone façade. The interior courtyard has been renovated recently and is quite attractive. The warm brick used inside provides an attractive contrast to the smooth limestone exterior.

(Continue westward to the southeast corner of Bishop Street, originally named Fulford after the Anglican bishop whose residence was two blocks south of here.) Bishop was one of the last streets to be established after the closing of the previously mentioned playing fields. By 1900, the block south of Ste-Catherine already had affluent houses, and construction was spreading to the block just south of here.

Concordia University was created by the merger of Sir George Williams University and Loyola College (in west end Montreal). Its name comes from Montreal's motto: *Concordia salus* (salvation in agreement). The **Hall Building**, at 1455 de Maisonneuve West (the university's main downtown building), is a 12-storey block which clashes with the rest of the street.

On the southeast corner (1463 Bishop is **Bishop Court Apartments**, saved from demolition by Save Montreal and local area residents. It now houses the administration of Concordia University.

Lyall House, at 1445, was designed by J.J. Browne with a remarkable façade by Henry Beaumont. The sculptures on this building are Beaumont at his most imaginative.

The Royal George Apartments, across the street, was built in 1912 by C.A. Mitchell. Its impressive façade is of glazed terra-cotta.

Concordia University was pressured to integrate the Royal George building into its library project. Unfortunately, the university could not permit the building to be maintained as housing. The library will be built around the Royal George, preserving the terra cotta facade. The university has said that it will replace the lost housing by converting some office space back to housing. Can the new units be as inexpensive as those lost?

At 1425 Bishop is another work of Robert Findlay, built in 1891 in buff sandstone for the interior decorator, Walter P. Scott.

7 The Coronation Building

The Coronation Building, on the northeast corner of Bishop and Ste-Catherine, displays a stone frame which sets off its large windows. The subdued decoration framed by a stone structure is typical of pre-First World War commercial architecture. Look up to see a superb cornice.

On the southeast corner in an Italianate building by Ross and MacDonald who are responsible for a number of buildings of this kind along Ste-Catherine Street. The old Post Office, across Bishop, was built in 1913 of pink granite and sandstone.

Further south are two buildings erected in 1889, 1234 and 1226 Bishop, which have been beautifully renovated. As you continue down Bishop, keep your eyes on the upper floors and let your imagination recreate the past. Bishop Street now rivals Crescent Street in bars and other night spots.

At 1176 is another interesting building which displays the style of H.H. Richardson. Darwin (1189 Bishop) is a bar with a close (small courtyard) frequented by the tweed-blazer-with-patched-elbows crowd. It is the only survivor of the row of houses which once lined the east side, for the others have been replaced by a parking lot.

Returning to Ste-Catherine, just west of Bishop is **Saint James the Apostle Church** built in 1863 near the cricket field. When constructed, it seemed too far from the city centre and was nicknamed "Saint Cricket in the Fields." At lunchtime its yard, the only patch of green in the area, is filled with office workers.

For a sweet end to this walk, drop into Toman's Pastry at 1421 MacKay (one block north, one block west) where rich chocolate and butter-pastry morsels are prepared daily.

The Guy metro station is located west of MacKay, on the corner of Guy and de Maisonneuve.

THE CHURCHES OF DOWNTOWN

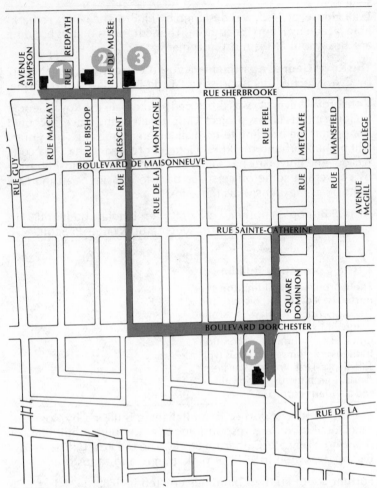

Because many of Montreal's churches are open only during services, this *two-hour tour* should be done on a Sunday. The start is at the Church of the Messiah, at the northeast corner of Sherbrooke Street and Simpson, at 10 a.m. The visit covers the adjacent churches on Sherbrooke. Since services will have begun by the time you reach Erskine American, you must sit down in order to admire the stained-glass windows.

1 Church of the Messiah

The Church of the Messiah houses Montreal's Unitarian congregation. This sturdy building reflects the English Gothic style through the purity of its lines, its elongated shapes and its sober design. It was designed in 1906 by Edward and William Maxwell who carefully interpreted the wishes of the minister, William S. Barnes. Reverend Barnes wanted his church to be both modern and traditional and requested that the design be both pious and poetic.

Everything was to be a work of art combining quality materials with careful execution. He contracted the work to the Montreal studio of the England-based Brownsgrove Guild of Applied Arts. The congregation was encouraged to commemorate their loved ones through the purchase of the church's furnishings. In addition to the 75 donations which he received from his congregants, a stained-glass window was donated by the Maxwell brothers.

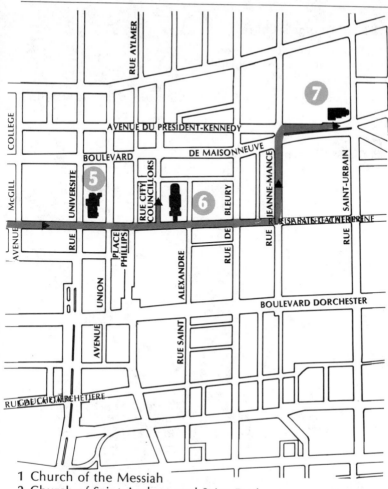

1 Church of the Messiah
2 Church of Saint Andrew and Saint Paul
3 Erskine and American Church
4 Saint George's Church
5 Christ Church Cathedral
6 Saint James United Church
7 Saint John the Evangelist Church

2 Church of Saint Andrew and Saint Paul

A visit to the church can be arranged by request at the church office, entrance on Redpath Street. For description, see Golden Square Mile tour.

3 Erskine and American Church

For description, see Golden Square Mile tour.

Walk down Crescent Street until Dorchester, turn left on Dorchester and walk until Peel Street. Turn right on Peel Street, the next church is on the northwest corner of Peel and de la Gauchetière streets.

4 Saint George's Church

This church is open every day during the summer. For description, see Downtown tour.

Walk up Peel Street until Ste-Catherine, turn right and walk until University Street.

5 Christ Church Cathedral

Located in the heart of Montreal's commercial district, this is one of the finest examples of Gothic architecture in Canada. It was designed by Frank Wills of Salisbury, England, who died in 1857 before the foundations were completed. Montreal architect Thomas S. Scott took over and the cornerstone was laid on May 21, 1857. Although this Anglican cathedral opened its doors in 1860, it was not consecrated until seven years later.

The building follows the cross-shape of 14th century English churches. Originally, a stone spire soared 127 feet (38 m) above the tower. This was one of the first stone spires constructed in Canada, but unfortunately the soil was not strong enough to support the load and it was removed in 1927. The present spire is made of aluminum treated with acid to imitate stone. Although the cathedral is often compared to the famous one in Salisbury because of the origin of its architect, the only similarity is the treatment of the spire where horizontal bands emphasize the change in shape. Inside are stained-glass windows from Morris' studio. The arcades of the nave are capped by leaves which represent Canadian indigenous trees.

Continue east along Ste-Catherine Street until City Councillors Street; entrance to Saint James Church is by the latter street.

6 Saint James United Church

Like many protestant churches in North America built in those days, this 1888 church designed by Alexandre F. Dunlop has a Gothic façade. However, the interior is unusual in its free interpretation of the Gothic vaulted ceiling, and by the horseshoe arrangement of the pews. The design is known as Akron since it was first used in Akron, Ohio. Stained-glass windows add to the richness of the decoration and the central chandelier, designed by the architect, is noteworthy. Stores were later constructed on Ste-Catherine Street which mask the attractiveness of this church.

The service at Saint John the Evangelist ends at 12:30 p.m. Saint John is about a 15-minute walk from Saint James. Continue along Ste-Catherine, take Jeanne-Mance north until President Kennedy Avenue, then turn left again to St-Urbain.

7 Saint John the Evangelist Church

This Gothic-style church is covered with greystone on the outside and red and white bricks inside. It was completed in 1879 following the plans of Frank Darling and W.T. Thomas. The unusual wood corbels which support the ceiling of the sanctuary had to be added because of a structural error in design.

The main rood screen was designed by M. Vaughan of Boston and executed by Montrealer Robert Reid. The sculpture is by Henry Beaumont. The stalls in the chancel were designed by P.B. William who was also responsible for the buildings around the church. The sculptures at both ends of the church were executed following earlier designs of Andrew Thomas Taylor. The screen in front of the chapel on the side was constructed in Henry Beaumont's Montreal studio. The pulpit was designed by Frank Darling and executed by Henry Beaumont.

Henry Beaumont (1853-1910) was a sculptor. His father, William Marsden Beaumont was a well-known businessman and Henry was still young when he took control of his father's stonemasonry. His artistic talent soon surpassed purely mechanical work and his creativity led him to study sculpture. He made rapid progress at school in London and he soon acquired a respected reputation. Beaumont came to Canada in 1888 and settled in Montreal. He sculpted the decorations on the façades of the New York Life and Sun Life buildings, the Museum of Fine Arts, McGill University buildings and private homes.

GOLDEN
SQUARE MILE

GOLDEN SQUARE MILE

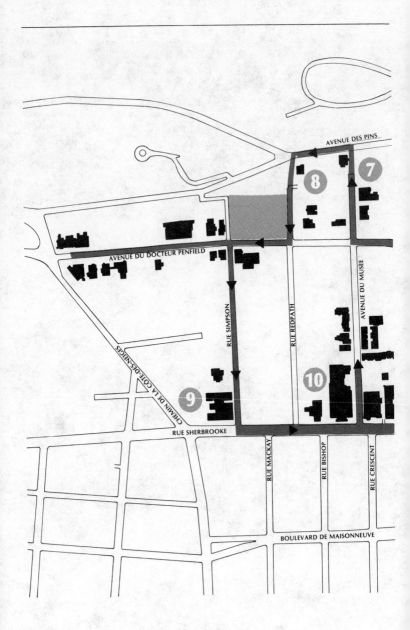

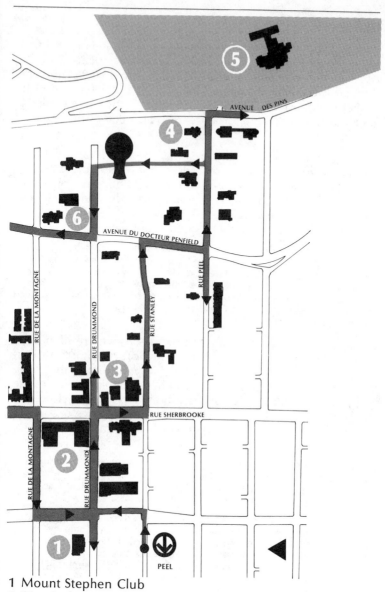

1 Mount Stephen Club
2 Ritz-Carlton Hotel
3 Corby House
4 Meredith House
5 Ravenscrag
6 Martlett House
7 Maison Raymond
8 Maison Cormier
9 Linton Apartments
10 Montreal Museum of Fine
   Arts

History

People began to settle in this part of the Sulpician lands north of Sherbrooke and east of Côte-des-Neiges after peace with the Amerindians was established in 1701. By the mid 1700s, large portions of the area were owned by influential citizens. After the British conquest of 1759, the prominent French names slowly gave way to the new English and Scottish families associated with the fur trade.

In the early 19th century, this area was filled with country estates and apple orchards. The orchards had a reputation similar to Mont Saint-Hilaire's orchards today; the estates belonged to prominent people such as Simon McTavish, **Alexander MacKenzie**, and James McGill. These men generally maintained city houses in the area we now call Old Montreal.

Sir Alexander MacKenzie, born in Stornoway, Scotland (1764-1820), came to Canada in 1778 after having lived in New York City. He ventured west, exploring Lake Athabaska and the Great Slave Lake (1789) and was the first European to reach the Arctic Ocean when he followed the river which bears his name to its mouth. During another expedition in 1792, he crossed the Rocky Mountains and was the first to reach the Pacific Ocean by land (1793). His account of his travels was published in London in 1801.

J. Cane's 1846 map of the area shows six or seven residences in the area between Côte-des-Neiges and McTavish, north of Sherbrooke Street. A few stones of the McTavish house may have been incorporated into the Duggan house (which is part of the tour) but no other vestige of these buildings remain. However, the street names of the area still reflect the presence of some of these early residents. Examples include **Drummond, McTavish**, and Redpath.

George Alexander Drummond, born in Edinburgh, Scotland (1829-1910), came to Canada in 1854. He founded the Canada Sugar Refining Company in 1879 and was successively director (1882), vice-president (1887) and president (1905) of the Bank of Montreal. He was named to the Senate in 1885.

Simon McTavish, was born in Scotland and became a director of the North-West Company which fought a bitter battle with the Hudson's Bay Company for control of the fur trade in northwestern Canada. He married Marie-Marguerite Chaboillez, daugher of a fellow fur trader. In 1803 he constructed an enormous mansion on the north of the intersection of Peel Street and Pine Avenue but his wife refused to emigrate from England and live in it. He died a year later, some say of sadness. The building was said to be haunted and his children never lived in it. He is buried near the château of his dreams.

By 1859, Montreal had developed westward along Sherbrooke Street and a map of that date shows 19 residences in the sector. Of these, the only ones remaining are No. 6 Ontario Place and Thomas Paton's coach house. Ravenscrag, now the Allan Memorial Institute, was built two years later.

Prince of Wales Terrace, a row of English-style town houses, was built in 1859 on the north side of Sherbrooke between Peel and McTavish by **Sir George Simpson**, then governor of the Hudson's Bay Company. The terrace was in the same spirit as the houses designed by **John Nash** in London.

Sir George Simpson, born in Loch Broom, Scotland, came to Canada in 1820 in service with the Hudson's Bay Company. He was active in the negotiations which merged that company with the North-West Company. He later became a director of the Hudson's Bay Company in North America and governor of Rupert's Land.

John Nash was an prolific architect and urban planner during the reign of George III (1752-1835). He designed Clarence House for the Queen Mother and the original part of Buckingham Palace. He designed Regent Street and conceived the row houses which developed along the main streets or around public squares. They were characterized by a main pediment, setback wings and other elements which were reminiscent of palaces.

By 1867 the sector had become desirable enough for J. Auld Jr., son-in-law of John McGregor, to begin subdividing the area between what is now Pine Avenue, Sherbrooke Street, Côte-des-Neiges Road and Simpson Street.

The completion of the Canadian Pacific Railway in 1885 ushered in Montreal's gilded age. The men made wealthy by the new prosperity chose to build their mansions on the pleasant slopes of Mount Royal. You will be coming across a number of their sumptuous homes which were built in a variety of styles and materials. The residential area of the city's élite was bounded by Dorchester, Guy, University and Pine. It was roughly a square mile in area and came to be known as the Golden Square Mile. It is estimated that at the turn of the century the 25,000 residents of the area controlled 70% of the wealth of all of Canada.

After 1900, congestion and pollution caused by the expansion of Montreal's commercial core to Sherbrooke Street considerably diminished the Golden Square Mile's prestige. Nevertheless, McGregor Avenue (now Docteur Penfield Avenue) retained its cachet in the first half of this century, becoming "Embassy Row" where many consulates were located. Even this small vestige of the Golden Square Mile began a slow decline when McGregor Avenue was extended eastward from Simpson to join Pine Avenue in 1957. As the very wealthy fled the congestion, the area fell prey to the building boom that occurred in Montreal in the late 1960s and early 1970s. All of the Golden Square Mile might have taken on the appearance of Drummond Avenue had the construction boom not ended; highrise towers began to lose favor with Montrealers, and urban planners began to suggest a return to construction on a more human scale.

Itinerary

This two-hour tour begins at the Stanley Street exit of the Peel metro station.

Walk to Drummond Street by following de Maisonneuve Boulevard under the **Drummond Court Apartments**. In 1957, Montreal's city council decided to enlarge Burnside Street and join it with Ontario Street to the east and St Luke and Western avenues to the west, thereby creating present day de Maisonneuve Boulevard. In order to do this, a tunnel was constructed under the office and apartment building at 1500 Stanley, and the private lane which ran north of it was expropriated. This was a complicated undertaking which required a number of delicate procedures as the mass of the building was shifted to 24 columns which support the eight upper storeys. (For more details, consult *Architecture-Bâtiment-Construction*, October 1958, pp. 64-70).

1 Mount Stephen Club

Robert Meighen took over the house of his cousin, Lord Mount Stephen, in 1888 (1908 photo).

Among the vestiges of the Golden Square Mile south of Sherbrooke is 1440 Drummond. The Mount Stephen Club was built in 1883 in Italian Renaissance style as a residence for **George Stephen**, head of the Bank of Montreal and the first president of the Canadian Pacific Railway. He returned to England in 1888 and was named to the House of Lords as Lord Mount Stephen in the following year. The gentlemen's club which bears his name was founded in 1926. The splendid period interior has been to a large extent maintained by the private club.

George Stephen, Lord Mount Stephen, born in Dufftown, Scotland, came to Canada in 1850 and was helped by his relation, William Stephen, an importer and manufacturer. He became a wool and cotton trader and made such a large profit during the Crimean War that William Stephen made him a partner. He took over the firm in 1860. He became chairman of the Bank of Montreal in 1876. He was the first president of the Canadian Pacific Railroad Company in 1881. He returned to Great Britain in 1888 with an enormous fortune and became a baron three years later.

At 2055 is the former Winter Club, a limestone and brick building designed by the Maxwell brothers, and later transformed into a recruiting centre for the HMCS Donnaconna. While this solid and attractive building has been somewhat spoiled by the addition of an incongruous mast and anchors, the details of the cornice are attractive.

Beside it is the former Emmanuel Congregation Church, (1906), designed by Saxe and Archibald in the Classic Revival style. It is used by the Salvation Army and has been integrated into Alcan International's headquarters which you will see later on the walk.

2 Ritz-Carlton Hotel

Sherbrooke Street, circa 1900.

At the southwest corner of Drummond and Sherbrooke is the Ritz-Carlton Hotel designed in 1911 by Warren and Whetmore of New York City with the collaboration of Montrealer Fred Garfield Robb. The capopy and the richly decorated façade make it one of the most elegant hotels in the city. Note how the ornamentation continues on the upper stories. This hotel was a favorite of residents of the Golden Square Mile and their guests and it still maintains a special aura of old elegance.

The Acadia Apartment Building (1924) at 1227 Sherbrooke West is an attractive example of early apartment buildings designed by David R. Brown.

Continue on Drummond to see where Theodore Labatt (of the brewery family) lived. The house at 3418 Drummond was designed by Robert Findlay in red sandstone. It displays a lovely portal in the Tudor style. Its two greystone neighbors are also attractive. Take at look at the detailing on the cornice and around the windows at 3429 and 3431 Drummond. On that side, nearer Sherbrooke, you can also see the coach houses of Corby House, dating from 1906. (Return to Sherbrooke Street and walk east. There are three excellent Victorian residences, side by side)

3 Corby House

Corby House, at 1201 Sherbrooke, was designed in 1882 by J.J. Browne for Thomas Craig. It was completely rebuilt by Richard A. Wait for J.R. Wilson some years later. Wait respected the original design and masonry and reused materials and the ornamentation of the original building. Corby's Distilleries Ltd. acquired this house in 1951. The United Service Club, at 1195, was erected in 1882 for Senator L.J. Forget, an important financier of the era.

The Mount Royal Club, at 1175, was built after a 1904 fire had destroyed an earlier building once owned by John Abbott, Prime Minister of Canada (1891-92) and legal counsel to Sir Hugh Allan.

The present building was designed by the American firm of McKim, Mead and White.

Van Horne House in 1920.

Until 1973, the picturesque and historic Van Horne Mansion was situated on the northwest corner of Stanley and Sherbrooke. Van Horne was director-general of the Canadian Pacific Railway during the construction of the railway, and later became its president. The Van Horne house was the most sumptuous of this group of mansions. Despite much public protest, the mansion was demolished in 1973.

At the southwest corner of Sherbrooke and Stanley is the Atholstan House which was built in 1894 in cut stone. Noteworthy are the sculpted panels on the upper part of the façades. Lord Atholstan was the founder of the *Montreal Star*, the city's largest English language daily paper until its lamented closing in 1979. The building, together with the neighboring greystone houses, has been carefully restored. They and the old Berkeley Hotel, as well as a well-mannered new building behind, form the international headquarters of Alcan Aluminium Ltd, done by the Arcop architectural firm (including Ray Affleck, Peter Rose, Peter Lanken and restoration expert Julia Gersovitz). A pleasant atrium (entrance at 1188 Sherbrooke) links the buildings to each other. Tours are available in the evening (inquire at the security desk, 2200 Stanley Street).

Just above Sherbrooke is a row of late Victorian houses on the west side of Stanley. At 3433 is the house once occupied by Andrew A. Allan, Sir Hugh Allan's nephew. The building is of imported red sandstone with copper framing the windows and balconies. It dates from 1890. Now it houses the École supérieure des arts et métiers of the Congregation de Notre-Dame nuns.

Across the street, at 3448, is the original home of **Massey Birks**, jeweller. It was built in 1887 and renovated 25 years later. The brick and greystone house at 3460 was once occupied by *The Gazette's* Richard S. White and is now used by the Hillel Foundation. Along with activities for Jewish university students, the building houses the Golem Coffee House.

Detail of Hugh Allan's house. Hugh was the last president of the Allan line, and the brother of Andrew A.

Among the other fine 19th-century houses on this street is the home of James Gorden, at 3489 Stanley, built in 1898. Although an architect himself, Gorden had Edward Maxwell design his red-brick and terra-cotta residence.

(Continue up Stanley, turn right on Docteur Penfield Avenue) Initially known as McGregor Avenue, this street was recently renamed to honor the pioneer neurologist Wilder Penfield who did brain research at the Montreal Neurological Institute.

(Make another right on **Peel** and walk to 3484 Peel Street).

Eugène Lafleur's house was constructed in 1902 by the Maxwell brothers. In fact, one of them used the identical design for his own home which has been demolished to make room for Peel Plaza. The two houses once faced one another across a circular lane. Unfortunately, the whole effect is now lost. This building is used by the Newman Centre which provides services to the Catholic students of McGill University.

On the east side is a row of greystone and sandstone houses which portray all the romance of the Victorian era. The four nearest Docteur Penfield were built between 1890 and 1906, while the others were built from 1860 to 1880. Although they were built decades apart, they fit very well together. It is vital that these buildings be conserved as a unit since their uninterrupted rhythm is unique.

Fortunately, McGill University has abandoned plans to put up a large building at the southeast corner of Peel and Docteur Penfield, which would have meant the disappearance of these houses.

It is interesting to compare 3644 Peel to 3647 Peel. The latter is soberly classic while the former is eclectic in style. Between 1893, when the former was built, and 1904, the date of the one on the east side, the vocabulary of architecture changed dramatically with the classical style becoming the vogue.

The Ross family in front of their home, circa 1910.

James Ross, engineer and entrepreneur during the construction of the railway across the continent, lived at the older house and his son at the newer. The father's was built of New Brunswick sandstone while that of John Kenneth, the son, had a brown limestone façade. Edward and William Maxwell were the architects for both houses. The father's house was enlarged twice, once in 1905 (by the brothers Maxwell), and again in 1922 (by Trobridge and Livingstone.) The majestic buildings now house the law faculty of McGill.

As you continue towards Pine Avenue, a fine house at 3611 stands out. At one time it was used by Marianopolis College (which has since moved to Côte-des-Neiges Boulevard) and now houses various divisions of McGill University.

Further on is the coach house of Purvis Hall. On the southeast corner of Pine and Peel (1020 Pine Avenue) is **Purvis Hall** itself. It was designed in the rigorous symmetry of the Beaux-Arts style, favored by Findlay and McGregor for Sir Mortimer Davis and was given to the University by A. Purvis, director of C-I-L Company and honorary rector of McGill. It now houses the Centre for Northern Studies and Research.

On the southwest corner of Pine Avenue and Peel Street is Meredith House, designed by Edward Maxwell for H.V. Meredith. This house is the most attractive of his work seen on this tour. Built in 1892, it is an example of eclecticism at its best: the details from various styles are in perfect harmony with each other. Note especially the line of the chimney, the play of the masonry and the stairway visible inside the round turret.

4 Meredith House

Meredith House, residence of a financier, now part of McGill University.

To the east, at 3740 McTavish, is **Duggan House**, yet another attractive Victorian mansion, built circa 1860 by O.S. Wood. Matthew Gault lived here between 1868 and 1911. G. Duggan lived in it for about 15 years, begining in 1930. Later, he donated the house to McGill University. Unfortunately, it has been stripped of the fine Carpenter's Gothic woodwork which once decorated the gallery.

5 Ravenscrag

Before returning to Peel, walk to Ravenscrag, at 1025 Pine Avenue. It was built for **Sir Hugh Allan**, the richest man in Canada during the late 1800s.

The ornate wrought-iron gates and the original gatekeeper's lodge are quite nicely done. This was perhaps the most lavish estate in the Golden Square Mile as befits the owner of the Montreal Steamship Line. From here, Allan could see his ships on the river. Actually, the house looks a lot like Osborne House, Queen Victoria's summer "cottage" on the Isle of Wight, whose Italian Renaissance style was frequently imitated. While this majestic house is perfect for its grand location, I wonder if it is not a bit too forebidding to its present occupants — it is now the Allan Memorial Institute of mental health.

Sir Hugh Allan, shipbuilder and founder of the Allan Line. Born in Scotland (1810-1882), he came to Canada in 1826 and joined the shipbuilding firm of William Kerr and Company five years later. He was named a partner in 1835. When William Kerr died in 1839, Allan formed a new company with Kerr's former partner, Edmonstone. Later he became sole owner of this large navigational firm. In 1852, the colonial government gave him a contract to establish a steamship line on the Saint Lawrence River. By 1856, four ships were offering biweekly service and by the following year eight ships were offering daily service. During the Crimean War, the governments of Great Britain and France used his steamships to transport troops. Allan became involved with railroads in 1870 and two years later he was given a contract by the federal government to construct a railroad across the continent to the Pacific Ocean. However, members of the opposition Liberal party accused him in 1873 of having bribed Sir John A. Macdonald, with some of the money coming from American investors. The disclosure of his correspondence with the Americans and his manipulation of the federal government caused the fall of Macdonald's government. Allan was knighted in 1871 for his services to Canadian industry. He was involved in banking companies and founded the Merchants' Bank of Canada. It was chartered in 1861 and managed like a family institution. Allan was also involved with iron and steel production, the pulp and paper industry, shoemaking and mining.

(Now walk down Peel until the driveway before 3690 Peel) The original McIntyre House is at 3690 Peel; its coach house is also worth a look.

Walk down the drive to the McIntyre Medical Building — that enormous round tower with an arm outstretched. The building's unusual shape is convenient for the medical library on the lower floors and the lecture halls, but its other occupants find it hard to arrange furniture in offices with a curved wall.

Directly across Drummond, at 3656, is the Davis House. James Davis was with the firm which constructed Windsor Station and bridges for the Canadian Pacific Railway. Although the Maxwells designed this brick structure in 1909, it seems more modern. The front faces not the street but the sunny south. Nearby, at 3630, is Hosmer House, a large red sandstone building designed by the Maxwells in 1907 for Charles Hosmer, head of the telegraph department of the Canadian Pacific Railway and developer of the entire Canadian telegraphic system.

The architect travelled to New York and Europe to select antique furnishings for the house. The effect of the interior is over-whelming. The main hallway gives access to several magnificent rooms. Plaster reliefs, cartouches and fanciful panels in the ostentatious Roccoco manner are featured in the drawing room and reception rooms. The library is finished in rosewood and the pilaster flanking its mantel is carved in arabesque patterns. Tiger-wood panels the breakfast room, while the dining room is domi-nated by an elaborately-carved stone fireplace which extends from floor to ceiling. Between the panels in the ceiling are plas-ter angels in a heavenly setting of clouds.

Hosmer house.

As Jean-Claude Marsan comments in *Montreal in Evolution*, this house: "well reflects the profound insecurity of this *nouveau riche* group, ready to reject original and creative ideas for the certainty and security of traditional values. They were apt to mis-trust local inspiration and welcome foreign input from Europe and the United States."

The view of Drummond Street from this point was once of an elegant avenue lined with magnificent elms. At the southeast corner of Drummond and Docteur Penfield is an old house which has been renovated for the Italian Consulate.

The houses which were once at 3459, 3465 and 3471 Drummond, were of a refined design with Dutch-styles gables and gently projecting windows: excellent examples of the Shaw style. Their demolition began illegally in 1974, without a city permit. The case was before the courts for a long time and the three houses stood there forelornly, their façades a pile of rubble. Eventually, demolition was allowed to proceed after payment of a small fine.

(Return to Docteur Penfield and walk to Mountain Street)

6 Martlett House

At 3605 Docteur Penfield is Martlett House, a rusticated-style mansion with a beautiful interior. It houses the McGill University Graduates' Society. You may want to try to go inside to discover the panels which depict medieval scenes of splendor. The building was erected in 1926 by Robert Findlay for B.M. Hallward of *The Montreal Standard*.

At the southeast corner of du Musée and Docteur Penfield are the offices of the Polish Trade Commission which renovated the 1910 residence of Senator J.M. Wilson. Primarily of brick, greystone was used as decoration and to visually strengthen the building.

Just east of du Musée is McGregor Place — row housing built in 1960 on land rented from McGill.

Herbert Molson had Robert Findlay build the house at 3617 du Musée in 1912. Its imposing façade is decorated with pilasters topped by Ionic capitals. The reason for the locked gate, and cameras on the lawn is that it is part of the Consulate of the Union of Soviet Socialist Republics. A 1987 fire gutted 3617 du Musée.

On the west side, at 3636 du Musée, was the de **Sola Club**. This was perhaps the only gentleman's club in North America which served strictly Kosher meals. A local movie star purchased it in 1979. Completed in 1923, this grey and chamois limestone building was designed by W.O. Hutchison for Melville Miller.

7 Maison Raymond

At 3685 du Musée was once the home of Senator Donat Raymond. It was constructed by J. Omer Marchand for Sir Rodolphe Forget, president of the Montreal Light, Heat and Power Corporation. Look carefully at the sculpture above the entrance and around the window on the second floor. The head of a woman surmounted by angel's wings was perhaps the sculptor's homage to Madame Forget.

Even though the stairs ahead seem daunting, the next part of the tour is worth the effort. You should not be so close to Cormier House without seeing that elegant residence. Soon you will be able to rest in a pleasant London-style park.

Once you have climbed the stairs, you will see immediately to your left (1374 Pine Avenue) the house of Clarence de Sola, son of the first Rabbi of the Spanish and Portugese Synagogue. Fittingly, the house was constructed of terracotta in the Spanish-Moorish style in 1914.

8 Maison Cormier

Cormier House is situated at 1418 Pine Avenue. Ernest Cormier designed the Supreme Court of Canada in Ottawa and the main building of the Université de Montréal. In 1930 he designed, decorated and furnished his home, a beautiful example of Art Deco. The outside is deceiving for the house is built on a slope, and a dramatic interior staircase leads from the hall at the entrance to more floors below. The large window on the right of the door illuminates a formal living room which is two storeys high. Prime Minister Pierre Elliott Trudeau now owns the building.

(Walk down the stairs just after the next house) Two impressive homes set in huge gardens are a bit to the north. Senator Molson lived at 3655 Redpath until the late 1970s. His residence is now part of a condominium complex. At 3627 Redpath is an elegant limestone building constructed in 1917. The third floor was added in 1930.

Residence of Sir James Ross, 1894. It was demolished in 1944.

Across the street is **Sir Percy Walters Park**. The park was formerly the site of "Rosemount", the home of Sir John Ross, first high commissioner from the United Kingdom. The Prince of Wales stayed here during his 1860 visit. The gates around the park may be remnants of Ross's estate.

Percy Walters, millionaire vice-president of Imperial Tobacco, gave the site to the city for a park in 1944. Despite legends to the contrary, the park was not donated for the needs of local dogs. In fact, in his deed, Walters stipulated that the Park "is primarily intended for young children and their parents and companions." Strangely, he directed that "no swings, chutes or other apparatus shall be erected...the city will discourage football and baseball games, in order to preserve the quietness of the park."

(Leave by the gate at the southwest corner) Look across Docteur Penfield to **Trafalgar School for Girls**. The school was founded in 1893 with funds donated by such people as Donald Smith, governor and chief commissioner of the Hudson's Bay Company, and member of the CPR syndicate. He also funded Royal Victoria College, the women's division of McGill University.

Trafalgar School was initially housed in Chalderton Lodge. In 1902, Taylor and Gordon added a wing, which still stands, on **Docteur Penfield Avenue**. Note its elegant entrance. In the 1950s the original lodge was demolished and a new wing built on the site. Funds for a new gymnasium were obtained from the sale of a large property located on the other side of Simpson Street, a bit below the school. This was the site of the elegant house of a Miss Galt whose garden was a definite asset to the street.

Now you can stroll down what was "Embassy Row". Actually, since Montreal is not a capital, the foreign offices were consulates, not embassies. The McGregor property was divided into lots in 1867, creating this street (which bore that name until 1978). The tour leads down one side of the street and then returns by the other sidewalk. At 1501 Docteur Penfield is a fine red sandstone mansion in the Queen Anne style, built for Benjamin Tooke in 1899.

Next door, at 1507 Docteur Penfield, is a classical mansion designed in 1930 by Robert and F.R. Findlay. It was later occupied by Alderic Raymond who owned the Windsor Hotel. It is in the protected zone provided by the minister of cultural affairs' classification of the mansion's neighbor at 1513 Docteur Penfield Since tax evaluation is based on the speculative value of the land, and not the actual value of the building itself, this house is too expensive as a single-family residence. It would be affordable if new, sympathetic construction set back from the street were added.

At 1513 is an elegant beige limestone house in the Classical Revival style. It was built in 1910 for Charles G. Greenshield, and later inhabited by James N. Greenshield who defended Louis Riel in his 1885 trial for treason. The house was enlarged in 1915 and was the home of Walter Molson until the 1950s.

The developers of the building at 1515 Docteur Penfield agreed to integrate the façades of some of this street's mansions. One was constructed by the architect K. Rea in 1923 for his own use. While its façade remains, the rest of the house, including a two-story tall room illuminated by an enormous skylight, is gone. The design you see fails miserably in integrating the façades since it has absolutely nothing in common with the original buildings.

As you have no doubt noticed, little mention has been made of the highrise apartment buildings which you have passed during this tour. Not only are they of little architectural interest, but they are interlopers as well in this area. Highrises might be necessary to house an expanding population, but they should not supplant buildings which are as beautiful as they are historic.

Continue walking until 1579-85. Georgian style homes in this row were built between 1905 and 1914 and have now been divided into moderately-priced small units, an example of harmonious reuse.

A row of Victorian red sandstone buildings erected between 1894 and 1897 stand at 1587-95. They are as important individually as they are as a group. Until recently, 1587 housed an architect's office on the ground floor with residence above. Note the interesting details on the façade. The house at 1589 was a private residence, and 1595 was once the Italian Consulate.

Now you can examine the south side of the street. The **Canadian Jewish Congress** building, at 1590 Docteur Penfield, was donated to the organization by **Samuel Bronfman** and was designed during the 1960s by Fred Lebensold. It is an interesting example of modern poured-in-place concrete construction. Of good architectural design, its size relates well to the scale of surrounding buildings and it fits its corner site nicely.

Samuel Bronfman, born in Brandon, Manitoba, was president and co-owner of the Seagram's multi-national distillery company. Founded Distillers Corporation in 1924 which he later merged with Joseph Seagrams and Sons (acquired in 1928). The company's operations extended into the United States beginning in 1933. Active in a great number of philanthropic works, he became a Companion of the Order of Canada in 1969.

At 1572 is the Swiss Consulate, the last foreign government office on the street. It portrays an attractive use of red sandstone with fine detail. Edward Maxwell designed it in 1893 for James Crathern; it later became the home of the McArthur family, important in the chemical and paper industries.

The United States Consulate used to be housed at 1564 and at 1558. The building on the right was designed by Edward Maxwell and built in 1893 for Joseph Learmont, a hardware merchant. The other house is in the French Renaissance style. It has unusual dormers piercing a slate roof; they look like witches's hats or the visors of a medieval knight's helmet. I.F. Dunlop designed the house for John Auld. The Hodgesen family later lived there.

The small private home at 1538 was built in 1891. For many years it was the home of a Mr. Snowball and will soon be integrated into a condominium. Make a mental note of its appearance.

At 1506 is Lauterman House, a Gothic Revival stone cottage built in 1871, making it older than most buildings in the area. It is now used by the Friends of the Hebrew University (located in Jerusalem).

The Charles Gettey House, at 1500 Docteur Penfield, was built in 1871 by J.J. Brown. It was renovated and enlarged in 1920, and now houses the **Saint Michael's Lutheran Church Home**. It should look familiar since it is a twin of 1506 Docteur Penfield. In all, four cut-stone cottages were built around 1875 when this street was opened between Côte-des-Neiges and Simpson. Before leaving, take a look at the charming carriage house at the rear, then turn down Simpson Street.

9 Linton Apartments

Linton House, with the garden as it originally looked.

Linton House, built in 1866 is on the right just before Sherbrooke Street. Originally, the garden extended to Sherbrooke Street where the namesake apartment building is now situated. Finley and Spence constructed the latter in 1907, using the Beaux-Arts style.

(Turn east and walk past Redpath Avenue) **The Church of Saint Andrew and Saint Paul** is used by two Presbyterian congregations which joined in 1918. This Gothic Revival building was designed by Harold Fetherstonhaugh who was selected after a world-wide competition. It is constructed in steel and reinforced concrete, with stone used both as skin and inside. This is the regimental church of the Black Watch of Canada (Royal Highland Regiment), whose flags are displayed near the vaulted ceiling.

There are two different types of stained-glass windows. The lower tier are memorial windows, mainly from the former Saint Paul's Church (located on Dorchester Street), which were carefully removed when it was demolished. Two windows donated by the Allan family (located near the back of the church, on the left) are believed to be the work of Sir Edward Burne-Jones, a follower of the Arts and Crafts Movement. There are two stained-glass windows by William Morris which can be identified by the garlands of leaves used to frame the subjects. The huge window over the altar symbolizes hope, it was originally installed in Saint Paul's in 1900. The delicate upper windows on the sides are the work of Lawrence Lee and were installed in the 1960s. Saint Andrew is emphasized in the western windows, while Saint Paul is prominent in those on the eastern side. Lee was successful in retaining most of the natural light in the nave while adding rich color and meaning to the church.

10 Montreal Museum of Fine Arts

The Montreal Museum of Fine Arts (1379 Sherbrooke) was designed by Edward and William Maxwell and completed in 1912. The classical facade is in Vermont marble. Majestic stairs lead to monumental doors. Fred Lebensold designed a new wing, completed in 1977. That expansion has created many problems for the museum.

Another renovation (Provencher Roy, architects) was completed in 1984. A aerial passageway links the museum to a house to the north.

The Montreal Museum of Fine Arts, founded in 1860, is the oldest established museum in Canada. Its diversified collection comprises not only sculptures, paintings, prints and drawings from Europe and North America, but a rich selection of decorative arts, including furniture, porcelain, stained glass, ceramics, textiles and silver and gold work. Treasures from ancient Egypt, Greece and Rome, China, Japan and Pre-Columian America, as well as western European art from the Middle Ages to the present; Islamic art and works from Africa and oceania are all on display in Montreal's largest museum. Early and contemporary Quebec and Canadian art, Amerindian and Inuit works are given prominence in the Museum's collections.

The Montreal Museum of Fine Arts has the oldest art library in Canada. Here, students, teachers and researchers can consult over 50,000 books and hundreds of periodicals pertaining to the visual arts. The library is open to the public Tuesday through Friday, from 11 a.m. to 5 p.m.

The Museum has plans for further expansion on the south side of Sherbrooke Street. Architect Moshe Safdie was directed to create a building for additional galleries which is sensitive to the special streetscapes of Crescent, Bishop and Sherbrooke. Local merchants and preservationists were anxious about the project and the city administration ensured that the public was consulted.

At the southwest corner of Sherbrooke and Crescent was the first apartment building in the city of Montreal. Built in 1888, it was demolished in 1983. This greystone and brick building had stood vacant since a 1980-fire had evicted its last occupants.

To the right, on Sherbrooke, is the Erskine and American United Church (built in 1893). Its Richardsonian façade provides a marvellous focal point for Crescent Street. Its interior, completely redone in 1938-39 by Percy Nobbs and G.T. Hyde, is unusual: The curved lines of the choir balcony and the arangement of the pews make it look like an amphitheatre. Stained-glass windows are from the Tiffany studio.

(Turn up du Musée Avenue) Note the old coach house at 3427 now part of a new row. Built in 1855, it is the oldest house in the area.

Richelieu Place, at 3437-45 du Musée, was built in the 1920s. The inner courtyard is quite elegant, with discreet space for parking provided by garages in the mews behind the houses.

On the west side in an elegant group of town houses and small apartment buildings. The large open spaces, the homogeneous buildings and the sparse traffic make du Musée Avenue one of the most beautiful streets of the Golden Square Mile.

Further east, at 1321 Sherbrooke Street, are Le Château Apartments (1925). The building was designed by Fetherstonehaugh, and Ross and MacDonald, in the Château style for Senator **Pamphile du Tremblay** (former owner of *La Presse*). The building imitates a castle on the Loire river, offering stone gargoyles, turrets and a romantic inner courtyard. It is a fine building for sophisticated living, offering superior accommodation — at corresponding rents.

Pamphile du Tremblay, born in La Pérade, Quebec, was a member of parliament for Outremont, and organized a francophone army brigade during the First World War. He became legislative councillor in 1924 and senator in 1942. He was chairman of *La Presse* in 1934 and also started a number of radio stations.

Continue along Sherbrooke Street until Mountain; the entrance to the Peel metro station is at de Maisonneuve Boulevard.

McGILL
and its Student Ghetto

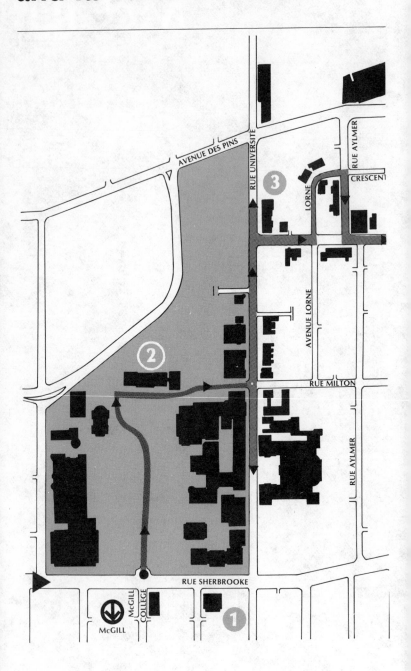

1 McCord Museum
2 The Arts Building
3 Burland House
4 3592 Durocher Street
5 Elm Avenue
6 3492 Dorchester Street

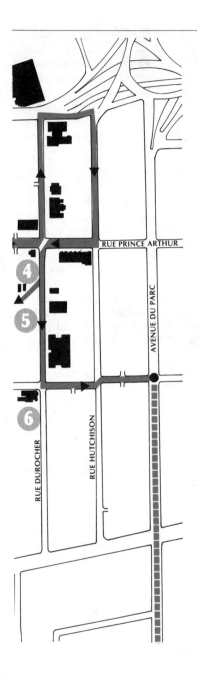

History

While this tour does not cover a very large area, there is much of architectural interest. Some early 19th-century buildings and many from the end of that century still stand on the campus and in the surrounding residential area. Their conditions vary from mint to mediocre. The tour lasts about an hour, and if you walk it when classes are in session you will see professors and students going about their daily life.

The McGill campus is an important green space for downtown Montreal to the south and the residential area east of the university (often called the McGill Ghetto). Since both these areas lack parks, many people use the campus as a place to throw footballs and frisbees while students read or chat, and children play in a protected corner reserved for them.

In 1813, the Scottish fur trader **James McGill**, bequeathed Burnside (his 46-acre estate), and 10 000 pounds to the Royal Institute for the Advancement of Learning. He directed the institute to establish a university or college bearing his name. The university received its charter in 1821 and officially opened eight years later, but legal complications made it impossible to erect the first building on campus before 1843.

James McGill (1744-1813), trader and politician, born in Glasgow, became a fur trader upon his arrival in Canada in 1766 and amassed a great fortune. He represented Montreal in the legislature (1792) and became a member of the Executive Council of the province in the following year. He was known for his philanthropy and civic spirit. He was one of three commissioners responsible for the demolition of the old city walls, director of the prison, head of the voluntary fire brigade, member of the committee for the construction of Christ Church Cathedral.

During the next hundred years, the area immediately to the east began to fill up with homes of affluent Montrealers, including a number of McGill professors. By the late 1940s, some students forsook the university residences and fraternity houses to live on their own in rooming houses or with classmates in the large flats of the area. More and more students moved here during the 1960s and 1970s and their youthful enthusiasm brought a unique atmosphere to the McGill Ghetto.

A new chapter in the ghetto's history is unfolding in the 1980s. The increased interest in centrally located old houses has initiated a return of the middle class to the area. Considerable rent increases make it necessary for the typical student to look elsewhere for housing. Many of these buildings were recently renovated and are now for sale as condominiums.

On this tour you will see the homes of two socio-economic groups — the students and others who live in rundown rooming houses and flats, and a more affluent group who have purchased recently renovated homes in co-ownership. It remains to be seen whether the distinctive qualities of this neighborhood will persist.

Itinerary

Access: McGill metro or # 24 bus

The Roddick Gates at Sherbrooke and McGill College were designed by Gratton Thomson in the Greek revival style, and erected in 1924. They honor Sir Thomas George Roddick, a McGill University benefactor.

Sherbrooke Street was the most elegant and desirable residential street in turn-of-the-century Montreal. Both sides were lined with the beautiful mansions of some of Montreal's wealthiest families. Many of these houses were set in spacious grounds and gardens. While most of them have disappeared, if you look to the west, you can still see some old houses among the office towers.

1 McCord Museum

The McCord Museum, at 690 Sherbrooke, was originally the McGill Union. Sir William Macdonald gave the funds for this building which was completed in 1907. Percy Erskine Nobbs was the principal architects.

At first, Nobbs proposed a *palazzo* of red brick and limestone. He wished to follow the ideal of the English architect Richard Normand Shaw who had, in the 1890s, designed two London buildings which Nobbs discussed in a letter published in the *Canadian Architect and Builder* in 1904: "Both these grand buildings stand on bases of hewn stone or granite. The upper storeys are constructed of brick with the occasional introduction of bands or members of stone, in such a manner as to make of this interchange of materials a decorative motif of distinct architectural value. The nobler material, thus, keeps helping out its humbler fellow all along, and together they form a unity and not a motley of elevations."

Benefactor William Macdonald suggested a building made completely of stone which was more expensive than brick. He wanted to outshadow the brick and stone Strathcona Hall which was built a block west of here. Nobbs agreed.

As director of McGill University's department of architecture, Nobbs wanted the McGill Union to be an example for his students to emulate. Shaw's influence does appear in the structure as built. Like him, Nobbs borrowed from a variety of styles. A Baroqe surround gives emphasis to the main

doorway, Gothic oriel windows distinguish the first storey, while slender classical mouldings grace the second floor.

Besides the structure itself, Nobbs designed the plaster decoration, draperies, furniture and even the cutlery used in the dining room. In this he was true to his training in the Arts and Crafts philosophy of William Morris.

The Union building was the focus of student life until the new University Centre on McTavish Street opened in 1965. Now it houses the McCord Museum, *open Wednesday through Sunday.*

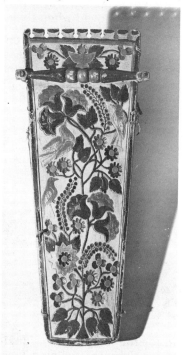

An Iroquois cradleboard.

The **McCord Museum** is *open Wednesday through Sunday from 11 am to 5 pm. For information phone 392-4778 or 392-4774.* It possesses the only major ethnographic collection in Quebec. It is one of the largest Amerindian and Inuit collections in Canada and contains artifacts from the four principal aboriginal cultures of the Arctic, the eastern forest, the Prairies and the northwest coast. The northwest coastal artifacts are particularly interesting since they were collected in 1878 by George Dawson of McGill University while he worked on the Geological Survey of Canada. The totem pole from Masset, B.C. which dominates the main stairway was brought by another McGill graduate, Frank Buller.

The McCord family began to collect paintings, drawings and engravings during the 1830s. The collection includes the works of such landscape and portrait artists as François Beaucourt, William Berczy, James Duncan, Théophile Hamel, Cornelius Kreighoff, Ozias Leduc. In the 1880s, David Ross McCord commissioned W.H. Bunnett to paint scenes which seemed liable to vanish; the more than 200 paintings by the former British officer form an excellent architectural record of the streets and buildings of Montreal and other cities. The costume collection was started in 1957 and has become one of the museum's most important sectors. It is one of the few collections of clothes in Canada. Decorative and popular art is represented by furniture, wood sculpture, cast iron, porcelain, pottery and jewellery. The artisanry in primitive religious art and children's toys is also on display.

William Notman was world-famous as an innovator in commercial photography. Most of the work produced in his Canadian studios are preserved at the Notman Photographic Archives housed in the McCord Museum. The archives are composed of about 700,000 glass negatives and proofs, a number of which pre-date Confederation.

Directly across the street from the Roddick Gates was, until 1982, **Strathcona Hall** a *palazzo*-style building designed by Montreal architects Findley and Spence in 1906. McGill University sold the site of Strathcona Hall to the developers of the silver-grey highrise, a bit to the south. The developers integrated Strathcona's façade, as well as that of the row of 1870s-greystones to the east, within the new construction. One storey of the greystone buildings was removed when their façades were put back.

The value of this reuse of architectural relics (as opposed to the conservation of entire buildings) is debatable. While some people feel that every element which can be preserved is to be treasured, others believe this to be akin to necrophilia. They argue that piecemeal preservation makes no valid contribution to our architectural heritage.

Inside the campus, **Burnside Hall** is that tall building immediately to the right. The building, which houses the computer centre, is in a modular design with no differentiation between the ground floor and those above.

The large tree stump with the plaque is Founder's Elm which was planted around 1790, perhaps by James McGill. It is unfortunate that it succumbed to Dutch Elm Disease in 1976 and had to be cut down.

To avoid magnetic interference, no iron or steel was used in the original construction of the **Macdonald Physics Building** in the early 1890s. This building by Taylor, Hogle & Davis was one of the last large buildings in Canada erected entirely of wood and masonry. It now houses McGill's science and engineering library.

Just a bit up from it is the original **Macdonald Chemistry Building** (designed by Andrew Taylor in 1896), now housing the schools of urban planning and architecture. Note the lions holding inscribed shields above the door.

The Macdonald Engineering Building was rebuilt in 1908 to replace an earlier one which had burnt down the previous year. Nobbs respected the original design and built on the original foundations, but extended the building further to the rear. Just below the roofline, on the south (right-hand) side, is a sculpture of a phoenix which Nobbs added to commemorate the building's resurrection after the fire. This is just one of the lovely sculptures which decorate Nobbs' buildings on the campus.

Reading Room of the Redpath Library, circa 1895.

The Redpath Museum, on the west side of the campus, is now open only to McGill students, but until the 1970s the public could visit the natural history collection; its shrunken head exhibit sent a shiver through many an elementary school child. This handsome structure, reminiscent of a basilica, was built in 1883 in the Greek Revival style. It was donated by Peter Redpath. The columns are in the Composite order — a hybrid of the Ionic and Corinthian orders.

To the left is **Morrice Hall**, originally used by the Presbyterian College. The polygonal annex was constructed for its library and is a miniature replica of the Library of Parliament in Ottawa, which was built around the same time (1875). The entrance to this once-independent college is from McTavish Street, through the belfry-topped pavilion at the rear.

Just to the south is **Redpath Hall**, also a gift from the sugar magnate who donated the Redpath Museum. Although it was too noisy and dark for its original use as a reading room, it is now appropriate, after careful restoration, for ceremonies and concerts.

The terrace and the smooth-stone building with the large windows were added in the early 1950s. Even this addition could not contain all of McGill's burgeoning library collection, and in the 1960s the **McLennan Library** — the modern building near Sherbrooke — was built.

Take the path to the right of the Redpath Museum. Behind the museum, and to the left, is the **Leacock Building**. This nicely designed edifice was constructed in 1963. The oriel windows on its north side and its green roof are a nod to older buildings on the campus. This used to be the site of the McGill Observatory which established the longitude here to be 60 degrees, 54 minutes, 18.67 seconds west of Greenwich. Now you know exactly where you are.

2 The Arts Building

Extending to the right is the original Arts Building, the first building on the campus, erected in 1839. As such it is the oldest school building in Montreal still standing. Before it was built, classes were held in Burnside, James McGill's residence which was located south of Sherbrooke Street. The Arts Building has been greatly modified: only the façade of the central building and the octagonal dome date from the original construction. It was designed by John Ostell, and resembles his Customs House on Place Royale (Old Montreal). A lack of funds prevented the construction of the colonnades until later; a wood porch was added in 1885 and replaced by the stone portico in 1926.

The urn-like monument in front of the Arts Building is James McGill's tomb. His remains were removed from the old Protestant cemetery, on the site of what is now Dominion Square, on June 23, 1875, a date which is observed annually as Founder's Day.

Standing at the **Milton Gates**, you are on the edge of the Student Ghetto, the neighborhood east of the campus. It is located between Sherbrooke and University streets, Pine and Park Avenues. In the mid-19th century, the orchards and fields on the mountain slope north of Sherbrooke Street made the area an attractive location for a villa or a home. The introduction of the horse-drawn tramway in 1861 improved the area's accessibility from the centre of the city. Modest-sized estates and single family rowhousing were built in the area.

University Street in the mid-1800's.

The suburb of one generation was engulfed by urban growth in the next. Wealthier property owners began moving west after the turn of the century. By 1945, owners of once grand homes had either sold or rented them and many houses were subdivided into flats and rooms.

Further down University is the buff-colored brick High School of Montreal. This building was constructed in 1914, following the design of Edward and William Maxwell. At that time, the school had acquired rivals to its pre-eminence as Montreal's first English high school. By hiring such prominent architects to erect a building of such majestic proportions (it extends the entire depth of the block) the high school was reasserting its dominance. Its classical revival style is most fitting in that the Classics were important in the curriculum of that era. The building now houses **Face** and **Mind**, two of the Protestant School Board's schools of alternative education.

The Montreal Diocesan Theological College, at 3473 University, is a marvellous reminder of a more contemplative era. Walk through the arches and stand in the courtyard of the religious college. There are sculptured angels on the label stops framing the windows, and near the roofline can be seen monsters and gargoyles. Alexander Galt had this college built. He also bequeathed to McGill University his Mont St-Hilaire estate and the Marlborough Apartments (a block to the east at 570 Milton). The latter is an attractive example of the Dutch gable style popularized in England by Shaw.

Compare the Diocesan Theological College with the Presbyterian College at 3495 University. Although this 1963 building is set further back on its lot than the others on the street, it is relatively well-integrated with its neighbors through the similar construction materials.

At the northeast corner of University and Milton is **Fisk House** built in 1909 on a narrow corner lot. It was designed by an English architect who failed to take Montreal's climate into consideration; a large skylight collapsed under the mass of the first winter snow. Its sculpted lion's head in the middle of a brick façade is a delight.

The house at 3521 University was built circa 1870 by the Reverend John Cordner. Since 1908 it has been the home of the descendants of Pierre Desbarats, the first Printer to the Queen, in Canada. The greystone façade has an attractive semi-circular bay. The curved-arch motif over the double-doors is repeated around the dormer windows. The design is distinguished, although austere.

On the other side of the street, at 3506 University, is Morris Wilson Hall. It was built in 1913 in the Collegiate Gothic style as a residence for McGill medical students and is now used by the School of Social Work and the School of Nursing.

Beside it stands the **William and Henry Birks Building**. Built in 1931, it was called Divinity Hall until 1972. It is also in the Collegiate Gothic style. McGill's buildings on this street form an ensemble which clearly distinguishes the academic from the residential.

The greystone rowhouses at 3533-3545 University were built around 1865. The exterior has undergone extensive alteration, but this block originally presented a coherent and dignified façade. These were home to H.J. Johnston, secretary of the North British and Mercantile Insurance Company; and A.M. Foster, partner in a straw and felt goods firm. Today, most of these houses are rented out as small flats and rooms.

The mansion at 3550 University was built in the 1870s. At that time, the whole west side of the street was occupied by magnificent mansions, most set within spacious grounds. This house was given to the Royal Victoria Hospital on the proviso that it never be demolished or sold.

The houses at 3583-91 University were built in the masculine, rather massive style which became characteristic of later 19th-century row housing in Montreal. Rusticated greystone was used for the façade, while the windows and doors were framed by smooth stone with carved decorations. Rounded and flat bays alternate across the façade, expressing the lay out of the interiors and enlivening the general appearance. A fur wholesaler, a leather merchant and an auditor of the Grand Trunk Railway lived in this row in 1880.

Other mansions were the property of McGill University, some acquired through the donations of generous patrons, others purchased. Regrettably, a number of them were torn down to erect the Rutherford Physics building, further north. One of the demolished buildings had been renovated the previous year at an enormous cost.

In the past, the McGill administration did not recognize the value of the old houses in its possession, choosing to see them solely as prime building sites, because the buildings seemed difficult to convert to academic use. However, McGill University has recently demonstrated a will to preserve its Victorian architectural heritage.

Between 3601 and 3623 is **Les jardins Prince-Arthur**, one of the first Montreal examples of building recycling. Members of the architectural firm of Desnoyers, Mercure, Lezy and Gagnon were convinced that renovation of old buildings such as these could be profitable, so in 1973, they acquired the five greystone houses as well as a vacant lot on a sixty-year lease from the university. The houses were completely renovated during 1974-75 at an average cost of $17,000 per unit. The fireplaces, arrangement of the original windows and other 19th-century details were preserved. The third-storey level on three of the houses was rebuilt.

The house on the corner is occupied by the offices of the architecture firm itself. In the summer of 1980, a fire did extensive damage which was soon repaired. The other buildings contain eleven deluxe apartments. At 3621 University is a three-storey infill apartment block. Its design, materials and setback from the street harmonize with its neighbors.

3 Burland House

The house at 3619 University is perhaps the most handsome mansion remaining on the street. It was built by George Burland in the early 1870s. Burland was president of the Burland, Desbarats Lithographic Company (later the Canada Engraving and Lithographic Company) which printed money. When he died, the house was sold to Colin Morgan, a member of the family that owned Morgan's Department Store for a number of years. In 1948, the property was donated to the university which housed departmental offices for a time. The elaborate details executed on the façade give the house a certain finesse. A sweeping ascent leads to a double-door and hides the basement entrance. Inside is a winding, Baroque staircase. Recent renovation has preserved the original fittings on the balustrade, the elaborately-carved wooden mouldings and numerous other luxurious decorative details.

Nobbs is responsible for **The Pathological Institute** on the northeast corner of University and Pine Avenue. His design illustrates a sensitivity to the urban landscape in the way it harmonizes with the massive Scottish-Baronial Royal Victoria Hospital, across the street, and the series of small row houses which continue along Pine Avenue. The gabled-end bay, which Nobbs placed at the corner of Pine and University, possesses sufficient visual strength to match the bulk of the hospital. On the other hand, the domestic scale of the attached house (originally the caretaker's residence) descends to meet the smaller row houses. His building nestles in the site as if it had been there for as long as its neighbors.

Renovation of the twin building at 645 Prince Arthur was completed in 1982. The rooftop addition which leads to a sundeck could have been designed to be less disruptive of the original design than the reptilian eyes you see. The renovator should not have changed the dimensions of the openings for windows and doors since this has disfigured the façade. Also, the subdivision of the windows is not in keeping with the original design of the house but comes from a different historical period.

The houses on the south side, 630-640 Prince Arthur, were bought in 1974 and slated for demolition. A last-minute attempt by three strong-willed, elderly tenants saved the buildings, but rents more than doubled after renovation. (Turn left on Lorne Crescent, walking until the curve)

In the early 1880s, A.M. Foster laid out Lorne Crescent and built semi-detached houses to create a lovely residential street. While several were demolished for the massive apartment tower on the west side of the curve, further along there still remains a group of similar houses which preserve a tranquil serenity. On the east side are several single-family dwellings which have been converted into rooming houses.

Aylmer Street, north of Milton Street.

As you walk along the curve you can see the towers of La Cité complex, looming over the rooftops of the 19th-century houses.

Lorne Crescent crosses Aylmer to end in an intimate tranquil cul-de-sac. The buildings on this block create an attractive quasi-courtyard.

(Turn down Aylmer) Aylmer Street, originally called Oxenden, used to run to the north of what is now Molson Stadium. Pine Avenue between University and Oxenden was opened at the turn of the century and ran through the Molson (beer) and Fro- thingham (hardware) estates. The two families owned much of what is now the McGill Ghetto. At that time there was a transition from large estates on the side of the mountain, through progres- sively smaller properties to the town below.

YMCA of McGill University is located at 3625 Aylmer. The orga- nization was founded in 1903 by philanthropist Lord Strathcona. It housed the Student Christian Movement from 1933-73. A non- denominational group, it serves the lonely senior citizens and troubled adolescents of the area. Downstairs is the Yellow Door Coffee House which dates from 1967 and is the oldest coffee house in Canada. A meeting place for American draft-dodgers during the Vietnam War, the Yellow Door saw the beginnings of Jesse Winchester's folksinging career. He still returns from time to time to perform.

Across the street is an attractive row of apartments and flats, in red brick articulated with stone decorations.

On the south side of Prince Arthur Street is a terrace of six grey- stone houses built in the late 1870s in handsomely subdued good taste (524-548 Prince Arthur). The dignity of the terraces is matchless. The house at 552 Prince Arthur was the home of James Morgan, another member of the department store family and founder of the Montreal Cement Company. He helped organize the Montreal Citizens' Association which worked for municipal reform in the early 1900s.

Here was once the heart of the student ghetto: most of the old homes had been converted into inexpensive rooming houses for students. In the last few years, the rooming houses have been converted back into more expensive residences.

On the north side of the street is the **Rigi Apartments** (3610 Prince Arthur Street), an impressive and well-maintained block. Note the mosaics beside the door. The units in this 1911 building are spacious and high-ceilinged.

The red brick and terra-cotta house at 481 Prince Arthur is interesting because of the ornamental detailing and because it stands apart, in its own yard behind a fence. A family named Benoit once lived here, and Madame Benoit was a prominent suffragist and fighter for women's rights in the early part of this century. The house had a varied history in recent years; it was at different times a fraternity house, a Hare Krishna temple, and a youth hostel. It is now privately owned and has been lovingly restored.

The Marché Campus, a little farther east, occupies an old stable. The hatchway into the loft was once used to load hay.

4 3592 Durocher Street

The old farm house at the opposite corner, 3592 Durocher, is one of the oldest houses in the district and probably dates from the early 1800s. Durocher Street is the oldest street in the neighborhood — Paul-Siméon Durocher put it through his farm in 1837 and, subsequently, ceded it to the city.

One of the oldest houses in the neighborhood.

At 3610 **Durocher Street** is the attractive Halcion Apartments. Note how the scrolls and other sculpted details continue to the roof. The halcyon was a legendary bird said to charm the wind and calm the waves during the winter solstice, so that it could breed in a nest floating on the sea. The owners were obviously appealing to lovers of tranquility. The Halcion was originally built as a hotel, but the owners went bankrupt before construction was completed. It was converted into an apartment building in 1915.

Between 3615 and 3625 Durocher is an ensemble of two-storey, red brick townhouses built in the early 1890s. The wood trim of the pedimented dormers and cornice, and the rusticated sandstone in the horizontal string courses pull together the expanse of the façade. Can you tell which unit suffered a fire on the upper floor in 1980?

The red brick house at 3635 Durocher is among the oldest in the McGill Ghetto. It was already standing when John Kerry, co-owner of the drug firm of Kerry Brothers & Crathern, purchased the lot in 1857. At that time the house had a veranda the width of the front and was surrounded by more land.

The apartment building at 456 Pine Avenue was designed by Finley and Spence in 1906, at the same time that they worked on Strathcona Hall.

Across Pine Avenue is the **Sir Arthur Currie Memorial Gymnasium and Armory**. Its design was the winning entry in a contest open only to McGill graduates. While construction began in 1939, it was interrupted by the Second World War and not completed until 1950; the stadium was added not long after.

As early as 1844, John Frothingham had his residence at **Piedmont House** situated at the head of Durocher Street (to the north of present-day Molson Stadium). Frothingham was a major landowner. At one time he owned part of present-day Mount Royal Park, as well as substantial property south of Sherbrooke Street. His hardware store on St-Paul Street was well-known to 19th-century Montrealers.

The turn-of-the-century apartment building at 418 Pine Avenue has been remarkably well-preserved. Look into the lobby to see the marble tiles, decorated ceiling and cast iron details which have been kept in good repair. The original elevator is still in use.

To the east can be seen the prominent dome of Hôtel-Dieu. North of Pine Avenue is the lush open space of Mount Royal. While it was directly accessible to pedestrians until the construction of the Park-Pine traffic interchange in 1958, it now takes quite a while to get across, either by braving the traffic or following the meandering sidewalks. While such a trek is not on the itinerary, you may not want to pass up the opportunity to enjoy the park.

(After, walk down Hutchison until Prince Arthur Street)

The row of greystone houses at 412-420 Prince Arthur Street is the consummate expression of late 19th-century picturesque architecture. The variety of textures and details in the façade seem to come to life when the sunlight plays over the checkerboard pattern of alternating smooth and rusticated blocks. Members of the wealthy Masson family bought this land and built this group in 1892. Senator Rodrigue Masson, once Lieutenant-Governor of Quebec, built himself the corner house in 1894. In the 1920s, these houses were the residences and offices of doctors; later they were subdivided into flats occupied by students and young professionals. Now they have been renovated and sold as condominiums.

(To get to Elm Avenue, you must turn left on Durocher and walk into the lane opposite 3567 Durocher)

5 Elm Avenue

Elm Avenue is a survivor from another era whose intimacy and peacefulness is a world removed from the noise and bustle of the city. The two houses are apparently old farmhouses which predate the urbanization of the district. The earliest references to the houses date from 1873, when the lane was called Foster's Lane, and a bookkeeper and two merchants lived here. More recently, the small two-storey building was inhabited by FLQ-member Marc Carbonneau who was involved in the 1970 kidnapping of James Cross.

Today, Durocher Street is a mangled mélange. There are old well-designed, low-rise buildings such as Parkdale Court (3525-15), modern apartment buildings (The Princeton at 3553); grey-stone row houses and a red sandstone with a lovely semi-circular window, built before the turn of the century. Grand old trees still line the street, a rarity in this part of Montreal.

6 3492 Durocher Street

The large house with the oriel window, at 3492 Durocher, was built in 1885. Originally a single-family house, it was later subdivided into flats. Its landlord during the 1970s allowed it to fall into disrepair, and the exterior wall began to crumble. In 1980, it was purchased by an architect who renovated it and added a sympathetic annex in the rear. The renovation of this building was given Save Montreal's *Prix Orange* for excellence in 1982.

Hutchison Street was the last in the McGill Ghetto to be developed. Although it had been surveyed into lots by 1890, extensive construction did not take place until around 1900. In contrast to the rest of the McGill Ghetto where houses were originally single-family dwellings, duplexes and other multiple units were built on Hutchison.

The house at 385 Milton was built in the late 1890s. It has a large stained-glass oriel window and plentiful decorative details. Interestingly, the original entrance door on Hutchison was turned into a window. It is the one in the centre, with the broken pediment. It was probably at the same time that the building was subdivided into a number of units. Now it is part of one of the Milton-Park housing cooperatives (see St-Louis tour), and was renovated in 1982.

The building on Hutchison beside this house is an apartment building of the 1940s. While many people might consider it the ugliest structure in the district, a case can be made for its bold vertical lines and rectangular negative volumes.

Park Avenue was developed shortly before the turn of the century as a residential street; business establishments began to move in around 1910. This section is the commercial street for the neighborhood. Within a two-block radius is every necessary sort of store and commercial establishment. Half-way down the block is the Pâtisserie Belge. More than just a pastry shop, it sells pâtés, bread, and many imported products. A restaurant to the side of the shop boasts a continental atmosphere. Henri Richard, celebrated Canadiens hockey player, had a brasserie nearby until 1986.

The building at the corner of Milton and Park was completed in 1986. Designed by Mario Biocca, who also renovated 3492 Durocher, its horizontal articulation, use of brick and stone and its rounded corner make it a sensitive insertion into the streetscape.

The tour ends here, one block north of Sherbrooke. All Park Avenue buses go to Place des Arts metro station.

CHINATOWN

CHINATOWN

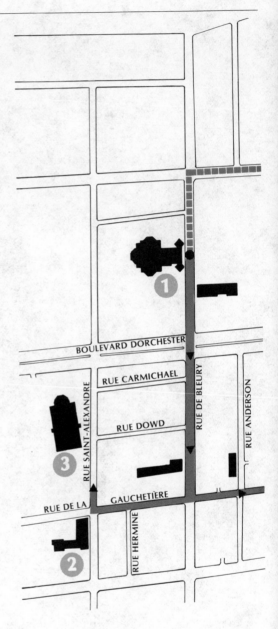

1 Église du Gesù
2 Unity Building
3 St. Patrick's Church
4 Mission Catholique
  Chinoise du Saint-Esprit
5 The House of Wing
6 Monument National

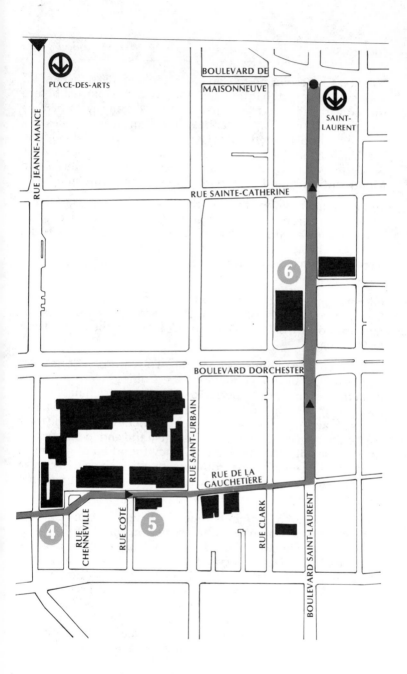

History

The first Chinese came to Canada in the mid-1800s. While it is generally believed that they did not arrive in Montreal before the construction of the Canadian Pacific Railway in 1885, a number of Chinese names appear in the mid-century files of a Catholic school located in what is now Chinatown. It is likely that the Chinese left the harsh working conditions of the gold mines of British Columbia to find a more acceptable life in the east. In Montreal they found employment as servants or in laundries.

Today, Chinatown comprises the area bounded by Jeanne Mance, St-Laurent, Dorchester and Viger streets. Much of it has been swallowed up by Place Guy-Favreau and the Palais des Congrès, as you will see. Consequently, these construction projects have inflicted serious social and economic costs on the Chinese community.

It is recommended that you take this tour on the weekend, when Chinatown is at its most vibrant. There are innumerable restaurants to choose from if you wish to savor more of the exotic flavor of the area.

Chinatown came into existence for two reasons — loneliness and fear. Of all our immigrants, the Chinese were probably maligned for the longest period of time. The first Chinese laborers came in the 1860s from the impoverished villages and farms around Canton. Lured by the prospect of riches, they made their way to the gold mines of British Columbia and ended up working on the Canadian Pacific Railway. They found employment in work considered too dangerous for whites which paid 75 cents a day. A particularly difficult stretch of track is said to have cost one Chinese life per mile.

The Canadian government imposed a head tax on Chinese immigrants which admitted only those who could earn a living, virtually excluding women and children. The men came because their families were starving and they hoped to eventually save enough to pay the head tax and bring their loved ones over. In 1923, the federal government passed the Chinese Exclusion Act which cut off all Chinese immigration (The United States had passed a similar law in 1882). This was probably the most racist action of Canada's none-too-open immigration policy. The men who were already here formed ghettos, staying together for safety and companionship. Most settled in British Columbia but some came east to the booming cities of Montreal and Toronto.

Inevitably, where there are a lot of single men there will be prostitutes, so "red light districts" soon sprang up alongside the Chinese settlements. Even today the Chinatowns across Canada are frequently adjacent to areas with flop houses, cheap clubs and gambling dens.

After a great deal of public pressure, the Chinese Exclusion Act was repealed in 1949. Ironically, as the number of families increased, the population of Montreal's Chinatown declined. Probably the men who had lived here wanted to escape bad memories. They set up their own businesses such as laundries (because they required little capital and were not in competition with white-owned businesses). It is said that they established restaurants because the aroma of their cooking enticed the other workers on the railway.

As they prospered, families moved uptown to the area near Hutchison and Fairmount streets and then out to the suburbs. The children were sent to universities, and today there are Chinese in almost every profession. While in 1840 there was only one Chinese doctor in Montreal, there are now more than a hundred. Most Chinese Montrealers are members of the middle class.

The Chinese are now scattered throughout Montreal and the population has grown from 3,000 in 1949 to about 25,000. However, there are only about 300 people living in Chinatown; most of them are either new immigrants who welcome the security of a familiar environment and the inexpensive housing available, or old men, those whose families never came to Canada.

Neverthless, Chinatown is far from abandoned. On weekends, Chinese families from all over the city come here to attend one of the churches, have lunch and shop. The stores are open Sundays, harking back to the time when the Chinese worked 12 hours a day, six days a week.

While speculators may look greedily at Chinatown's redevelopment potential, many Montrealers treasure it as a living witness of history. Chinatown bears witness to the valiant efforts of the first Chinese immigrants to fight adversity and establish themselves in Montreal.

Currently, their descendants must fight to maintain this neighborhood as the focal point of their culture. Without a viable resident community, the area will always be threatened.

On this tour you will see Chinatown's origins, its recent past and present problems. We can only hope that the recent truce in demolition activity will permit Chinatown to maintain its place in Montreal history.

Itinerary

1 Église du Gesù

Gesù Church is on Bleury Street, near Dorchester Blvd. (#80, #129 and #150 buses). Strictly speaking, the church is not in Chinatown, but it is included in the tour because of its nearby location. It was built in 1864-65 by the Jesuit Fathers who directed the Collège Sainte-Marie which used to be located just to the south. They had wanted to build a church on the scale of Notre-Dame when the college's chapel became too small. As the price asked for the land by its Protestant owner was more than they could afford, it was not until 1863 that they acquired the lot through a dona-

tion from a wealthy benefactor named Berthelet.

The Jesuits have always had a reputation for academic brilliance. They taught the Classics: Latin, Greek, theology, rhetoric. These were the subjects which the French-Canadian élite thought necessary for the cultivated man. Among the pupils at Sainte-Marie was the well-known poet Émile Nelligan. The Jesuits relinquished control over the college's curriculum in 1955 because they were vastly outnumbered by the lay staff. After being used by the Université du Québec a Montréal

for a number of years, Collège Ste-Marie was demolished in 1977. Place Félix Martin, a multi-storey office complex ironically named after the architect of the college, now rises on the site.

The Gesù church is in the Italian Baroque style. Although the Jesuits had planned a 12th-century Gothic Revival church, they were over-ruled by the Bishop of Montreal, Monseigneur Bourget, who insisted that a Jesuit church must be based on the Gesù in Rome, a symbol of the Counter-reformation.

The church you see was designed by a Brooklyn architect who claimed to be familiar with the namesake in Rome. His design resembles the original, only in the use of trompe-l'oeil decoration inside. While the architect had planned two bell towers, only their bases were completed. The only resemblence this façade has with Rome's Gesù is its vaguely Italian Baroque style which was common in later-Victorian architecture. The adjacent buildings make it difficult to see the latin cross shape from the street.

Like most other churches in Montreal, the Gesù is in severe financial straits. Attendance has dropped and the church is in need of major repairs. The Jesuits are reputed to be a wealthy order, but much of the wealth is tied up in buildings such as this one.

The Gesù's interior is notable for the number of carvings on the main altar and in the smaller chapels off the nave. The statue of the Virgin Mary was made in France in

1793 and brought to Canada in 1857 by a Canadian Jesuit who was studying in France. Called Notre-Dame de Liesse, the statue is a replica of an earlier one dating from the Crusades which was destroyed during the French Revolution. Legend has it that three crusaders brought the original sculpture back from Cairo in 1134. They said it had been carved miraculously as a sign to encourage the Sultan's daughter to convert to Christianity. The village in France to which it was taken took its name from the statue rather than the customary reverse. Liesse means joy in French, so her name is Our Lady of Joy. The plaques around the chapel are testimonials of miracles, some of them recent.

In front of the sanctuary is the original parquet floor, made of a variety of woods. The cupola bears the name of Jesus while scenes on the ceiling portray his life. The magnificent oil paintings on either side of the sanctuary are by the Gagliardi brothers of Rome.

Théâtre du Gesù opened in 1865 as an auditorium where students held debates and peformed religious plays. No women or professional troupes were allowed on its boards until the 1930s. After that it became so successful that it took away business from the larger Monument National which had acquired a reputation as being the site of radical political speeches. Many a Québec playwright and singer made his or her debut at the Gesù.

The building at 1179 Bleury Street is in the Classical Revival Style which was popular in the mid-1800s. It has a severe and ordered façade.

The Southam Building is at 1070 Bleury, just before the corner of de la Gauchetière. It was built in 1912 and the Southam Company sold it in the late 1960s to a group of small businesses. It still bears the Southam name on the sides and has a lovely terra-cotta and brick façade. The sculptures of four women represent cultures or, perhaps, the continents of Africa, Europe, Asia and North America. The laughing faces at eye level and the other sculpture near the cornice are delightful.

2 Unity Building

No. 454 de la Gauchetière is a 1913 skyscraper which was designed according to the principles of the Chicago school. Such a building has a definite base, shaft and capital: the ground and first floor are a sort of pedestal upon which sits the main portion of the building which is crowned by a projecting cornice. The Unity's Art Nouveau cornice is unique in Montreal. In *Montreal in Evolution*, Jean-Claude Marsan compares the Unity Building with the Wainright Building of St. Louis (1890) and the Guaranty of Buffalo (1894), both designed by Louis Sullivan.

3 St. Patrick's Church

This part of the city used to be known as "Little Dublin" in honor of the Irish that settled in this area when they came to Montreal to build the Lachine Canal in the early 1820s and the Victoria Bridge 30 years later. Each wave of immigrants settled first around the docks and the railway yards because this was the area no one else wanted. As they moved out, they left a reminder: The Irish left St. Patrick's; the Jews, their shops and restaurants on the Main, while the Chinese are still here.

The first Irish Catholics were given a church by the Sulpicians in Old Montreal which they soon outgrew. By 1841 there were at least 6500 Irish Catholics in the city. Consequently it was decided to build a larger church. Land was acquired with help from the Sulpicians, and St. Patrick's was begun in 1843. At that time, this was a magnificent site. Pierre Louis Morin designed this church with the help of the Jesuit Félix Martin. Part of the property was sold to a developer for the construction of Place Air

The central chandelier of Saint Patrick's Church. The church is open only when mass is celebrated.

Canada building to the east of the church whose exterior is remarkable for its simplicity and pragmatic use of materials. The heaviness of the bell-towers might be criticized, but the architects are not to be faulted: plans for a smaller building without towers were overridden by Quiblier, the Sulpician Father Superior, who made the final decision. Even then, the architect suggested taller towers than the ones which were built, which appear unfinished. Actually, this Gothic church has little in common with the Gothic Revival churches of Europe.

The buttresses on the left side of the church are stained green. This must be from the copper patina roof which has begun to dissolve, and is probably due to acid rain. Air pollution has damaged historic buildings all over the world.

The Honorable **Thomas d'Arcy McGee**, one of the Fathers of Confederation, was assassinated in 1868 and his funeral was held in this church. Just inside the vestibule hangs a plaque to the poet Émile Nelligan who was baptized here.

Il you go inside, you will be impressed by the vastness and elegance of the interior. Volume is the dominating feature of this church. The oak wainscotting around the nave is inset with paintings of 150 saints. The walls above the wainscotting are painted to resemble damask, and are decorated with the shamrock and the fleur de lys, which symbolize the old homeland and the new. Halfway down the centre aisle can be seen the white enamelled tag of d'Arcy McGee's pew. Each pillar is made of a single length of pine over 80 feet long (24 m) and is said to be without a flaw. However, the latter detail is not verifiable since the pine has been painted to resemble marble. The Fourteen Stations of the Cross are by the Italian artist Patriglia.

Thomas d'Arcy McGee (1825-1868) was born in Ireland and was active in that country's struggle for independence. He immigrated to Canada and became a popular politician among the numerous Irish immigrants living in Montreal. He represented Montreal-West in the colonial legislature and in 1864 he was one of the representatives for Canada East (Quebec) at the first conference on the confederation of British colonies in North America. During his campaign for re-election in 1867, he condemned the Fenians (a brotherhood of Irish living in the United States which wanted to use military force to eliminate the British from Canada). He was re-elected, but not without creating enemies among Irish Montrealers. On April 7, 1868, after returning from a day at Parliament in Ottawa, he was shot and killed while entering his hotel on Metcalfe Street. His assailant was never identified but was believed to have been a Fenian. His funeral was the most impressive that Montreal had ever seen.

Chinatown is well worth visiting on Sunday when it is at its liveliest.

(Go east along de la Gauchetière) At 1037 Bleury is a building which is a typical late-18th century construction. During that era, rowhouses were built along the entire length of a block, with the roof at each end in a distinctive style. This sort of building has almost completely disappeared from the city. In front of you is a remnant, with eight of the original 10 houses demolished, and the two you see, drastically modified. There are very few buildings in the city — even in Old Montreal — which are older than these houses.

4 Mission Catholique Chinoise du Saint-Esprit

(Continue along de la Gauche-tière to the corner of Jeanne Mance Street) As far north as Ste-Catherine, Jeanne Mance used to be known as St-George Street, but the name was changed to conform with the portion above in the early years of this century. This is the western boundary of Chinatown and from here can be seen Complexe Desjardins and Complexe **Guy-Favreau.**

Before demolition for Complexe Guy-Favreau began, there were three churches in Chinatown. The Presbyterian Church still stands on Chenneville and may become a community centre. The Pentecostal Church on Côté was demolished and the congregation now worships in a new building located on the southwest corner of de Bullion and de la Gauchetière streets.

The Chinese Catholic Church and its presbytery were classified as historic monuments in 1977, and thus escaped demolition. The church has been greatly modified since its original construction. It is supposed to be recycled, perhaps as a Chinese cultural centre, although the government buildings are now a barrier between it and Chinatown.

The church has had a varied history. Constructed in 1835, it was initially used by the Récollets (Notre-Dame-des-Anges). It later became the second Scottish Secessionist Church of the city. In the area now occupied by Complexe Guy-Favreau was once the Spanish and Portuguese Synagogue (1838), the first Jewish house of worship in British North America.

Guy Favreau (1917-1967) was a lawyer and politician. He was called to the Quebec Bar in 1940 and became a member of numerous commissions such as the Royal Commission on patents and royalties in 1954. He was co-author of the Fulton-Favreau formula on bilingualism and biculturalism. From 1955 to 1960 he was associate deputy minister for justice. He was elected member of Parliament for the riding of Papineau in 1963 and became minister of citizenship and immigration. In 1964 he became minister of justice and solicitor-general of Canada and in 1965 he was elected president of the Privy Council.

When the federal government announced construction of Complexe Guy-Favreau in 1975, there was a great deal of concern expressed by the Chinese community and the general public. It was feared that such a large complex of office buildings would eliminate a large part of Chinatown and disrupt the local economy. In addition, the consolidation of federal services in one place would leave empty offices elsewhere, destabilizing the Montreal rental market. The project was designed to create an impressive federal presence in Montreal and also to provide employment for construction workers during the lull after construction of the 1976 Olympic installation was finished.

The evolution of the project was lengthy and tortuous since the public was not kept informed of plans and also because its conception was changed a number of times, responding to elections, budget cuts, etc. Save Montreal and members of the Chinese community lobbied for the creation of a consultation committee which could provide some public input on the $200 million dollar project. Although this committee was not as effective as had been hoped, it does include residential buildings and an interior space which serves as a gathering place for the Chinese community. The YMCA also has a branch in the complex.

Near the Presbyterian Church was **Dufferin Square**, named after the Earl of Dufferin, Governor General of Canada from 1872 to 1878. Originally a Protestant cemetery established in 1779, the land was expropriated by the city in 1871 to make it a public square. A fruitless petition in 1878 requested preservation of the cemetery as a history site.

On the right, across from the Catholic Church, was an enclave made up of the oldest buildings of the sector. The houses were decidedly primitive construction.

Palais des Congrès, Montreal's convention centre, is of a disappointing design. Instead of linking Old Montreal to Chinatown and the rest of the city as had been hoped, it acts as a barrier. The outdoor plaza is sterile and uninviting.

5 The House of Wing

The House of Wing (at the corner of Côté and de la Gauchetière) is reputed to be the oldest building in Chinatown and was used by the British and Canadian School at the time it was built, in 1826. Towards the end of the last century, an additional storey was added by converting the roof into a false mansard. As a city's population increases, this is an efficient way to provide more housing in limited space. The building now houses a noodle and cookie factory.

The Montreal Chinese Community Service Centre and the **Chinese Restaurant Association** are located at 112 de la Gauchetière. The latter is responsible for setting standards for its members. Built around 1864, this was originally a middle-class home, as were many others on this street. Later it became the Chinese Hospital. Since the rooms were cramped and poorly ventilated, the hospital's move in 1965 to St-Denis Street was a good one for the patients.

Until 1982, there was a small park on the northeast corner of St-Urbain and de la Gauchetière which was graced with a pagoda. The park was eliminated to allow for the widening of St-Urbain Street.

Four of the larger family clans of *tongs*, to which anyone with the same family name can belong, have headquarters on the south side of de la Gauchetière. They help settle immigrants, act as banking associations, and house the old men who have no one to take care of them. If you look up, you might see an elder watching the street activities. Most cannot speak English or French, are illiterate, and do not know how to use phones or public transport. While the Tongs had a criminal reputation in some American cities, in Canada they are solely concerned with the welfare of their family. At Nos. 94 and 92 are the Lee clan houses; No. 90 houses the Tam clan, No. 88 the Chan, while the Wongs are at No. 76.

This part of de la Gauchetière Street is the heart of Chinatown, where most of the restaurants are located. Many of them have two menus: one in English and one in Cantonese. If you are adventurous, you might ask your waiters to recommend something from the latter.

Sun Sing Lung Grocery (72A de la Gauchetière) opened in the 1960s and specializes in roast pork, chicken and duck. Families come from all over town to buy their specialty meats here.

If you browse around various stores, you will notice that some sell goods from the People's Republic of China only, while others sell produce just from Taiwan. While political affiliations are strong in Chinatown, the Chinese tend to respect the opposing point of view. Each group celebrates its own national holiday with a banquet and parade without interference from the other.

Leong Jung at 999 Clark Street is a kind of Chinese supermarket which sells everything from vegetables to glassware. You will find things here that are difficult to get elsewhere in Montreal: bitter lemon, jackfruit, horn nuts, breadfruit, abalone, dry white jelly fungus, fresh Chinese fruits and vegetables.

Blocked by development westward by government buildings, Chinatown began to spread east of St-Laurent Boulevard, but the city administration wants that area to be primarily residential.

St. Lawrence Boulevard (Boulevard St-Laurent) was know as *The Main* because it was the longest street running north to south, and the main commercial boulevard of Montreal. This area is Montreal's skid row and you will notice a lot of taverns, flop houses, and second-hand stores. However, the police cannot abandon the street to derelicts because there are so many government buildings nearby.

Take a look at the row of stores on the west side of the street. These flat-roofed buildings with detailed cornices were built at the turn of the century. The windows are nicely designed and the use of different materials adds pleasing contrast.

6 Monument National

Monument-National in the mid-1900s.

The Monument National at 1182 St-Laurent was built in 1894 and was one of the first theatres in Montreal.It was also used for political meetings and acquired a reputation as the site of inflammatory speeches. The National Theatre School purchased it in the early 1970s and the building is now used to train actors and to build sets. The building, classified as a historic monument 10 years ago, looks rather run down now but the theatre itself is still attractive. Student performances are free and often extremely good.

The enlargement of Hydro-Quebec's head office (built a block west of here in the 1950s) means substantial change to this part of St-Laurent Blvd. Architectural firm Cayouette et Saïa's plans include conservation of the existing streetscape along St-Laurent, the creation of a public park, integration of the Monument National and a modernized playhouse for Théâtre du Nouveau Monde, thanks to Hydro-Quebec and Fonds F-I-C Inc. In keeping with the commercial nature of the street, ground floor space is given over to stores. This new construction, together with improvements which the city administration plans for St-Laurent Boulevard, will soon encourage new investment to the area.

As you continue up the Main, note the West Indian Food stores. The corner of Ste-Catherine and St-Laurent is the centre of Montreal's red light district. There are a number of strip-tease bars and pornographic theatres on this block. *One block north of Ste-Catherine is the St-Laurent metro station and that is why our tour ends here.*

ST-DENIS STREET

ST-DENIS STREET
Quartier Latin

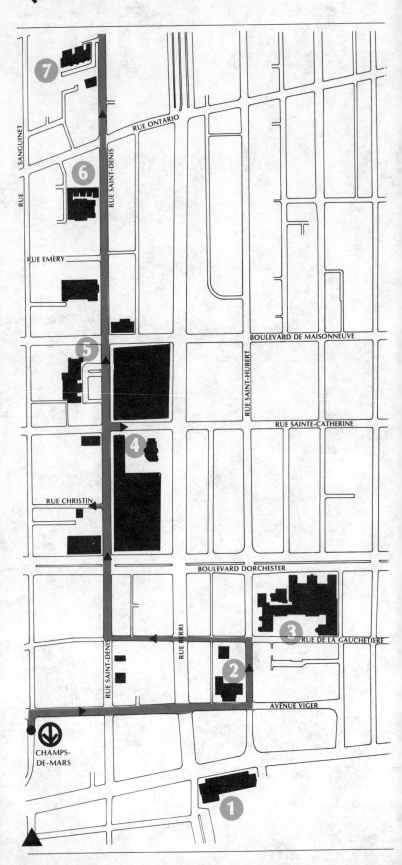

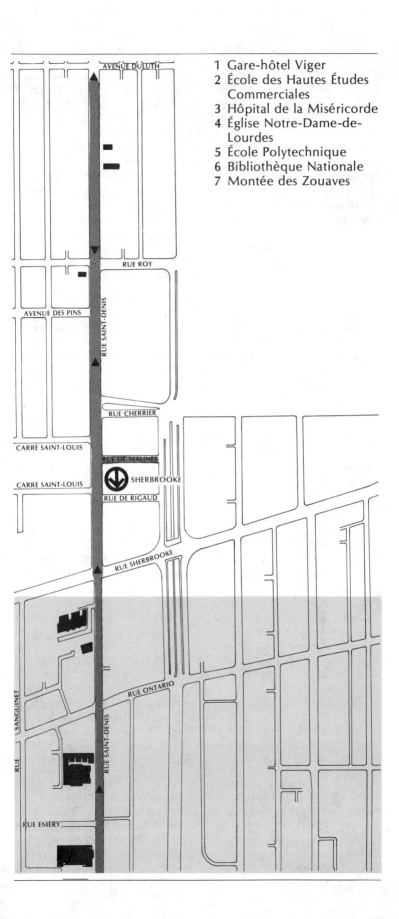

1 Gare-hôtel Viger
2 École des Hautes Études Commerciales
3 Hôpital de la Miséricorde
4 Église Notre-Dame-de-Lourdes
5 École Polytechnique
6 Bibliothèque Nationale
7 Montée des Zouaves

History

Like a kaleidoscope, the St-Denis area is made up of a myriad of pieces: sidewalk cafés, art galleries, intimate restaurants, rows of romantic Victorian façades. The area explored in this tour (bounded by St-Antoine, Duluth, Sanguinet, and St-Hubert streets) has a rich and colorful history. While for many years it was a prestigious suburb where wealthy French-Canadian families lived, it underwent a decline in the middle of the 20th century, only to be revitalized in the recent past. Although reminders of the 19th century remain in the architecture, the forces of transition and growth have altered much of the physical and social make-up of the area. The neighborhood now fulfils a combination of commercial, institutional and cultural functions. As one proceeds north along a half-mile of St-Denis Street, the kaleidoscope shifts and the images change.

Over the past 20 to 25 years, this area has witnessed many changes within and around its borders. Such projects as Maison Radio-Canada, Télé-Métropole, the Ville-Marie Autoroute, Cegep Vieux-Montréal, Place Dupuis, Place du Cercle, the Université du Québec à Montréal and a number of hotels have left their mark. While we can praise, condone or criticize the quality of the changes that have been imposed on the community, this is unarguably a vital and exciting part of the city.

Starting in 1671 and continuing until 1746, this area was composed of farms and seigneuries. Large open fields and stone quarries were found in the unsettled land north of Sherbrooke Street. At that time, de la Gauchetière Street was a dirt path leading to the Seigneurie de la Gauchetière. In the latter half of the 18th century, Sir John Johnson's farm ran north of what is now Ontario Street.

As the city grew beyond the fortification walls in the mid-19th century, the area became an affluent residential suburb, Faubourg Saint-Laurent. The first street to be laid north of the old walls was Viger Avenue (then known as Dubord Street) in 1818. That same year, Denis-Benjamin Viger (father of Jacques Viger, first mayor of Montreal) ceded to the city the site which was to become Viger Square. In 1821 the soil obtained from the levelling of the hillock near Quebec Gate, was used to fill and level this marshy site. A cattle market was established to the east of Viger Square in 1823. Construction of the first Cathédrale St-Jacques, at the corner of St-Catherine and St-Denis, began that year. The cathedral, like so many of Quebec's churches, accelerated and focused residential growth. By 1830 the land north of Viger Avenue had been subdivided into the long narrow estates of Louis-Joseph Papineau and Denis-Benjamin Viger both of whom played an important role in the istory of Quebec. By this time, St-Denis Street was a dirt path leading to Cathédrale St-Jacques.

Through the donations of Denis Viger and another land-owner, Marie Lacroix, Viger Square was enlarged in 1844. By 1851, St-Denis Street had become a main residential artery marking the boundary between Quartier St-Louis and Quartier St-Jacques. During the following 50 years, the population of the area was to more than double.

An awesome fire struck the St-Denis area in 1852, leaving 10,000 people homeless. The majestic greystone façades were built as a result of the subsequent restriction in the use of wood as a building material. Abundant amounts of grey limestone were extracted from the quarries located north of Mont-Royal Boulevard. Elegant examples of residential construction built with this stone can still be found in the many Victorian homes fronting St-Louis Square, Viger Square and St-Denis Street itself.

As grey stone replaced green trees, the demand for public squares grew. Public parks were created to add a bit of color and breathing space to the urban tissue. Viger Square was landscaped in 1855 and St-Jean Baptiste reservoir was transformed into St-Louis Square in 1880. Middle- and upper-class Montrealers built houses around the square, attracted by the proximity of a park.

The corner of St-Denis and Ste-Catherine streets at the end of the 19th century.

The area's tree-lined streets and rows of homogeneous residential units remained much the same until the beginning of the 20th century. At that time, St-Denis Street became attractive to commercial entrepreneurs with the establishment of tramway lines along Dorchester, Ste-Catherine and St-Denis streets. Its transformation was a result of the appearance of a number of commercial enterprises, educational institutions and cultural facilities.

The establishment of schools of higher learning transformed the area into a lively *Quartier Latin*. Construction of École Polytechnique commenced in 1905 and it was followed by the École des Hautes Études Commerciales five years later. The student population soon expanded with the appearance of the medical and law faculties of Université Laval de Montréal (the university became the Université de Montréal in 1919).

The demand for increased educational and cultural facilities brought a wave of innovative construction into the Quartier Latin. Wealthy residents began to move north, leaving many of the row houses to be subdivided for conversion into student lodgings.

By the 1920s, St-Denis was the intellectual and cultural mecca of French Canada, attracting priests, poets and philosophers. However this Golden Age was not to last long: in 1943, the Université de Montréal left St-Denis Street for the north slope of Mount Royal. Many local merchants suffered a loss in income and the area began to deteriorate. While some large Victorian mansions were converted into rooming houses, inexpensive hotels and even brothels, others were simply demolished. A ghostly image settled over the area. The district deteriorated drastically. Viger Square was cut in half for the widening of Berri Street, neglected by the city and left to derelicts.

In the mid-1960s, St-Denis Street underwent a rebirth. Restaurants, bistros, and boutiques sprung up in many of the houses situated between de Maisonneuve Boulevard and Ontario Avenue. Youthful people (of all ages) flocked to the district to enjoy its intimate and relaxed atmosphere.

The area is still evolving. It appears that, for the time being, most of the destructive elements of demolition and negligence have been tamed, but not without the eviction of a large part of the previous inhabitants of the neighborhood. A row of lovely greystone houses situated on St-Hubert Street between de Maisonneuve and Ontario was demolished in 1981, and nothing has been constructed on the empty lot.

Itinerary

The tour begins at Champs-de-Mars metro station, named for the army parade grounds that were once located east of here. The stained-glass window which illuminates the station is by Marcelle Ferron.

At the northwest corner of St-Denis and Viger streets is the former Holy Trinity Memorial Anglican Church which was built in 1864 in the English primitive Gothic style. It is now used by an eastern-rite Catholic congregation.

Square Viger was officially opened in 1860. Originally it was quite large and the city greenhouses were located here for 30 years. Weekly concerts and firework displays attracted Montreal society to the park in its early years. People would stroll under the proud maple and chestnut trees and admire the well-designed flowerbeds, fountains and ponds. (Please note that the correct French word for an open place surrounded by houses is "square" and not "carré")

The 1898 inauguration of the Viger Hotel (still standing south of the square) bought with it glorious days. However, the park soon entered a decline from which it has not risen: one by one, the affluent families who lived around Square Viger moved to the shaded slopes of Mount-Royal. Streetcar service along Dorchester, St-Denis and Ste-Catherine streets brought an influx of commercial establishments. During the subsequent 75 years, the square was used for parking, divided in two by the prolongation of Berri Street south, and gnawed at by the Ville-Marie Autoroute. In 1981 its stately trees were chopped down, and the entire area became a construction site for the extension of the expressway. The attempt to re-establish the square resulted in three sorry plazas, very poor examples of public space design.

Once the extension of the Ville-Marie Autoroute is completed, the city will close St-Antoine and Viger streets to traffic, so that Champs-de-Mars and Viger Square can be re-established as the public squares they once were.

The Union française, a cultural centre for French citizens and francophiles, is located at 429 Viger. Fittingly, the building is in the Second-Empire style, named after the mid-19th century empire of Louis-Napoléon.

1 Gare-hôtel Viger

Viger Station and Hotel, circa 1920.

To the south of St-Antoine Street is Viger Hotel and Train station. Bruce Price designed this building in the same Château style that he used for the Château Frontenac in Quebec City. The hotel closed in 1935, victim of the westerly displacement of Montreal's downtown core. The building has been used for the last 30 years by the municipal administration.

2 École des Hautes Études Commerciales

École des Hautes Études Commerciales is a Beaux-Arts building whose façade is reminiscent of those of the homes of ambitious wealthy Parisians of the early 20th century. Note the sculptures in particular. The building was completed in 1910 and housed the business school established in 1907 by the Chambre de Commerce. The school (now located on the Université de Montréal campus) is the Montreal equivalent of the renowned Paris school of the same name. Dawson College moved into the building in 1970.

The library of the former École des Hautes Études Commerciales in 1966.

3 Hôpital de la Miséricorde

The Centre Hospitalier Jacques Viger is at the corner of St-Hubert and de la Gauchetière. Its oldest section, built in 1853, was the Hôpital de la Miséricorde (hospital of mercy), a maternity hospital for abandoned women. The orphanage wing was added in 1958. Some of the other buildings on de la Gauchetière Street still retain their charm.

The heart of the Quartier Latin is St-Denis Street, north of Dorchester Boulevard. Before we enter it, take a look at St-Denis below de la Gauchetière. The old Académie St-Denis (at 1037) is how renovated, and occupied by offices. On the opposite side is a row of greystone houses with much of their original allure intact.

Above de la Gauchetière, it is the east side which boasts a superb row of houses with many well-kept façades. Although the one-family homes have been subdivided, many still retain their residential use. Hôpital St-Luc was built on the west side of the street in 1930, with a projecting pavilion added more recently.

The Old Munich (1170 St-Denis) is a rather Teutonic introduction to the Latin Quarter. It has hardly been modified since its original use as a furniture warehouse and store, but now houses a rollicking beer garden — a year-round Oktoberfest.

One block further north, and to the left, is 330 Christin Street, an early example of reinforced concrete construction. When this building was erected in 1910, Christin was a calm and pleasant street.

Artist and architect **Napoléon Bourassa** lived at 1242 St-Denis. The house was built in 1878 on land owned by his father-in-law, Louis-Joseph Papineau, leader of the 1837 Rebellion. Do you see the "B's" and "P's" which adorn the façade?

Napoléon Bourassa architect, artist and novelist, was born in L'Acadie, Quebec (1827-1916). He married the daughter of Louis-Joseph Papineau and was the father of Henri Bourassa. He studied in Rome and Florence. In addition to being the creator of such buildings as Notre-Dame-de-Lourdes, he was a portraitist and designed church decorations and sculptures. He was also a historical novelist and one of the founders of *Revue Canadienne* (1846).

The Dandurand Building is named after its owner, Ucal-Henri Dandurand. When designed in 1913, by Ross and MacDonald, this 10-storey building was the only skyscraper east of St-Laurent Boulevard. Dandurand was a real estate promoter and the first Montrealer to sell land on credit. He was responsible for the 1904 subdivision of the Rosemont district, named for his mother, Rose Philips. He also subdivided the village of Verdun in 1909.

4 Église Notre-Dame-de-Lourdes

Notre-Dame-de-Lourdes Church was consecrated in 1876. Napoléon Bourassa used an unusual form for this church: its height is not much less than its length. While its dome and other details are in the Byzantine style, it also has Romanesque features.

Église Saint-Jacques before construction of the Université du Québec à Montréal.

In 1823, the first **Cathédrale St-Jacques** and Bishop's Palace was built northeast of here on land donated by Denis Benjamin Viger, a relative of the bishop of Montreal. His generosity was rewarded by the naming of the street after his patron saint. The cathedral succumbed to flames in 1852 and the bishop of Montreal, Monseigneur Bourget, decided to build the new cathedral at Dominion Square in what was rapidly becoming Montreal's downtown.

With the construction of Complexe Desjardins, one block west of here, and Université du Québec à Montréal, there has been a deliberate effort to make this area a rival to the traditional downtown.

After the fire of 1852, Irish-American architect John Ostell erected a majestic parish church in the Gothic Revival style on top of the original foundations. Only part of the façade on St-Denis Street (rising part way up the bell tower) survived a second fire in 1858.

Victor Bourgeau was responsible for the third church (1860). He incorporated the walls which had survived. In 1880, Curé Sentenne followed Ostell's plans in raising a steeple which is still the tallest church steeple in Montreal. Ten years later, Perrault, Mesnard and Venne designed a new façade for the Ste-Catherine side. Another fire in 1933 required the reconstruction of the interior, which was undertaken by Gaston Gagnier two years later.

The steeple and façade on St-Denis are all that remain after demolition for the university buildings. The façade of this church now shares the block with the Pavillon Judith-Jasmin of the Université du Québec à Montréal (UQAM). Dimitri Dimakopoulos designed both this building and Pavillon Hubert-Aquin which contains the other half of UQAM. He was also responsible for Complexe Desjardins and Salle Wilfred Pelletier of Place-des-Arts.

It is indisputable that the influx of 25,000 students has had positive economic and cultural effects. Still, the university's implantation has evicted much of the population. Most of the remaining residents live on limited incomes; they would have great difficulty in finding a new place to live if evicted from their present homes.

An attempt has been made to integrate the forms of the university buildings into the surroundings, with four storeys on St-Denis, rising to eight storeys on Berri. However, inside these structures is a labyrinth. A maze of indistinguishable, lifeless corridors make it difficult to find one's way around. Even within the open galleries it is very difficult to get from one end to the other, or to find the correct exit. The value of preserving only the spire and south transept of the St-Jacques Church is debatable.

5 École Polytechnique

École Polytechnique was founded in 1873 and was originally housed on Sherbrooke Street, across from Lafontaine Park. Architect and engineer Émile Vanier (one of the school's first graduates) was responsible for this building, completed in 1905. Vanier also designed the St-Louis-de-Mile-End city hall which is on the Plateau Mont-Royal tour. The building is part of the latest phase of the UQAM campus, which includes surrounding new construction.

At the northeast corner of de Maisonneuve Boulevard and St-Denis Street is the Quebec headquarters of the St. John's Ambulance whose cool expanse of dark glass does not blend in with the rest of the street. From the sidewalk, the Maltese cross-shaped roof looks like a nun's hood. You may want to take a seat to rest on the concrete wall surrounding the building, as many people do.

Théâtre Saint-Denis shortly after its 1916 construction date.

The 2500 seats of **Théâtre St-Denis** make it the second largest concert hall in Montreal, after Place-des-Arts. Sarah Bernhardt and other famous actors performed in this theater. The marquee and entrance are recent, and if removed they might reveal the magnificent original façade designed by Ernest Barott.

During the summer, Place Émile-Borduas, east of St-Denis, is a small pedestrian mall where painters and craftspeople sell their works.

6 Bibliothèque Nationale

At 1700 St-Denis is the National Library of Quebec. It was built in 1914-15 in the Beaux-Arts style by Eugène Payette and is reminiscent of a Parisian town house. Payette is also responsible for the municipal library on Sherbrooke East (Terrasse Ontario Tour). In the early 1960s, the Sulpician fathers donated the building, along with their priceless collection of Canadiana, to the province.

Glasswork in the concert hall.

At 1714 St-Denis is a reinforced concrete structure built in 1908 by Omer Marchand. The versatility of Marchand is evident in this apartment building where he explored the possibilities of reinforced concrete. The closed arcades and cantilevered central balcony structure are in the Art Nouveau style. Marchand also designed St-Cunégonde Church (Little Burgundy tour), the Grand Séminaire Chapel (Lincoln-Tupper tour) and the Mother House of the Notre-Dame Congregation at Sherbrooke and Atwater (Westmount tour).

Like Beaux-Esprits across the street, the restaurant-bar La Côte à Baron at 2070 St-Denis is an excellent example of renovation.

7 Montée des Zouaves

In 1867 a great many pious French-Canadians met at Montée des Zouaves, officially known as Terrasse Saint-Denis, to discuss joining the Zouaves, an army which defended what were then the Papal States in Italy. Towards the end of the century, the building was the headquarters of a literary circle which included 17-year-old **Émile Nelligan.**

Émile Nelligan, poet, was born in Montreal (1879-1941). He was an undisciplined student who at a young age showed a talent for poetry which bordered on the genius. He was influenced by Baudelaire, Verlaine, Mallarmé and Rimbaud. His most important works were Le Vaisseau d'Or and La Romance du Vin.

(Cross Sherbrooke Street to reach the Sherbrooke metro station or to continue northward). There are a number of examples of fine renovation work on Sherbrooke Street, east of St-Denis. If you look to the right along Sherbrooke, you will see the Club Canadien (438 Sherbrooke east) with its green copper patina roof. This delightful Victorian house was originally the home of Dandurand, the affluent real estate investor mentioned above.

The Institut des Sourdes-Muettes, located north of Cherrier Street, is discussed on the Plateau Mont-Royal tour.

The former École d'opérette at 3774 St-Denis Street should be mentioned because here was founded the respected intellectual journal, Parti Pris. It is also noteworthy because here was the office of Save Montreal, from 1978 to 1981.

On the left side of St-Denis, between Roy and Duluth, is a group of antique stores. Take a look at the roofs of the buildings further north, a lively array. The reasonably priced restaurant-bar L'Express at 3927 is an excellent Art-Deco renovation. A Moorish touch is added to the street by the pink stucco building at 3903 St-Denis.

ST-LOUIS

ST-LOUIS
Montreal's mosaic

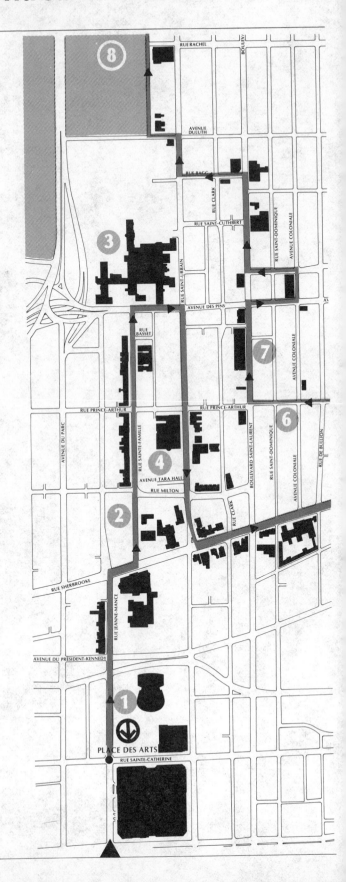

1 Place des Arts and
  Complexe Desjardins
2 Le Cour Ste-Famille
3 Hôtel-Dieu
4 École d'Architecture
5 Square St-Louis
6 Prince-Arthur Street
7 Boulevard St-Laurent
8 Parc Jeanne-Mance

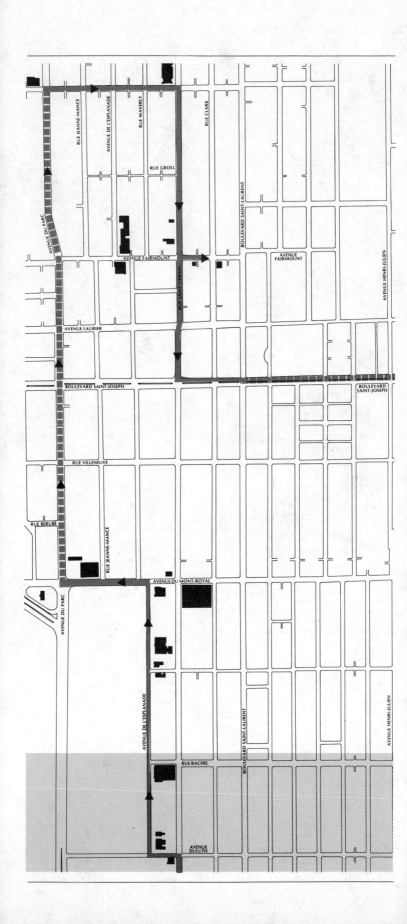

History

The area covered by this tour is a microcosm of Montreal. During this walk you will see the remnants of two prosperous late 19th century neighborhoods, one French and one English. Set between them, and extending further north, is the heart of Montreal's immigrant district. The walk is divided into two sections and takes about three hours. Probably the best day to explore the area is on a Saturday, when the commercial streets are the busiest. However, any bright morning will entice residents to sit on their front steps and balconies to chat with their neighbors passing by.

The walk goes through distinct zones which share a palpable sense of community. People do not live next door to strangers, for neighbors become friends. This is due to cohesive factors: residents are linked by ethnic origin, similar vocation or simply because they have lived side by side for many years and have shared their sorrows and successes.

Until 1867, when Ste-Famille Street was laid out, the western part of this district was made up of quiet fields and orchards. The first greystone row houses were built in the early 1870s and were inhabited by such people as Alex Leslie, hardware merchant; Joseph Lafrenière, flour and grain merchant; John Parlow, bookbinder and stationer; William McLaren, shoe manufacturer; A.F. Dunlop, architect; and the Reverend Wright.

At that time the area between University Street, Sherbrooke Street, Pine Avenue and St-Laurent Boulevard, was a suburb of Montreal. It rapidly filled with English-speaking, upper middle-class inhabitants as more row housing was built on narrow lots in the 1880s. Many of these people were involved with McGill University, a 10-minute walk away.

The 19th-century suburbs differed from those of today. Victorian three-storey row housing used space more economically than present houses do. Since walking was the primary mode of transportation, housing was relatively dense and all the services necessary for daily life were to be found within a small area.

After the First World War, Montreal's middle class began to move from the eastern side of the mountain to the new suburbs, made accessible by the automobile. St-Louis was no longer considered a prestigious place to live and was left for the working class.

In the mid-1960s, many university students and young professionals returned to the houses in which their grandparents had lived. Like the McGill Ghetto area to the west, this area is becoming fashionable, as more affluent people return to the inner city, purchasing newly-revitalized housing stock.

The houses located between Hutchison, Milton, Ste-Famille and Pine have been converted into co-operatives by many of their residents. With non-profit housing co-operatives, tenants who cannot afford to buy their own homes individually can do so by joining together and obtaining subsidies from the federal and provincial governments for necessary renovations. This is especially needed in Montreal, where about 60% of the population is made up of tenants, a proportion much higher than elsewhere in Canada.

The lovely Victorian woodwork was preserved during the renovation of these houses.

Some residents tried to organize housing co-ops in the late 1960s, even before developer demolished much of the houses in the area to build a series of apartment towers, named La Cité.

In 1976, Save Montreal in alliance with residents managed to persuade the city to pass a zoning by-law limiting construction in the area to four-storey buildings. Prevented from further construction by this down-zoning (and also because the first apartment complex was not profitable) the owners of LaCité abandoned plans to add supplementary towers to the four already built. The local residents, with the support of the urban conservation group Heritage Montreal, persuaded the Canada Mortgage and Housing Corporation (the federal government housing agency) to buy all the remaining Victorian row houses with the aim of converting them into non-profit residences. About 700 units have been renovated and their management turned over to their inhabitants. Co-operatives and other non-profit organizations such as senior citizens' homes have been established. This is an example of neighbors getting together and taking control of their community.

As you walk through this area, you will see signs of gentrification. The middle class, which first settled this area, have returned. Prince-Arthur Street, east of St-Laurent Boulevard, has become a restaurant-lined mall which rivals downtown for activity on a Saturday night. Parts of St-Laurent Boulevard and Park Avenue have seen the addition of chic bars, cafés and boutiques.

Itinerary

Leave Place des Arts metro station by the exit marked Place-Des-Arts in order to see the artwork which is located in the main lobby of that cultural centre. Then walk through the Ste-Catherine Street exit. Complexe Desjardins is directly opposite.

1 Place des Arts and Complexe Desjardins

Place des Arts is composed of two buildings containing three concert halls/theatres. The provincial government has postponed plans to construct the Musée d'Art Contemporain on the site.

Salle Wilfred Pelletier, the large, ornamented building, was designed by the architects Affleck, Desbarats, Dimikopoulos, Leben-sold, Michaud and Sise. The inaugural concert was held on September 21, 1963. Salle Wilfred Pelletier is the home of the Montreal Symphony Orchestra and is also used by the Grands Ballets Canadiens. The Opéra du Québec also puts on productions here.

A number of works of well-known Canadian artists are on display in the main lobby or *Piano Nobile*. Most prominent are two tapestries. One was designed by Robert LaPalme and executed by Aubusson. It represents the meeting of Orpheus and Dionysius on the banks of the river Styx; the second is the work of Micheline Beauchemin and was inspired by the legend of the fatal flight of Icarus. An imposing sculpture on the west side of the upper foyer is by Anne Kehane. Made of brass sheets, *Anges Radieux* by Louis Archambault, dominates the main stairway. Julien Hébert was responsible for the large aluminum mural of the lower foyer, while Jordi Bonnet created the ceramic tympana which adorn the entrances to the corridors leading to the orchestra seats. In the upper part of the lobby is a large marble swan executed by Hans Schleeh, as well as a work by the Inuit sculptor Innukpuk. Two important paintings were donated to Place des Arts in 1976: *La Bolduc* by Jean-Claude Riopelle and *Hochelaga* by Fernand Toupin.

Two theatres are housed in a stepped building to the east, which was designed by the firm of David, Barott and Boulva. Its official opening occured on April 30, 1967. The two theatres are placed one above the other and soundproofed through the suspension of the floors and ceilings from thousands of springs. This ingenious construction permits the use of both halls at the same time.

Théâtre Maisonneuve is located on the upper level, in the part of the building which is visible from outside. Drama, recitals, and dance are presented on its vast, adjustable stage. The lobbies contain many works of arts which were especially designed for this building. A sculpture by Charles Daudelin and a painting by Louis Feito decorate the entrance; the mural is the work of Peter Gnass, and the mezzanine tapestry is by Hélène Baranyna. The magnificent acrylic curtain is by Micheline Beauchemin.

Théâtre Port-Royal located below grade level, is used almost exclusively for drama. Of an unusual design, the theatre is made up of long parallel rows of seats and a very wide stage, which measures 100 feet (29 m) in width. Its foyer has a large terra-cotta mural, the work of Jean Chartier, and two paintings by Jean McEwen and Paul Beaulieu. There are also two enormous photographic murals by Michel Saint-Jean.

Place des Arts: Salle Wilfred Pelletier.

The airy interior of Complexe Desjardins.

Across from Place des Arts is **Complexe Desjardins**, a joint project of the Quebec government and the Mouvement Desjardins
credit unions. The complex is made up of a multi-levelled structure, a hotel and three office buildings grouped around a *Galleria* or enclosed space. Complexe Desjardins was completed in
1976. The theme and overall plan were developed by the Société
La Haye-Ouellet, the principal architect and planner of the
project.

The basilican structure rises three storeys and respects the scale
of the street. The many exhibits, shows and other activities which
are on view have made it an important meeting place in the central city. In the centre of the *Galleria* is a work by Pierre Granche
who has designed and assembled a three-dimensional stabile
whose central cube marks time with a slow back-and-forth
movement.

(Walk up Jeanne-Mance Street, past President Kennedy Avenue)
On the left is a group of 65 housing units at 2020-2092 Jeanne-
Mance which are on the boundary between commercial downtown and residential St-Louis. In the early 1970s these attractive
19th-century greystone houses were bought by a developer who
wanted to replace them with a highrise. But the city refused to
issue a demolition permit and Quebec's Ministry of Cultural
Affairs classified the façades, thereby preventing their demolition. In 1975, tenants united to buy the houses as a co-operative.
These buildings are noteworthy for the pleasing harmony of the
roof detail.

Across the street is the former **Institut de technologie de Montréal** (now part of the Université du Québec à Montréal) also
known as the Montreal Institute of Technology. The building

was designed by J.S. Archibald and Maurice Perreault and completed in 1910. The architects were inspired by a number of American public buildings such as the New York Public Library and Washington's Union Station. An imposing entrance dominates the structure, and its principle façade is majestically treated in the Beaux-Arts style. The rear displays elements of industrial architecture. The architects have designed the façades and forms to follow the functions of the building. The most prestigious portion housed the classrooms where theory was taught, while the workshops in the rear were designed in a more restrained manner.

Hydro-Québec's announced plans to build a new head office on the east side of Jeanne-Mance, below Sherbrooke, have been put aside, much to the relief of local residents who feared further encroachment of downtown on their residential area.

A collection of nightclubs was once located on this part of Sherbrooke Street. Montreal's counter-culture gathered here during the decades when the Fine-Arts school was located in this area. Beatniks were suceeded by hippies and flower children at La Hutte Suisse, Le Chat Noir, La Casa Espagnole and Le Mât des Oliviers.

The northeast corner of Sherbrooke and Jeanne-Mance is an undefined triangle of grass. Until 1979, this part of Jeanne-Mance had five traffic lanes which merged into three, halfway up the block. The replacement of two lanes with a bit of vegetation was a result of pressure from residents. Members of the Jeanne-Mance and Ste-Famille street committees have been strongly assertive of their rights to decent housing in a safe neighborhood since the early 1970s. They organized a number of demonstrations to protest the use of this street as a major north-south traffic artery. One imaginative tactic they used was a *die-in*, complete with ketchup-bleeding children to underline the danger of crossing a residential road-turned-autoroute.

(Turn right and walk up **Ste-Famille Street**) Benoît and Gabriel Basset gave the area around here, known as Mont Ste-Famille, to the nuns of Hôtel-Dieu in 1730. In 1860, the nuns built the hospital, which you can see at the head of the street, as a replacement for their buildings on St-Paul Street which had become surrounded by commercial establishments. Mont Ste-Famille was then the outskirts of the city.

Later the nuns sold the land on either side of the street to developers, and by the end of the 1870s most of the western side of Ste-Famille was filled with what were then single-family homes.

The houses at 3417-25 Ste-Famille form a fine ensemble of greystone apartments whose façade is in mint condition. Those are probably the original stained glass panels from the Art Nouveau period of the late 1800s at 3417 and 3421.

2 Le Cour Ste-Famille

Inner courtyard.

Le Cour Ste-Famille is a new group of buildings designed by architects Cayouette & Saia. This insertion was built of brick and concrete. The architects used sloped roofs and a dormer window motif to reflect some of the traditional architectural details of the street. They were able to create a courtyard between the houses which face the street, and an additional row in the rear of the lot. This format has eliminated interior corridors and maximized the usable space. Le Cour Ste-Famille was awarded Save Montreal's *Prix Orange* for successful integration in 1983.

On the northwest corner of Milton is the Café Commun-Commune, a worker-managed restaurant. Most of the row housing on the street was built in the last three decades of the 19th century. The buildings on the west side of the street are part of the Milton-Park housing co-operative project. They were renovated in stages, beginning in 1981. The ornamentation, the quality of the stone, the bay and dormer windows and the elaborate ironwork, give all these houses an irreplaceable quality.

Despite a couple of unfortunate intrusions, Ste-Famille Street still has the allure of an architectural ensemble. The street terminates nicely with Hôtel-Dieu on Pine Avenue and the École Technique de Montréal on Sherbrooke. A city's charm is gained not so much from the architectural importance or beauty of particular buildings, but rather from the harmonious effect generated by a cluster of simple, yet complementary buildings.

The shorter, squatter house at 3548 Ste-Famille looks different from the surrounding row houses. In fact, Mrs. Ransom's mansion stood alone for almost a decade until around 1880.

The houses at 3561-75 are an example of good infill architecture. They were designed by Mario Biocca, who also renovated 3492 Durocher, and did the building at Milton and Park (McGill tour).

The last seven houses on the southeast side below Prince-Arthur were built around 1880. They are noteworthy because of their excellent condition as well as their gardens. Isn't the rounded wing at 3599 impressive? In the last 10 years, one by one, these houses were renovated and now they form a very attractive group.

The house at 3626 is distinctive because it is built of polished stone and is taller than the others. Joseph Vanier, an accountant and the cousin of Canada's first French-Canadian Governor General, lived in this house from 1905 to 1940. This house, like so many others in the neighborhood, was later subdivided and is now a rooming house. Fortunately, the beautiful plaster decorations of its parlor ceiling remain intact.

Across the street is **Roxy Court** (3655-3675), a European-style apartment group built in the late 1920s. This group was designed to fit in with the rest of the buildings, to be a positive contribution to the street. A feeling of community, a connection with the street and with neighbors is encouraged by such construction.

In the early 1900s, the eminent physicist Ernest Rutherford lived at 3702 Ste-Famille, while he taught at McGill University. His revolutionary research into the structure of matter and the nature of radioactivity earned him the 1908 Nobel prize for chemistry. The building is now used by the nuns of Hôtel-Dieu.

3 Hôtel-Dieu

Hôtel-Dieu, circa 1910.

Hôtel-Dieu (209 Pine Avenue West) was designed by Victor Bourgeau and completed in 1860. It is made up of a main portion flanked by two lateral wings. The chapel wing projects from the main building towards Ste-Famille Street. A number of additions have been made over the years and, although they are in different styles, most of them are in harmony through the use of similar colors and materials. The pavilion on the right is a residence for retired priests, while the nuns live in an attached building on the left which is surrounded by a garden and a thick stone wall. Paladian windows and the accentuated pointing of the stones add a classical note to the building. Hôtel-Dieu is imposing through its austere, yet harmonious appearance. The impression of power is created by the imposing dome and the large size of the complex, made possible by the size of the property.

The section of St-Urbain between Prince-Arthur and Sherbrooke was formerly called Upper St-Urbain. The pleasant row at 3679-65 St-Urbain is a reminder of the original elegant houses which once lined the entire street.

As you walk south down St-Urbain, note the terrace of greystone houses at 87-99 Guibault. Their present deteriorated state cannot hide their inherent beauty.

St-Urbain Street was widened to become a major north-south artery, partly to accommodate the hospitals. The noisy increase in traffic volume damaged the street environment and led to a decline in the quality of housing.

The first hospital to appear on St-Urbain was the Hôpital Hôtel-Dieu. On the southwest corner of Pine Avenue and St-Urbain is the Institut de Recherches Cliniques de Montréal, a research institute and clinic affiliated with Hôtel-Dieu. To the south, on the same block, is the Montreal Chest Hospital. Further, at the southwest corner of St-Urbain and Prince-Arthur, is **Hôpital Ste-Jeanne-d'Arc**, established by a religious order from France.

Prince-Arthur Street used to be called Bagg Street after Stanley Clark Bagg, one of Montreal's largest landowners in the late 19th century. This part of the street first appeared on 1853 maps. The street was renamed in 1890 to honor the Duke of Connaught, third son of Queen Victoria, and Governor General of Canada at the time.

At the northwest corner of St-Urbain and Prince-Arthur, where there is now a parking lot, was St. Martin's Anglican Church, completed in the autumn of 1874. This church was one of the numerous English Protestant churches in the area. It was demolished in the 1960s.

The southeast corner was the site of the Home for Friendless Women, in the late 1800s. Appropriately, the last occupant of the building now on the site was the Women's Information and Referral Centre. This building had been used as a nursing school by the Hôpital Ste-Jeanne-d'Arc until the early 1970s when nursing education was transferred to the colleges. The hospital tried to evict the Women's Centre in 1973. The women's group fought the eviction in the court until 1976 when the building was damaged by fire, and the group was forced to move to the mansion next door. The Société d'Hypothèque du Québec has renovated the structure for use as low-cost housing.

The present Women's Information and Referral Centre is at 3585 Prince-Arthur, one of two mansions remaining on this block. This house was built for Trefflé Berthiaume, founder of *La Presse*. It was purchased by Victor Morin (president of the notary society and the Royal Society of Canada) at the turn of the century.

The mansion at 3567 St-Urbain was designed by J.W. Hopkins in 1875 for Sam Burland, the printer of several atlases of Montreal. Later, the Young Men's and Young Women's Hebrew Association used the building. It is now the **Chinese Baptist Church.**

The Centre Multi-Ethnique St-Louis, at 3553 St-Urbain, is a multicultural centre founded in the beginning of this century by middle-class citizens for members of the working class. It was set up in connection with McGill University and was part of a chain of University Settlements in many North American cities. It acquired its present name in 1979.

The St-Urbain Community Centre, as it is also called, is involved in important issues that affect local residents. It houses an artist's workshop, a daycare centre, an old-age club, a café, and offers many other services.

Walk down St-Urbain to Milton. You will note a street sign, Tara Hall. This is one of a number of "phantom" streets in Montreal.

4 École d'Architecture

The former School of Architecture is at 3450 St-Urbain. It was designed in 1922 by Omer Marchand and Ernest Cormier. École des Beaux-Arts de Montréal, at 125 Sherbrooke Street West, was founded in March 1922 by the government of Quebec. These two buildings share a number of characteristics: monumental dimensions, symmetry of articulation and decorations adopted from classical architecture. The École des Beaux-Arts building is no longer an art school, but houses the Quebec national archives. It was built in 1907 according to the plans and specifications of A.F. Dunlop.

Across St-Urbain, at 81 Sherbrooke Street, is a classical residence built in the 1830s. A developer acquired the mansion in 1975 and planned to replace it with a twelve-storey office tower. However, the classification of the house by the Ministry of Cultural Affairs disrupted the plans.

Stanley Clark Bagg was one of the first residents of this area. His house, "Fairmount Villa," was located at the corner of St-Urbain and Sherbrooke. Charles Brydges, managing director of the Grand Trunk Railway, lived on the other side of St-Urbain.

The Élysée Cinema, on the northeast corner of Milton and St-Urbain, shows first-run films, mainly from France. The Élysée is a good example of adaptation of a building for a new use: from 1904-54, this was the Austrian-Hungarian synagogue.

The Popliger Building is two blocks away, at 3548-3564 Clark. It was built in 1909 as flats to cater to a major influx of Jewish immigrants fleeing Eastern Europe. The owner proudly inscribed his name, as well as the date in Arabic numerals and the Hebrew equivalent, on a commemorative plaque set into the central roofline. The red brick is articulated with dressed stone. The impression of symmetry is strong despite the interesting differences between the two sides of the façade. A striving for grandeur, a concern with status is conveyed. Purchased by a co-ownership group in 1980, its rehabilitation won the 1982 Crédit Foncier/Héritage Canada award for private renovation.

At the northwest corner of Clark and Sherbrooke is the former **residence of William Notman**, built around 1852. It is a beautiful building of simple, clean lines with a façade of dressed limestone. Notman was one of Canada's most important photographers and his work is a remarkable record of Victorian Montreal. A substantial part of it is preserved by McGill University at the Notman photographic archives, located at 690 Sherbrooke Street West. John Molson Jr., chief accountant of Molson's Bank, lived in a mansion located where the gas station now stands.

In 1864, the **Sherbrooke Street Methodist Church** was built near Clark Street. Its triangular shape, rough stone envelope and the windows over the three entrances give this building, designed by C.P. Thomas, a very elegant appearance. It has been a Greek Orthodox Church since 1925. It is hoped that the church will be restored, repairing damage suffered in a 1986 fire. On the corner of St-Laurent and Sherbrooke is a concrete apartment building designed by J.A. Godin in 1910, in a union of Art Nouveau and modern architecture. Concrete was a new material at the time this was constructed and Godin made exemplary use of it, creating arches, rounded angles and other features of Art Nouveau. This was one of the first reinforced concrete buildings in Montreal. Two other early ones remain, they are on the St-Denis — Quartier Latin tour.

At 2115 St-Laurent (below Sherbrooke Street) is the building which housed **Eckers Breweries**. Its façade is a powerful design in the style of the American architect Henry Hobson Richardson.

East of Saint-Laurent Boulevard stand five attached apartment buildings, once gutted by fire. They were saved by private renovation and turned into a condominium in the early 1980s.

In 1846, the **Notre-Dame de la Charité du Bon Pasteur** sisters had a convent constructed on the south side of Sherbrooke. The nuns were involved with the reforming of delinquent girls and women. The main building of the Couvent du Bon Pasteur is based on 17th-century French convent construction and is one of the few Montreal religious buildings which are faced in cut-stone. It is made up of a number of wings which were built between 1846 and 1894. The exterior walls are smooth, with no delineation of the different storeys. Hipped roofs are punctuated by dormer windows and the main building is crowned by a turret.

The chapel is located in the central part of the building. Designed in 1878 by Victor Bourgeau, it is made up of four naves grouped around a central chancel, the only such arrangement in Montreal. The stone fringe on the corbie-stepped gable of the central projection highlights the inset statue.

SIMPA, a municipal agency, oversaw the renovation of the building (which began in 1982) including the restoration of the chapel, and conversion of the remainder of the complex to a mix of condominiums and subsidized housing.

Between Hôtel-de-Ville and Sanguinet streets is the former Mont-Saint-Louis, designed in 1887 by Jean-Baptiste Resther. This long horizontal building has projecting pavilions which are capped by true mansard roofs. The central mansard is in the form of a square dome. This design was based on the Palais des Tuileries in Paris, a 17th-century residence of the kings of France.

The treatment of the substructure and the mansard roofs diminishes the height of this building. The architect treated the windows on each of the main storeys differently: semi-circular arches on the ground floor, basket arches on the second floor and lintels on the third. The lateral pavilions are pierced by double windows, while those of the main projection are in the Palladio style. They interrupt the horizontal effect of the rest of the building. Unfortunately, the original monumental staircase has disappeared and the 1906 extension on the western side has destroyed the symmetry of the facade. In 1987, work began to recycle the building into market-rate housing.

(Follow Laval Street north to Square St-Louis) Originally, the houses on **Laval Street** between Sherbrooke Street and Pine Avenue were inhabited by French Canadian doctors, lawyers and other professionals. Many of the buildings on the street have retained their original character and, as you walk, look closely at them to appreciate the finely worked stone, elegantly carved doors and the opulent mansard roofs.

5 Square St-Louis

In 1848, the City of Montreal bought the property which is now St-Louis Square to install a reservoir. By 1879, the municipality's population had increased to such an extent that the reservoir was no longer adequate and it was transformed into a park. In the following year, the square was named after two brothers, Emmanuel and Jean-Baptiste St-Louis who were important businessmen living nearby. (The correct French word for this sort of open place surrounded by houses is *square* and not *carré*).

A western view of Square St-Louis.

The first houses around the square were built in the 1870s. They became the homes of Montreal's French-Canadian upper middle class. Artists were also attracted by the square: In the past, the poets Albert Lozeau, Émile Nelligan and Louis Fréchette lived in the area. Nelligan lived at 3686 Laval, between 1887 and 1892. In the last couple of decades, Gaston Miron, Claude Jutras, Pauline Julien, André Gagnon and many others involved in music, film, painting, writing, and drama have moved here.

If your French is very good, read the poem by Michel Bujold, which is painted on the side of the house at 336 Square St-Louis.

St-Louis Square is one of the most beautiful in Montreal. An ideal example of the residential square, it achieves a coherence made up of exuberant decorative elements. Take a look at the diversity of building details. Exterior staircases, dormer windows, wrought iron railings, flagpoles—each competes with the other behind the majestic old trees. It is clear why architecture is said to be frozen music. Note the stained glass at 284 and 312, the castle roof of 357 and the miniature railing fence around the shaped roof

towers at 301-317 (a picturesque adaptation of a style used in 17th-century castles in France).

The users of the park match the exuberent architecture. A public square such as this creates a place where social activities can occur. It makes it possible for people to relax, look at the trees, watch and talk to other people. During the summer, the Square is the apex of the Prince-Arthur Street pedestrian mall, while in the winter, the paths around the central area are flooded for skating. The first such rink was established in 1879.

Of course, the square is no longer a bastion of the French-Canadian bourgeoisie. There are, for example, the Hôpital Voghel on the south, and the Chinese Youth Centre on the west. However, the great majority of the residents are still francophone Québécois and, recently, some of the rooming houses have been bought and renovated to become, once again, large flats. A recent example is on the corner of Drolet, beside the building with the castellated tower. While the majority of the residents are young — about two-thirds are under forty — there is also a large group of older people who have spent their whole lives in the neighborhood.

The tall black and grey building just to the east of the square was given the *Prix Citron* by the Montreal Society of Architecture, for being the ugliest building of 1974. The **École nationale d'Hôtellerie**, one of the few professional hotel schools in the world, is located there.

6 Prince-Arthur Street

In the 1960s, counter-culture people were attracted to this area by the low rents, stimulating cultural diversity, and inner-city location. Towards the end of the decade, encouraged by the modest rents for locations on Prince-Arthur Street, several of them opened boutiques selling old clothing, hashish pipes and leather goods. Like Crescent Street downtown, the counter-culture was followed by the avant-garde who were followed by the people you see today. The city of Montreal helped this evolution by establishing a pedestrian mall in 1981. Generally, restaurants have been able to pay higher rents than the original boutiques, most of whom have moved elsewhere.

On **Coloniale Street** are renovated houses painted in vivid colors. The buildings were bought during the 1970s by their Portuguese owners who did much of the repair work themselves. The **Portuguese community** was given a Montreal Society of Architecture award of excellence in 1975 in recognition of the improvements they made on these buildings.

At 3601-29 Coloniale is an example of in-fill housing built by the city of Montreal which has abandoned the idea of large housing projects. The city now constructs smaller buildings such as this one, which are designed to suit the specific needs of the district and are in scale with the surroundings.

7 Boulevard St-Laurent

St-Laurent Boulevard has always been an important street in Montreal. It is the dividing line for the city: addresses for east-west streets begin here, just as north-south streets start numbering at the Saint Lawrence River. Traditionally, anglophones lived west of here, while francophones lived to the east. In English it is known as Saint Lawrence Boulevard or as "the Main," because for many years it was the main street of the St-Louis district. The street was established in the early 18th century during the French Régime and extended north from the city, all the way to Sault-aux-Récollets on the Rivière des Prairies.

By the 1830s, the road passed through many fertile farms and orchards. Several wealthy people owned mansions on long narrow farms stretching north from Sherbrooke Street. Stanley Clark Bagg, who would become the largest landowner on the island of Montreal and for whom Clark and Bagg streets are named, owned the land just west of St-Laurent extending one mile north from Sherbrooke. Houses began to appear in the countryside in the 1850s. For the most part, these mansions lined Sherbrooke Street. It was a middle-class area, inhabited primarily by English-speaking merchants, businessmen and tradesmen.

For a time, the physical barrier of the slope below Sherbrooke Street was a social barrier as well. However, the barrier was weakened when the Montreal city Passenger Railway Company opened a line of horse-drawn tramways extending as far north as Mont-Royal Boulevard. As two horses had quite a hard time negotiating the hill, an extra team of animals was added. Once the tramway was electrified, in 1892, it was no longer difficult to climb the slope. A new wave of working-class immigrants came to this area when pogroms in Russia started a stream of fleeing Jews, in the early 1880s. The stream soon became a flood, and by the 1920s Yiddish was heard everywhere around St-Laurent. We will see many remnants from the Jewish era in our walk along the street. Wealthy Jews established textile factories in this area, but most Jews were poor working people struggling to survive. The factory owners employed whatever cheap labor they could hire, making no distinctions in their exploitation.

During the 1930s the centre of the Jewish community moved northward, past Mount-Royal Boulevard. After the Second World War the Jews moved even further away, to Côte-des-Neiges, Côte-St-Luc and the other suburbs northwest of the city.

The Greeks followed one step behind. They settled first on St-Laurent, near Sherbrooke, and later moved northward. Park Avenue became an axis of the Greek community along its entire length.

Of course, Jews and Greeks are not the only immigrants to Montreal — this part of the walk will point out evidence of people from every continent. Many Hungarians and Slavs moved to the St-Laurent area after the Second World War, and in the 1960s they were joined by the Portuguese and Latin-Americans. A cluster of Chinese families live on Clark and St-Dominique streets, just to the west of St-Laurent.

These immigrants have made St-Laurent an exciting and exotic place to shop. Each ethnic group craves its own distinctive foods, and there are now specialty stores catering to every culinary taste. The only major ethnic groups

A 1890's photograph from the foot of St-Laurent Boulevard.

which do not find their culinary heritage on the Main are the Chinese who still have Chinatown, and the Italians. Actually, the Italian area is not too far from here. Jean-Talon Market, about two miles (3 km) north of here (at the intersection of Casgrain and St-Dominique), is the focal point for the Italians of Montreal.

In the last couple of years, more upscale "trendy" products are taking over many commerces on St-Laurent.

It is possible that the ethnic flavor which makes the street unique in the city will be eliminated, giving way to yet another chic artery.

The Toronto-Dominion Bank at 3590 St-Laurent was originally the Dominion Bank. It was designed in 1909 by A. Cox and W.A. Amos and enlarged in 1928 and again in 1949. Apparently, before its merger with the Bank of Toronto, the Dominion Bank did not have many branches in Montreal and this is one of only two remaining.

The large airy lofts of the buildings on St-Laurent are an attraction to designers and artists. A number of New-Wave clothing designers and retailers have moved to the street. This influx of new tenants has begun to pressure the rents upwards.

Walk on the east side to admire the magnificent and massive **Baxter Block**, (3640-3712) extending along the block. This building retains its original common heating system. Note the impressive bay window which projects above 3650. Factories were once located behind the superbly arched windows of the upper floors, explaining the large number of wholesalers and dry goods stores which once lined the Main. Stores on the part of St-Laurent between Milton Street and Pine Avenue have changed most rapidly, equalled only on St-Laurent north of Laurier Avenue.

At 3622 is the office of a local Greek-language newspaper, a holdover from the time when most of the Greek community lived near here. The brightly-colored pottery display at 3556 is the showcase of Arka, a Ukranian specialty store. Many Ukrainians have now moved to the Rosemont area, northeast of here.

Cinéma Parallèle is at 3684 St-Laurent. In addition to running a restaurant, Café Meliès (named after an early cinematographer), this organization shows intellectual and experimental films, runs a distribution centre and organizes the Festival International du Nouveau Cinéma de Montréal.

All along the street, among the clothing stores, you will find a number of delicatessen and other speciality food stores, some of whom offer take-out meals. Many of the stores are part of the Village St-Laurent, a merchants' association which lobbied the city to include The Main in its beautification program; hence the flower pots, benches and distinctive lighting. Probably their most successful venture is the annual ethnic festival and food fair, a week-long event which welcomes about 200,000 people in the early summer.

Guilbault's Zoological Gardens were located between St-Laurent, St-Urbain, Guilbault and Bagg (now Prince-Arthur) in the 1860s and 1870s. The gardens included wild animals, sideshows and acrobatic performances. Their great popularity for group picnics and other outings did not prevent the disappearance of the zoo in 1885, during a construction boom.

The City and District Savings Bank at the corner of Pine and St-Laurent used to have signs in the windows boasting that its clientèle could be served in nine languages. While these were removed in 1980, another bank, located further north, still claims to be quadrilingual.

(Turn right on Pine Avenue) At 100 Pine Avenue is the **Théâtre de Quat'Sous** founded by Paul Buissonneau, one of Montreal's pioneers in drama.

(Go north on Coloniale to Roy Street) **Roy Street** was named in the memory of Marguerite Roy, wife of Jean-Marie Cadieux de Courville who named the east-west streets he laid out on his property after his wife and daughters.

Waldman's Fish Market (74 Roy Street East) is a fresh fish emporium, run by the sons of the founder, Max Waldman. It is reputed to be the largest wholesale/retail fish market in North America. If you like fish and seafood or if you like watching an interesting mix of people, you will enjoy browsing through it. (Return to St-Laurent Boulevard)

Warshaw's Supermarket is owned by a Jewish family whose origins are in Poland. They started business selling fruit and vegetables in the back of a butcher shop, in 1935. The customers are mostly immigrants or the children of immigrants. Many return from the suburbs to combine their shopping with nostalgia.

Schwartz's Delicatessen (officially the Charcuterie Hébraïque de Montréal) opened in 1927 at 3895 St-Laurent. It is said to be the only restaurant in Montreal that makes its own smoked meat. Schwartz's uses the Romanian way of pickling and smoking beef brisket which makes it the best smoked meat in the world, according to many self-appointed experts.

Don't expect a menu; the waiter will tell you what is available (mainly smoked meat and steak). The decor and the seating arrangements are as perfunctory as the waiters, many of whom have been there for at least 20 years.

Further north is Moishe's Steakhouse (3961 St-Laurent Boulevard). It was opened by Moishe Lighter in 1938 on the site of a restaurant where he had been a busboy.

The Cooper Building, at 3981, houses more than just needle trade businesses. Radio Centreville, (102.3 FM) a community station which broadcasts music and news in many languages, has its studios there.

Across the street, at 3960, is the Caisse Populaire Ukrainienne, a credit union for that ethnic group.

Just before walking west on Bagg, take a look at the Schubert Baths. Built in 1931, 3950 St-Laurent was used not only as a recreation centre but also for basic hygiene. In those days, many a home lacked a bath or shower. Also, during hot summer days the pool enabled many poor children to escape the city's humidity and pollution. The pool is still open.

Walking along Bagg you will be able to discern the original prosperity of these homes. The small Jewish **synagogue** at the southeast corner of Bagg and Clark was constructed no later than the 1920s and is still in use. Like the Jewish monument maker which you have just passed, it is a link with the sizable Jewish community which used to live in the area.

Straight ahead is a solitary house, on the west side of St-Urbain, whose cheerfully-painted dormer windows seem appropriate for a survivor. The rest of the row was levelled to provide parking for Hôtel-Dieu Hospital. In the distance, you can see Mount Royal, "the mountain" as it is fondly (if grandiosely) called by Montrealers.

Café Santropol is a restaurant furnished in a Victorian Revival style with charming bric-à-brac, tin ceiling and a room divider formed of old doors. The sandwiches, going by such names as Midnight Spread and Sister of Jeanne Mance, are unique. One consists of ham, pineapple, chives, cream cheese placed between two slices of thick bread and buried under alfalfa sprouts, grapes, slices of watermelon, and any other fruit or vegetable that is handy. The balcony on the first floor is of a design not often seen in Montreal. (Turn left and walk to Esplanade Avenue)

8 Parc Jeanne-Mance

A Canadian motif adorns the roofline of one Esplanade Street house.

In French, esplanade means an open plain providing an impressive vista; Esplanade Avenue certainly lives up to its name. From here you can see the woods on Mount Royal and the cross on the summit of the mountain. Jeanne-Mance Park is right in front of you, and its benches are probably quite inviting at this point in the tour.

Traditionally, Jeanne-Mance Park was known as Fletcher's Field and is thus immortalized in Mordecai Richler's novels. It is still extensively used by "neo-Montrealers" — and soccer is at least as popular as baseball on the playing field.

Many of the buildings on this street are worthy of their view. As you walk along, look especially at the parapet crowning 4052-71. The red sandstone at 4085 has delightful little sculptured heads which are known as label stops. The label frames the windows and doors.

The Grenadier Guards of Canada maintain a **military building** at 4171 Esplanade. The medallion to the right of the door is Quebec's coat-of-arms, a rare sight nowadays. On the left is the old coat-of-arms of Canada, which then consisted of the quartering of the shields of the country's four original provinces. The building was constructed in 1913.

Looking down Rachel, you can see a massive grey building which towers 14 storeys above the street. Local residents complained when this building was planned in 1975, fearing the new offices would make the street too dense, and harm the character of the area. Only recently has it begun to be occupied.

The **statue** capped by an angel honors George-Étienne Cartier. As a French-Canadian Father of Confederation, he worked to ensure that Quebec's linguistic and cultural heritage would not be lost in the federation of Canadian provinces. The monument was sculpted by George Hill.

A "green thumb" must live at 4323 Esplanade — vines have been trained up the pergola and some of the more adventurous branches have even made it up to the second storey of the house.

The terra-cotta house with bow windows, at 4351, was a private hospital for a long time. It is believed to be the only Montreal house faced in this shiny, white material. The brown brick building at 4373, originally housing the Jewish Old People's Home, has been taken over by a Catholic missionary order.

At 4499 Esplanade is the former **Jewish Public Library**, now used by the Bibliothèque Nationale du Québec. The Jewish library remained here for quite a while after the Jewish community moved west of the mountain and into the suburbs, to the northwest. In 1973, the library was transferred to a building on Côte-Ste-Catherine Road, not far from the Young Men's-Young Women's Hebrew Association. The YMHA used to be located on Mont-Royal Boulevard in what is now a pavilion of the Université de Montréal. It was designed by Ross and MacDonald in the palazzo style, in 1928. Note the arched windows, majestic entrance and the treatment of the corners.

Just east of St-Urbain stands what was Mount Royal Arena, home of Montreal's other professional hockey team. Although only a memory now, the Maroons once beat their cross-town rivals, the Canadiens, to win the Stanley Cup.

Beauty's (93 Mont-Royal West) is a hang-out for people who have eaten breakfast there for the last 30 years.

(If you wish, you can end the tour at the corner of Park Avenue and Mont-Royal, taking the #80 southbound or the #97 eastbound to the metro.)

In Jeanne-Mance Park, at the intersection of Mount-Royal and Park avenues, is a fountain with a plaque commemorating Louis Rubenstein, the first Jewish city councilor in Montreal. He was also an accomplished athlete and a world champion figure skater.

This is the beginning of the Greek village in Montreal — Plato Language School and the small Greek Orthodox church a few blocks away are indicators. You can take the bus (#80) up to the next part of our tour or you can stroll by the interesting shops. Cafés, bars and clubs have recently sprung up in the buildings on Park Avenue.

During the 1940s, young Jewish Montrealers spent their Friday evenings walking up and down the east side of Park Avenue. It was a chance to be with friends or to meet someone new. Nowadays, on a Friday night, more people are in bars and cafés than walking down the street. Many of the children of the suburbs have returned to this area, and now live on the streets north of Mont-Royal, as their grandparents did.

Get off the #80 bus at Park Avenue and St-Viateur. The International YMCA (5550 Park) was built in 1912 and is a neighborhood centre for social and cultural activities. The building contains a gymnasium, a small pool in the basement and numerous classrooms and offices. There is a also a little playground to the right.

(Turn right and walk along St-Viateur) The Bagel Shop, at 263 St-Viateur, was founded in 1956. Its owners proudly display newspaper clippings extolling the merits of their product. You can observe the technique of the bakers while waiting in line. There is another bagel bakery a few blocks from here: opinions vary as to which provides the tastier roll.

This area houses a sizable percentage of Montreal's **Hassidic community**. The Hassidim are an extremely religious Jewish sect. The women are clothed in long-sleeved dresses and wear wigs (so as not to attract men other than their husband). Following the fashion in Poland and Lithuania where the sect originated, the men wear long dark coats and hats which are sometimes trimmed with fur. There are a number of *Yeshivas* (religious schools) in the area. A large part of each day of a Hassid is spent in study and prayer.

As you walk along St-Viateur, note the small shops and other establishments which cater to the residents whose tastes and habits were developed in the "old country". Side-by-side are a kosher butcher and an Italian meat shop. They share few customers and are more complementary than competitive.

Saint Michael the Archangel is a Byzantine-looking church. The design was suggested by Pope Pius X who wished to stress Christianity's origins. Erected in 1915 by the architect Aristide Beaugrand-Champagne, the impressive dome rests on pendentives and there is also a minaret. The interior was painted by Guido Nincheri. The initial congregation was predominately Irish — see the shamrocks in the stain-glass windows? This was the second largest anglophone parish in the province of Quebec before the Second World War. But, in 1964 the church faced closure as many parishioners moved to the suburbs; as a result, it

affiliated with the Polish mission. Now masses are celebrated in both English and Polish.
(Turn right on St-Urbain Street)

Many of the houses have been renovated by their occupants and this is one of the most pleasant simple residential streets of the city. You can identify the Portuguese homes by the religious portraits at the entrance.

At 5250 is the **Montreal Buddhist Church**, while next door is a Christian place of worship. Further down, at 5214 St-Urbain, is a synagogue which contains a *mikveh*, a bath which is used for ritual cleansing by Orthodox Jewish women.

The intersection of St-Urbain and Fairmont streets was once the heart of Montreal's Jewish community. The building with a semi-circular roof which looks like an arena was once the Beth Jacob Synagogue. It has been taken over by the **Collège Français**. The new front that was added in the 1950s was a poor graft.

On the northeast corner of Waverly, in a greystone house, was the first **Jewish People's School**. Unlike the *Yeshiva* which is primarily religious, this school emphasized Jewish culture, literature and history. The dark brown building to the west was the second school. It too, is now part of the Collège Français.

Walk left on Fairmount, past the Bagel Factory. It was founded in 1929, in a building located a few blocks to the south of here, and moved to 74 Fairmount in 1950. The shop closed in 1959, upon the death of its owner Itzak Shalfman. The founder's son and grandson reopened the factory in the late 1970s.

At 5167 is Wilensky's Light Lunch which dates from the 1930s. The store was originally located across the street and moved here in 1952. Wilinsky's achieved celebrity in the book *The Apprenticeship of Duddy Kravitz* by Mordecai Richler who grew up in this neighborhood.

The #51 bus going east on St-Joseph Boulevard goes to the Laurier metro station, while the #55 bus southbound on St-Urbain leads to the Place-Des-Arts metro station.

OUTREMONT

OUTREMONT

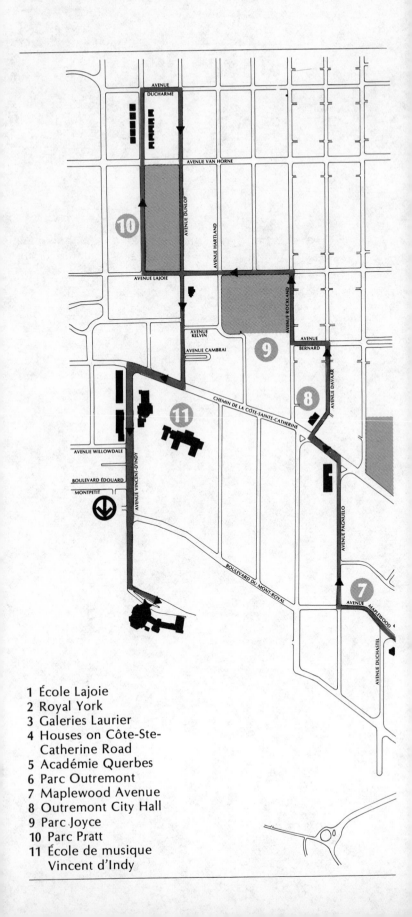

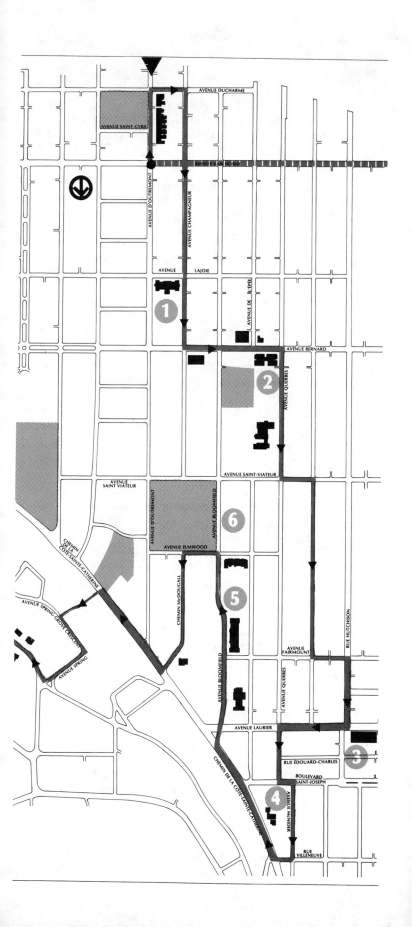

History

The Sulpicians gave out the first concessions along what is now Côte-Ste-Catherine Road, even before the signing of the 1701 peace treaty with the Iroquois. At that time the road was a simple Iroquois path skirting the northeast slope of Mont Royal. In the beginning, development was very slow — the 1778 map of Jean Péladeau (a surveyor) indicated only 12 landowners.

The first farmers and market gardeners, most of whom were from Great Britain, arrived in the mid-1800s. Côte-Ste-Catherine Road began at Tancrède Bouthillier's land, know as Outre-Mont ("over the mountain") which marked the boundary of the area. In addition to working farmers, the area also attracted some of Montreal's wealthy merchants and businessmen who liked the notion of gentleman farming as well as the speculative potential of their property. Donald Lorne McDougall, financier, acquired the Bouthillier property in 1856. The noted physician, politician and landowner, Pierre Beaubien acquired some land on Côte-Ste-Catherine as a honorarium. His son Louis moved there with his family in 1866.

During this time, Côte-Ste-Catherine farms produced what were known as "Montreal melons" in the restaurants of New York City's grand hotels. Eventually, orchards and market farms spread along the old road, forming one of the most pleasant settlements on the island. The village of Outremont was incorporated in 1875.

The northern districts of Montreal began to develop in the 1880s, causing a great deal of land speculation. Brother Arsène Charest, who was in charge of the financial affairs of the St-Viateur religious order, realized that this demand for land would sooner or later reach Outremont. During the late 1880s, he purchased more than 200 arpents of land including the McDougall farm, which was used for the training of deaf-mutes. The St-Viateur order became the largest landowner in Outremont.

Communication with the city improved with the construction of a railway by the Atlantic and North-West Railway Company, reaching the northern limits of the central district. Canadian Pacific later established a railway yard in Outremont. By 1894, a streetcar connected Côte-Ste-Catherine with Pine Avenue and the city core. As a result the population grew, as affluent Montrealers moved to the area.

Outremont's municipal council began to establish a system of waterworks and sewers. Owners ceded the land necessary to extend the existing streets in order to virtually complete the grid plan which exists today.

While some rural attributes remained, Outremont began to look more and more like a residential suburb. Its population quadrupled between 1901 and 1911, reaching 4820 inhabitants. Housing was no longer limited to Côte-Ste-Catherine Road, but was established further to the north. Newly-constructed triplexes attracted working class French-Canadian families.

The urbanization of Outremont began, housing construction accelerated and the face of the town changed with the influx of

French-Canadians and the arrival of a new ethnic group. The
Jews first lived on Hutchison Street before moving northward to
Van Horne Avenue. Their shops and *shuls* changed the appearance of that part of the town at the same time as Roman Catholic
establishments were being built on the pleasant slopes of the
mountain.

Judging by the compostion of the town council, political power
in Outremont remained for many years in the hands of the oldest
families of the area. Joseph Beaubien, grandson of Dr. Pierre
Beaubien, was mayor of the town between 1910 and 1949. In
response to the rapid urbanization of Outremont, the town
council decided to preserve and beautify the residential character of the town. The councillors formed a beautification commi-
tee whose enthusiastic work increased the reknown of Outremont. The best example of this is undoubtedly the agreement
signed with the utility companies in 1914 to place telephone and
electrical wires underground. Thus, Outremont became the first
city in Canada to light all its streets with tungsten-filament lamps
powered by underground cables. The municipality also began to
acquire land for parks and distributed trees and bushes to its citizens at cost price. Consequently, Outremont developed the
garden appearance it retains today.

Itinerary

*Until the Outremont metro station opens, take the # 161 bus
from Rosemont station to the corner of Van Horne and Outremont avenues to begin this two-hour tour.*

Van Horne Avenue is one of the three main commercial streets
of Outremont, serving the densely-populated northeast sector.
Recently, new shops have given a sophisticated appearance to
what was for many years the heart of the traditional Jewish quarter. The Jews are gradually moving away.

Although Outremont is no longer considered an industrial town, the triplexes and factories of the area near the railway yards are reminders that, at the turn of the century, this was a working-class area. Each flat occupied an entire floor and generally contained six rooms. The façades are of brick, and many, especially those north of Van Horne Avenue, display exterior winding staircases — a characteristic element of Montreal architecture. The houses on the blocks south of Van Horne do not share this feature, since a 1911 by-law made exterior staircases illegal on new construction in Outremont.

Take Champagneur Avenue to enter the Van Horne-Bernard-Wiseman-Hutchison area which was designated a special renovation zone in the 1971 Lajoie planning report. Although this plan was never instituted, many buildings in this area have been renovated by a young, affluent population; this was encouraged by the simplification of provincial laws governing the co-ownership of buildings. Apparently, few modifications to the buildings have been made, except for the replacement of railings and windows.

Champagneur Avenue south of Van Horne Boulevard is a typical Outremont street with its densely-built triplexes fronted by large trees. Note the original stained glass in the transoms above the doors. The mini-park near 773 Champagneur provides some sorely needed green space for this part of the town.

1 École Lajoie

To the right, at 1276-80 Lajoie, is the École Lajoie, built in 1914. Originally, there were two schools separated by a firewall in this building, one for boys on the Champagneur Avenue side and one for girls on the Outremont Avenue side. Architects Viau and Venne used cut stone to accentuate the ground floor and frame the main entrance. The projection of the two wings well-articulates the entire façade. The windows are also framed in cut stone. The cornice is accentuated through the use of a contrasting string course. These features were common in school design of that period. It is interesting to note that the right side is decorated with sculptures whereas the left side is bare.

At Bernard is the Cinéma Outremont which became a repertory theatre in the early 1970s. Its sale in 1987 created concern that its ornate interior, one of the remaining few designed by Emmanuel Briffa, would be lost. While the city of Outremont has recognized the importance of the building, only the minister of cultural affairs can protect its interior.

The cinema attracts film buffs from all over the island to Bernard Avenue, enhancing its commercial vitality. Evidence of this can be seen at 1227-1203 Bernard where boutiques have supplanted dwellings on the ground and first floors. An interesting example of recycling is evident at 1169 Bernard. An indoor parking garage, built in 1924, has been transformed and now contains boutiques and apartments.

2 Royal York

The Royal York (1120 Bernard), across the street, was built the year before at a cost of half a million dollars. It was then one of the most luxurious apartment buildings in the area. Multi-storeyed construction on Bernard Avenue and elsewhere required zoning changes. They were contested by a number of people who wished to preserve the residential character of the town.

The footbridge crossing the pond in **St-Viateur Park** is a symbol of the tranquility reflected in most Outremont parks. This park was established in 1930 on land given to the municipality by the clerics of Saint-Viateur. The headquarters of the order are still nearby, at 450 Querbes.

Take St-Viateur and Durocher avenues. At the corner of Fairmount (5210 Durocher) is a remarkable early example of recycling. It was built as the Temple Baptist Church in 1911, then converted into the Alfred Joyce High School in 1920.

Hutchinson Street leads to Laurier Avenue. In the last 10 years, Laurier has become a very chic commercial artery, due to the influx of a young, discerning populace. As you can see, art galleries, bookstores, gourmet shops and clothing boutiques now line this street which is the last commercial artery on the itinerary. You might like to take this opportunity for a pause before the remainder of the tour.

3 Galeries Laurier

Les Galeries Laurier is another example of an indoor parking building which has been converted to other uses. Strictly speaking, it is outside of Outremont's boundaries.

The pleasant rows of houses along Querbes and McNider avenues lead to **Côte-Ste-Catherine Road**. As you walk along this route you will see apartment buildings of different eras. The recent highrises built on the slopes cut off the view of the mountain and change the scale of the streets.

Virtually all of Outremont was built up by 1940. Therefore, construction of newer apartment buildings means demolition of older buildings. These older buildings contribute to the special atmosphere which attracts Montrealers to Outremont. Their loss alters the harmony of the town.

4 Houses on Côte-Ste-Catherine Road

Of the houses which do remain among the recently constructed highrise apartment buildings, two particularly stand out. The first, at 137 Cote-Ste-Catherine, was inspired by the Norman style. It was designed in 1930 by architect Henri S. Labelle.

The house at 143 Côte-Ste-Catherine is an attractive Italianate villa. Two portions of the roof are separated by a unusual square belfry. The overhanging eaves, the harmony of the forms and the large porch are characteristic of the Italianate style.

Save Montreal was successful in preserving this house.

Returning to Laurier, you come to **Église St-Viateur.** Consecrated in 1913, it was designed by E.C. Daoust and L.Z. Gauthier in the Gothic Revival style. Its cut stone façade is capped by two towers of different heights, which are topped by pinnacles in the English Gothic style. The imposing portico is topped by finials behind which is a decorative gable. Delightful sculpted angels complete the decor. You will notice that the fieldstone sidewalls are not as well executed as the front of the church. This is often the case when the architect concentrates on the façade. Inside, numerous frescos and wood sculptures were designed by famous Québécois artisans.

Unfortunately, visits to the church at times other than when mass is celebrated is by appointment only.

5 Académie Querbes

Académie Querbes, at 215 Bloomfield, displays the lofty ambitions of Outremont's leaders. This theatrical-looking, Beaux-Arts building was designed by J.A. Godin and completed in 1915. Its flamboyant horseshoe-shaped entrance is like those of mansions in Copenhagen. It was built at the same time as Montreal's fantastic movie theatres such as the Imperial and the Loews. The façades on all three sides of the school (Bloomfield, Fairmount and de l'Épée avenues) are not to be missed. The lintels above the windows on the de l'Épée Avenue side form a lovely frieze, and even the fire escape is a piece of architectural sculpture. Académie Querbes's indoor pool was considered the most modern of its era and was a source of great pride for Outremont residents.

Lionel Groulx, father of Quebec historiography, lived at 261 Bloomfield from 1939 to 1967. Now the building houses his archives, as well as those of other important Québécois.

6 Parc Outremont

Bloomfield Avenue leads to Outremont Park. The land for the park was ceded to the city by Brother Charest in 1895. But it was only in 1915 that the park was actually established and a concrete basin built to provide a skating rink in the winter and a wading pool in the summer. Before that time, the land was a plateau where water from Outremont brook collected in a bog. This terrain was unsuitable for construction, and its development as a park enhanced the value of the surrounding area.

(Walk down McDougall Avenue, the first street to the left) You will soon see an impressive house at 221-223 McDougall Avenue. This was formerly Maison Bouthillier, then McDougall Manor and was used by the pupils of the Outremont farm-school. The first mass in Outremont was celebrated in this building in 1887. **Henri Bourassa**, founder of the prestigious daily newspaper Le Devoir, lived in this house at the turn of the century.

Henri Bourassa (1868-1952), journalist and politician, was born in Montreal. One of the most powerful Canadian speechmakers, he was a member of the House of Commons for many years. His opposition to the South African war caused him to quit Laurier's Liberal party in 1899. He opposed all participation in the wars of the British Empire and was convinced that a nation's permanent interests must always govern its policies. He opposed obligatory military service during the First World War. In 1926 he declared that he was in favor of a link with Great Britain since this was the sole obstacle to Canada's absorption by the United States. He supported Mackenzie King against the Governor General in the constitutional crisis of 1926 but refused a portfolio in King's cabinet. Although he defended Catholicism, he himself was a non-conformist. He also played an important role as representative for Saint-Hyacinthe in provincial politics. He was the author of numerous works, including Que devons-nous à l'Angleterre? (1915), Le Canada Apostolique (1922), Patriotisme, Nationalisme, Impérialisme (1923).

A return to Côte-Ste-Catherine Road is a return to the opulently decorated mansions which contrast with the design of the old manor.

The rise of the lane near 366 Cote Ste-Catherine permits a side trip up the mountain. Here the topography has dictated the road plan and adds to the aloofness of the houses.

7 Maplewood Avenue

The house at 160 Maplewood Avenue sits well on its site, but is rather rigidly designed. Unfortunately, the entrance is timid and is not in the same scale as the main part of the house.

Across the street, the house at 159 Maplewood has features borrowed from the American *stick style*, characterized by wood strips on the exterior walls which echo the interior layout of the building. Also note the magnificent carved wood door. Its Norman-inspired roof harmonizes with the design and gives it a cosy, intimist look.

The Tudor Gothic house at 161 Maplewood has windows with a rhythm much like a small New England college residence. The chimney is a miniature version of the turrets of a Medieval castle.

(Proceed west along Maplewood to Pagnuelo Avenue) At the foot of Pagnuelo Avenue is **Strathcona Academy**. It was constructed in 1898 by the Protestant School Board of Greater Montreal. Its closure was a result of the decline in the English-speaking population of Outremont during the late 1970s. It has been used by the geography department of the Université de Montréal since 1980.

The well-designed playground in Beaubien Park, across Côte-Ste-Catherine Road, was established in 1970. The equipment and hills give full freedom to a child's spirit and imagination.

8 Outremont City Hall

Outremont City Hall (543 Côte Ste-Catherine Road) occupies one of the oldest buildings in the area, probably built in 1800. This square, English colonial style building is believed to have once been a Hudson's Bay Company fur trading post.

(Take Davaar Avenue to Bernard Avenue, turn left on Bernard and walk to Rockland Avenue) It may seem ironic that Outremont's two finest parks are near here, where each house seems to have its own sumptuous yard. Simply because it was available, or to further enlarge Outremont's prestige, the land was reserved for public space as part of the city's beautification program.

9 Parc Joyce

The Joyce property in 1920.

In 1926, the city of Outremont acquired the house and yard of Alfred Joyce to convert into a park. His gardens were already celebrated for their beauty. After his death in 1937, his house was demolished and the whole property became Joyce Park. (Cross Joyce Park and take Lajoie Avenue to Pratt Park.)

10 Parc Pratt

At the northwest corner of Lajoie and Dunlop avenues, is Pratt Park, probably the loveliest green space in Outremont. It was acquired from the Pratt estate in 1931 in a fashion similar to the acquisition of Joyce Park. Its diversified design is an accurate rendering of the English natural plan where the slopes and other features of the land are maintained. This provides space for many different activities, each of which can be conducted in relative isolation. Consequently, Pratt Park is very popular at all times of the year.

(Take Pratt Avenue to Ducharme Avenue, thence Dunlop to Van Horne Avenue) The semi-detached houses on Pratt Avenue, north of Van Horne, are the most attractive houses of this kind in Outremont. The stones framing the openings are linked together in an unusual way. The white or pastel-painted balconies brighten the somewhat austere façades. The replacement of some of the wood railings and window frames by other materials requiring less upkeep has damaged the unity of the ensemble.

There is a fine example of the Chateau style at 675 Dunlop Avenue — note the pitched roof with multiple dormers and many vertical elements. While it is large enough to have been built for some institution, it seems to have always been a private residence.

11 École de musique Vincent d'Indy

Through the trees at the corner of Cote Ste-Catherine Road and Dunlop Avenue can be seen the Pensionnat du Saint-Nom-de-Marie. The building was designed in 1903 by Resther. It has an imposing portico with classical elements, above which is a dome complete with a cupola on top. The 1986 addition should have been set back to be less obtrusive. The east wing of the original building houses the École Vincent-d'Indy, an internationally acclaimed music school

Église Saint-Germain on the corner of Côte Ste-Catherine Road and Vincent d'Indy Avenue was built in 1931. David, Tourville and Perrault were the architects. The wide arches of its portal are unusually large. The bell tower is modelled on those of the monasteries of the Middle Ages, but it overpowers the rest of the building.

Walking along Vincent-d'Indy Avenue means an end to the shaded quiet of Outremont's streets and a return to a major traffic artery which is lined with the repetitive façades of apartment buildings designed to suit the needs of the marketplace, not Outremont's traditional appearance.

From the slope which leads to the Université de Montréal's music school can be seen Outremont's lush greenery surrounded by the metropolis.

Until the Edouard Montpetit metro station opens, the #51 bus goes east to Laurier metro station. The route goes along Cote Ste-Catherine, giving you a final look at the city of Outremont.

PLATEAU
MONT-ROYAL

PLATEAU MONT-ROYAL

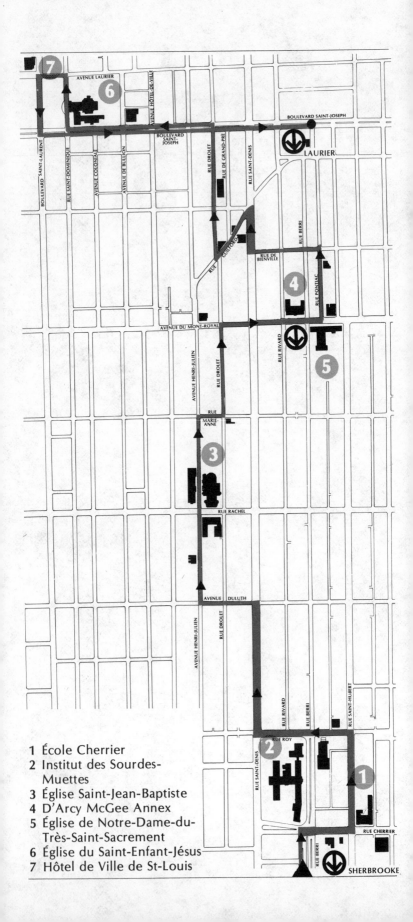

1 École Cherrier
2 Institut des Sourdes-
   Muettes
3 Église Saint-Jean-Baptiste
4 D'Arcy McGee Annex
5 Église de Notre-Dame-du-
   Très-Saint-Sacrement
6 Église du Saint-Enfant-Jésus
7 Hôtel de Ville de St-Louis

History

Plateau Mont-Royal comprises the area north of Sherbrooke Street, between the mountain and the Canadian Pacific Railway tracks (approximately Frontenac Street). Sherbrooke Street marks a historical boundary in the evolution of the city as it was only after the establishment of the streetcar line that the city developed on this plateau. Thus most of the buildings on this tour date from the 1890s, at the earliest.

The walk covers mainly the area originally known as Côte-St-Louis. This sector, north of Duluth Street, developed as a result of the limestone quarries which were discovered here at the end of the 1700s. By 1846, the area officially became the village of Côte-St-Louis. In 1870, the population of the area was 8,000 and four municipalities had been formed. North of Mont-Royal Avenue lay St-Louis du Mile End and Côte-St-Louis, which were separated by Henri-Julien Street; between Mont-Royal Avenue and Duluth Street was the village of Saint-Jean-Baptiste. Côte de la Visitation was north of Mont-Royal Avenue and east of Côte-St-Louis.

Members of the working class populated the area once the tramway lines were established in the 1800s. The streets steadily filled with houses and by 1930 there was little open space aside from a few parks. In addition to migration from rural Quebec, people came from eastern and Mediterranean Europe. By 1940, the population had swollen to around 65,000.

After the Second World War, many people left the neighborhood for the new suburbs. The area began to deteriorate — 23% of the housing units of Plateau Mont Royal needed renovation in 1950. Many of these buildings burnt down or were replaced by new construction. Some of the remaining ones were renovated by conscientious landlords, while others underwent major repairs by individuals who had bought the units for their own use.

The area is a diverse community, with its own commercial and entertainment streets and a great deal of housing. Some of Montreal's most attractive churches and religious properties can be seen along the route.

The tour lasts about two hours and covers three of the former villages. If you do not wish to complete the entire walk at one time, Mont-Royal metro station is a convenient point to interrupt the tour.

Itinerary

(Leave the Sherbrooke metro station through the exit marked Berri Street, turn right and go to Cherrier) On Cherrier Street are a few fine greystone buildings trimmed with the decorative Victorian woodwork known as "Montreal gingerbread". Some display the original decorations, mansard roofs pierced by dormer windows, and painted woodwork.

The three buildings at 520, 522, and 528 Cherrier demonstrate tastes from different eras — the first is in the typical Victorian style characterized by painted wood and shingles; the second highlights the natural hues of the wood but the windows are an anachronism taken from the 1700s; aluminum siding is the no-nonsense jacket at 528. The balcony at 546 Cherrier is also note-worthy.

A horn-of-plenty motif adorns the portico of the Palestre Nationale.

(Continue along Cherrier to St-Hubert Street) **La Palestre-Natio-nale**, at 840 Cherrier, is an Italian Renaissance style building completed in 1918. It was originally used by the Association athl-étique d'amateurs and is now the physical education building of the Université du Québec à Montréal. Note the ornamented entrance.

1 École Cherrier

École Cherrier, circa 1940.

Across from it is the Cherrier School built in 1931 in the Art Deco style, as demonstrated by its dominant vertical lines, geometric details (especially in the wings), and set back volumes.

Once on St-Hubert Street, take a look at the alleyway coach house. St-Hubert Street contains many prosperous houses of the late 19th century which boast decorated balconies, turrets, dormer windows and mansard roofs.

The church on Roy Street is **Saint-Louis-de-France**. It was built in 1936 to replace one erected a few blocks to the west during the 1890s. While the original church burnt down in 1933, the stately presbytery remains on Laval, between Roy and Napoléon (not on the itinerary). The parish of Saint-Louis-de-France now comprises the area between Laval Street and Lafontaine Park.

As is quite common in Quebec, there is a Caisse Populaire bearing the same name as the parish. While the caisse is frequently housed in the church basement, this time it is located across the street. Traditionally, Caisses Populaires, a kind of credit union, were more trusted by the Québécois than the primarily English banks. They were founded in 1900 by Alphonse Desjardins. (Continue west on Roy to St-Denis Street)

2 Institut des Sourdes-Muettes

A number of streets were unpaved at the turn of the century.

The first institution for deaf-mutes was built around 1864 on land given by Côme Séraphin Cherrier. Clay makes up a large portion of the land on Plateau Mont-Royal, and the building sank little by little. Therefore, the main section of the present structure is supported by 1700 stakes added in 1882 and is on a two-feet (0.6 m) thick concrete block. The nuns ran a kindergarten as well as educating deaf-mute girls.

Joseph Michaud was responsible for the construction of this H-shaped complex during the 1880s and 1890s. The building on St-Denis Street is connected to the one on Berri by a wing which contains the chapel. The first phase of construction (executed by the firm of Maison Philippe) was begun in 1882, starting on the Berri Street side. Later, in 1891-93, the chapel wing was raised. The large building on St-Denis completed the group in 1898.

The buildings are in embossed stone, crowned by mansard roofs with corner towers at each end, a characteristic of the Second Empire style. On the Berri side, note a double projection in the centre which is surmounted by a pinnacle. The façade on St-Denis is much more opulent. In the centre is a classically inspired detail: a triangular pediment supported by pilasters. From the centre of the building rises a dome surmounted by a lantern.

During the last five years, **St-Denis Street** between Sherbrooke and Mount-Royal has blossomed into a variegated collection of restaurants, bars, clothing boutiques.

As the only street linking La Fontaine Park and the slopes of the mountain, **Duluth Street** offers a pleasant view at both ends. This once residential street has been transformed into a landscaped commercial street. The change is resented by local residents who must put up with substantially more traffic and night-time noise: most of the restaurant-goers bring their cars to the area.

Henri-Julien is a typical street of the area with its hodge-podge of old buildings never renovated, modernized housing, and recent in-fill structures. There is a nice ensemble of houses at 4102-4118. The fan-design brackets above the doors were probably carved by machine and not by hand, as they are repeated elsewhere. It was a standard model that was relatively inexpensive and quite convenient.

Saint-Jean-Baptiste Village was centred at Henri-Julien and Rachel. It was separated from Côte-Saint-Louis and incorporated in 1861. It covered the area north of Duluth to Mont-Royal, between Park and Papineau, and was later truncated at Christophe-Colomb Street.

In 1880, horse-drawn streetcars began to go up St-Denis as far as Mont-Royal Avenue. But many of the other north-south streets were largely unsettled. Before that time, most of the population worked in the quarries of the area as it was difficult to commute to work in the city itself.

By 1883, the village had increased its population to 8,000 — making it one of the largest of the villages around the city of Montreal. Saint-Jean-Baptiste became a town in 1884 and was annexed by Montreal two years later, due to a debt of $60,000. The debts which the town owed were paid from taxes subsequently collected. Many of the previous municipal council were creditors!

3 Église Saint-Jean-Baptiste

Nincheri and Dalfour decorated the interior of this church.

The church you now see on the northeast corner is the third on the site. The first was built in 1873 on a lot which had previously been the site of quicklime furnaces. The land was donated by four rich citizens, one of whom was Gustave-Adolph Drolet, owner of building lots on the street which bears his name. His motivations were not entirely spiritual in nature: building a church increased nearby property values during the speculative 1870s. After a fire in 1898, the church was rebuilt, only to be damaged by fire once again in 1911.

The present Classical-style edifice was designed by Casimir St-Jean in 1912. It was then the second-largest church in the city. A projecting portico such as the one on this building is not common in Montreal churches. Each entrance is framed by double columns, and on each side of the façade is a recessed bell tower crowned by a cupola. Paccard bells were imported from France in 1909 and survived the fire of 1911. In 1976, John Bland renovated the interior whose most interesting feature is a superb baldaquin.

Across the street is the Institut des Saints-Noms-de-Jésus-et-de-Marie which later became the **Académie-pensionnat Marie-Rose**. It was built in 1876, primarily in the Classical style, but with a steeply-sloped mansard roof in the Italian Renaissance style.

Just west of Henri-Julien is the **Hospice Auclair**, built in 1894-96. Now know as the Centre d'Accueil Auclair, it is a live-in facility for young people. Casimir Saint-Jean also designed this building, completing the grouping of religious buildings around Saint-Jean-Baptiste Church. Its construction in stone and concrete was innovative at the time. The rectangular building is well-anchored to the ground and has a modernist, functional look to it now. However, when it was built, an imposing stone balustrade ran the length of the roof. In the middle of the east and south faces, a false pediment was added over the galleries. The portico is of stone and uses a horseshoe arch shape.

Before leaving Rachel Street and continuing on Henri-Julien, look west to Mount Royal. The angel on top of the monument seems frozen in flight.

The presbytery behing the church at 4237 Henri-Julien was built in 1901 and was not damaged by the fire which destroyed the second church. Its sober, ordered façade is pierced by a distinctive entrance.

(Once at Marie-Anne, turn right and walk a block to Drolet) The building on the southeast corner has been bricked over up to the roofline. It is as if an elegantly-coiffed 19th century lady were wearing jeans.

The Art Deco style Clinique Laurier at 305 Mont-Royal East was designed in 1932 by Fetherstonhaugh and is still occupied by municipal services. Its clean, pure lines lend it majesty.

Mont-Royal Avenue used to be the main shopping street for the Plateau. Now St-Denis Street and St-Laurent Boulevard have more commerces, including clothing chains and designer boutiques which up until now were located only downtown. Many of the stores on Mont-Royal seem somewhat shabby. The new, more affluent residents of Plateau Mont-Royal tend to ignore this commercial avenue, although it is still patronized by the many recent immigrants who live in the area. (Walk past St-Denis to Mont-Royal metro station which is the mid-way point on the tour, should you wish to postpone the rest)

4 Maison de la Culture

Directly across the street from the metro station (465 Mont-Royal West) is what was initially Pensionnat St-Basile, a boarding school. This symmetrical greystone building was constructed between 1895 and 1896. J.B. Resther was the architect.

The building is U-shaped with two wings at right angles to the main section. The latter is four storeys-high, with a flat roof surrounded by a balustrade. Emphasis is placed on the central portion of the building — note the pronounced setback of the surface, the raised portico, and flat roof. A double-lanterned belfry bordered by pinnacles, rises above.

A number of schools have been housed in this building at different times. The first was established by the Religieuses de Sainte-Croix who taught anglophone and francophone girls from kindergarten right through high school. When the Saint-Sacrement Church was built, this building became the parish school under the name Académie Notre-Dame du Saint-Sacrement. In 1951, it was renamed the École Normale Ignace Bourget. Later, the Catholic school board used it as an annex for D'Arcy McGee High School.

The building sat empty for years until the city finally converted it into low-cost housing and a cultural centre comprising a library and amphitheatre.

(Continue east on Mont-Royal) If you wish to extend the tour to see "showcase" streets, continue east four blocks to **St-André.** Walk down it for two blocks, turn right (east) to return to **St-Hubert,** then up this broad street to return to Mont-Royal Avenue.

5 Église de Notre-Dame-du-Très- Saint-Sacrement

The interior has been carefully restored after a fire in 1982.

Notre-Dame-du-Très-Saint-Sacrament is a complex of buildings housing the monastery, church and novitiate of the Holy Sacrament Fathers. The complex was begun in 1892 when the order purchased a house on the site from one Monsieur Barré to form the "Sanctuaire de l'exposition et de l'adoration perpétuelle". The house was modified by adding a high flat-ceilinged nave and a second storey, followed two years later by the part of the building extending east, which was used as a monastery. The novitiate in brick was added in 1896.

(Cross the street and walk north along Pontiac) This street has an example of almost every traditional kind of Montreal house: there are small painted brick houses, more prosperous cream-colored brick with the old address in stained glass, a row of greystones with tin parapets at the roof, some diminutive bay windows, some squat two-storey buildings. There is even one token example of an exterior spiral staircase. The proprietors of the small one-storey "Depression houses" at the end of the block intended to add another floor when prosperity returned.

(Turn around for another view of Très-Saint-Sacrement before you turn left at Bienville.)

At 4664 St-Denis is the **Théâtre du Rideau-Vert**. This is one of Montreal's most important theatres, for many of the most celebrated names of the Quebec stage have performed in productions here. The "green curtain" first went up on February 17, 1949 for the play *Les Innocents*. (Walk to the intersection of Gilford, Villeneuve and St-Denis streets.)

Gilford Street marks the boundary of the quarries which were the incentive to developing the area. The name is a corruption of Guibord which was printed in Henry W. Hopkins gazeteer of 1879. Somehow the name of the street was never corrected. The **Guibord affair** helped define church-state relations in Canada.

Gilford is one of a small number of Montreal streets which deviate from the grid pattern. Since these streets meet other streets at an angle, there are some oddly-shaped buildings such as those at 361, 365, and further west at 466. The diagonal streets generally correspond to the original service roads which followed the natural topography.

Guibord Affair: Since the city had no French university, the Institut Canadien de Montréal was founded in 1844 to provide advanced learning for the graduates of the classical colleges. The radical young men who studied there were supportive of freedom of speech and thought, ideas which were becoming popular in Europe at that time. Consequently, they soon met the opposition of Monseigneur Bourget, Bishop of Montreal, who feared conversions to Protestantism and the tolerant, non-conformist attitude of the Institut.

Many of the leaders of the Institute were also involved with the Rouge political party. Their opposition to Bourget was caused in part by the official alliance between the Catholic hierarchy and the conservative party. The Rouges believed in the new republican ideas which were threatening the strength of the Church in Europe. They openly espoused the concept of separation of Church and State, a doctrine which was anathema to the Catholic tradition and horrified the conservative and monarchist French-Canadian clergy. In addition, the Rouge party sympathized with the American ideal and favored annexation by the United States, something the clergy feared would mean the loss of French Canadian Catholicism.

The Institute's position was weakened in July 1869 when its publications were condemned by the Vatican and placed on the Index of proscribed literature. Monseigneur Bourget read a pastoral letter from Rome which stated that adherance to the Institut Canadien, or simple possession of its works, would mean exclusion from the Holy Sacraments.

Until then the quarrel was a private one. However, the death in November 1869 of Joseph Guibord, a printer and former vice-president of the Institute, set off a scandal which became international in scope. In accordance with the bishop's orders, he was refused a Catholic funeral, and the burial party was prevented from entering the Roman Catholic cemetery. Instead he was interred in the Protestant cemetery.

Legal measures were taken and the case grew into a public debate on the allegiance of a nation's church, freedom of speech, French and English legal codes, ecclesiastical and civil law, and, finally, the connection between Church and State. The case went through all levels of appeal till it reached the Privy Council in London, which ruled that under the French régime, ecclesiastical law was subject to French authority and the right to appeal religious decisions in civil courts had been recognized. It decided that the Quebec Act had perpetuated this right and the Index was never legally recognized in France or Canada. Therefore, Guibord could not be subject to an ecclesiastical decree which would prevent his receiving a Christian burial. Thus, after six years of litigation and agitation, Guibord's remains were buried in the Catholic cemetery on September 2, 1875.

This is the western border of **Côteau-St-Louis**. The limestone quarries of the area were first discovered around 1775. By 1870 a village had sprung up which became the autonomous parish of Saint-Enfant-Jésus. The 1891 census indicated that there were 100 quarrymen, 12 stonecutters, 79 laborers, 11 carpenters, 12 blacksmiths and six bakers living here. In addition to the quarry, a sugar refinery and a door factory were located here.

The building at 4820-4850 Grand Pré was completed in 1980. It is a good example of new residential construction since it fits in with the houses already built, due to the choice of a complementary construction material.

Elegant architectural details of the turn of the century are still apparent on the buildings on this street.

St-Joseph Boulevard is a pleasant street of the 1920s and 1930s lined with stately homes and public buildings. Notice the detailed craftsmanship which is still appreciated by the doctors and lawyers who maintain their offices here. At one time there were two rows of trees to shelter the 28-foot (8.50 m) wide median. They were sacrificed so that two more lanes of traffic could be added. (Turn left on St-Joseph Boulevard.)

Académie du Boulevard, at 155 St-Joseph, was built in 1906-07. Dalbé Viau was the architect of this building, as well as that of

École de l'Enfant-Jésus which is on the south side of the street, at 102 St-Joseph Boulevard. The two buildings are similar in style, using stone in the portico section of the façade, with brick on either side. Both buildings are unoccupied at present. Viau also collaborated with J.A. Venne to design École Lajoie (Outremont tour).

The residence St-Dominique, at 95 St-Joseph, is partially housed in an old greystone building which has been substantially changed. Although it is almost impossible to tell, originally the building had only three storeys. As each floor was rather high — about 14 feet (5 m) each — it was not difficult to retain the exterior envelope, while modifying the interior to house this residence. The work was so well executed that the greystones look as if they were never modified.

LaHaie Park was named after the first curé of the Church of Saint-Enfant-Jésus. Grouped around this square was the heart of the town of St-Louis du Mile End. The town hall and church were joined by two banks, the presbytery and a Catholic school.

6 Église du Saint-Enfant-Jésus

The Church of Saint-Enfant-Jésus is one of the finest in the city. Architect Joseph Venne was commissioned in 1898 to enlarge the old church whose original cornerstone had been laid by Monseigneur Bourget in 1857. Venne was noted for his rich façades and this church is a masterpiece. While the portico was inspired by the sober Italian Renaissance style, the treatment above is reminiscent of the Baroque architecture of Latin-American churches. There are trumpeting angels, cherubs, niches, colonettes, and other highly-decorated stonework. The climax of the church is a pinnacle turret surmounted by a cross.

Inside there is an impressive vaulted ceiling supported at eight points. It covers the original 1857 nave, the choir and the side galleries. The frescoes of the Sacré-Coeur Chapel, though greatly reworked, are also interesting. They were done by **Ozias Leduc** between 1917 and 1919.

7 Hôtel de Ville de St-Louis

On the northwest corner of Laurier Street is the St-Louis Town Hall and Fire Station. This building was constructed in 1905, five years before St-Louis du Mile End was annexed by Montreal. Most assuredly it helped to contribute to the municipal debt that forced this action. The engineer and architect J. Émile Vanier took his inspiration from late Medieval or early French Renaissance styles — hence the arches, turrets, balcony with parapets and the delicate detail of the stonework on St-Laurent Boulevard.

The original building accommodated a fire station, stables, sleeping quarters for the men, granaries, post office, council assembly hall, mayor's office and a prison. Three years after the building was constructed, the masonry façade had to be replaced. It was converted into a fire station in 1951. In 1980, $186,000 was spent on renovations.

This ends the tour of the Plateau, the Laurier metro station entrance is a few blocks back on St-Joseph.

TERRASSE
ONTARIO

TERRASSE ONTARIO

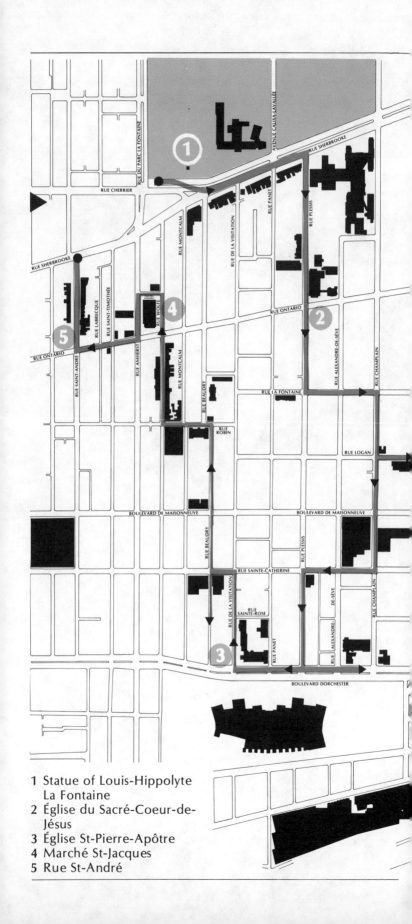

1 Statue of Louis-Hippolyte
 La Fontaine
2 Église du Sacré-Coeur-de-
 Jésus
3 Église St-Pierre-Apôtre
4 Marché St-Jacques
5 Rue St-André

History

The neighborhood called Terrasse Ontario is the western portion of a larger area known as Centre-sud and covers the area roughly between the streets of Sherbrooke, Dorchester, St-Hubert and Papineau. This section of the city, located as it was on the outskirts of the old town and on the road to Quebec City, used to be known as Faubourg Québec. Its development began in the second half of the 19th century when many textile, shoe, tobacco and food manufacturers established factories here. These factories employed for the most part people from rural areas, who had come to Montreal to find work. Houses, schools and churches were quickly built to accommodate this new population.

Terrasse Ontario was a flourishing area until the 1950s. However, with the passage of time, equipment in the factories became obsolete. Foreign competition, primarily from the Far East, rendered local factory output unprofitable. Consequently, the industrial strength of the neighborhood declined rapidly.

Since Terrasse Ontario is situated near the expanding centre of Montreal, a new vocation was found for it. In 1970, the federal, provincial and municipal governments proposed a "Terrasse Ontario Neighborhood Improvement Program" to bolster the residential character of the area. It was decided to demolish approximately 1000 housing units and renovate over half of those remaining.

Most of the demolition is finished now. Small contractors were attracted to the goldmine of renovations, especially the subdivision of large units. Subdivision was more profitable because government subsidies are calculated in terms of number of flats, not by square foot. The new housing is being rented or sold to a new, more affluent population who can afford the higher cost. Housing has also been constructed by the city; some of these buildings will be seen on the tour.

While the area is populated primarily by low-income francophone families who rent their homes, in recent years there has been an influx (especially near Maison de Radio-Canada) of some more educated and more affluent individuals. Still, most of the population is unemployed and welfare recipients, with average per capita incomes lower than in the rest of the city. The proportion of elderly women has increased recently and there has been an influx of young men moving into the area, as it becomes known as a mecca for gay men from all over the province. A variety of different types of stores and restaurants have sprung up.

With its mixture of delapidated housing and recently renovated condominiums, its motorcycle bars and *chi-chi* cafés, this area is primarily of interest for people interested in urban evolution.

Itinerary

Access: Sherbrooke metro station and # 24 bus east.

1 Statue of Louis-Hippolyte La Fontaine

Our walk begins on the outskirts of the neighborhood, at the Statue of Louis-Hippolite near Amherst and Cherrier streets, four short blocks east of the Sherbrooke Metro Station (#24 bus).

Louis-Hippolyte La Fontaine was, with Robert Baldwin, joint Prime Minister of the union of Upper and Lower Canada in the 1840s. The statue was designed by Henri Hébert and erected in 1930.

La Fontaine Park, like Montreal's other major parks — île Ste-Hélène and Mount Royal — was established towards the end of the 19th Century. This park was part of James Logan's farm which stretched from Mont-Royal Boulevard to a few blocks south of here. The British government bought the farm in 1845 and used it for military exercises. Twenty years after Confederation in 1867, the Canadian government ceded it to the city for use as a park at the nominal rent of $1 per year. The land, then, was dotted with tranquil ponds and meandering brooks.

The western portion of the park was originally landscaped in the English style with irregularly-shaped ponds, slopes and paths following the original topography. The eastern half is a formal park, done in the French style. There, straight walkways divide the lawns into geometric shapes with paths flanked by ordered rows of trees. While the original lay-out reflected the bicultural nature of Montreal, later construction has spoiled the original plans of the country garden portion.

The École Normale was once located near Sherbrooke Street. It was destroyed by a fire in the late 1940s and replaced by a buff brick building, now used by the Université du Québec à Montréal.

Across the street from the statue is the **Bibliothèque municipale de Montréal**. The provincial government ordered the city to establish a municipal library in 1914. At that time the only library open to the public was the Fraser Institute, and most of its books were in English. The Sulpician Fathers, the first religious order in Montreal, were opposed to a secular library and they decided to establish the Bibliothèque Saint-Sulpice on St-Denis Street which would contain only the books they approved of. It is now the Bibliothèque Nationale du Québec.

The municipal library was inaugurated on May 13, 1916 by the mayor, Médéric Martin, and the French Marshal, General Joffre, resplendent in his blue military dress. Eugène Payette was the architect. It is interesting to note that he was at the same time the architect of the Sulpician library. He made use of the Beaux-Arts style. The façade of this unusually-shaped structure is neo-classical with 10 monolithic columns of granite from Stanstead, Que. The stained-glass windows of the entrance hall depict the founders of New France, recall the home regions of the French settlers and the provinces of Canada. Precious manuscripts dating from the beginning of the French colonization of North America are kept here.

Imposing greystone houses march eastward along Sherbrooke. In the past, the elegant homes on this street, as well as those on St-Hubert and St-Denis, formed a middle-class shell around the working-class neighborhood. As a major traffic artery, Sherbrooke Street is no longer suited to residences. Consequently, many of these houses have been transformed into offices for doctors, lawyers and other professionals.

Maison Radio-Canada looms into view at Panet Street. In the late 1960s, real estate developers, with the help of some city councillors, planned to turn this street into a "Champs-Élysées" leading from LaFontaine Park to the Cité des Ondes where two television stations were to be located. The developers managed to convince French investors to finance the project (named Allée des Ondes). Luxury apartment buildings with glamorous boutiques were to line the avenue. This would have required the demolition of the houses on both sides of the street.

As you turn down Plessis, take a look at the **Hôpital Notre-Dame**. This hospital was established in 1880 on Notre-Dame Street. At that time, francophone doctors (supported by some dissidents from McGill University) decided to create a French-language faculty of medicine in Montreal. They hoped to initiate the development of a new university in Montreal. The Université Laval in Quebec City claimed that since it had been sanctioned by the Pope, it alone could offer higher level learning in Catholic Quebec and established a rival medical school. The hospital moved into this glazed brick building when it outgrew its original one in 1924.

The present building was designed by Lapierre (of Montreal) and Lee and Stevens (Boston). Details are in Eschambault stone, while the base and shafts of the columns are in Stanstead granite. Wings were added subsequently and this modern hospital now has 1100 beds. The Université de Montréal's medical students do their internships here. The hospital has an additional building, Pavillon Louis-Charles Simard, on Alexandre de Sève Street.

At 2144 Plessis stands one of the few houses remaining from the time of Logan Farm. When it was built in the early 1880s it stood alone but was later joined by other houses.

During the industrial revolution the population of the city increased dramatically, and developers constructed houses in the courtyard behind these homes.

Homes on Plessis Street illustrate **typical housing construction** of the late 1800s. The house at 2098-2108 contains four flats, two on the ground floor and two above. Since each room has a window, the flats are quite bright. Because there is no back lane, a porte-cochère pierced the building to provide access to the back; consequently the lower units have only three rooms. The balconies are in the rear since the house was built flush with the sidewalk. Access to the upper floor is via an interior staircase. The house is a wood structure with a red brick covering. It is poorly insulated and provides inadequate protection against harsh Montreal winters. Indoor plumbing was added decades after its construction with a consequent loss of living area.

At the corner of Ontario and Plessis is the traditional nucleus of the Quebec parish: church, presbytery, boys' school and girls' school. École Plessis, at 2075 Plessis, was built in 1877-1881. It is the second oldest school building remaining in Montreal (only

McGill Unversity's Arts Building is older). It was run by the Frères des écoles chrétiennes. Now the municipal chief returning officer uses the building.

2 Église du Sacré-Coeur-de-Jésus

Sacré-Coeur-de-Jésus church is the pride of the area. The parish was founded in 1874 when Ste-Brigide church became too small for its growing congregation. The new parish of Sacré-Coeur embraced the area that is now Terrasse Ontario. The mill of Logan farm was used as a chapel. This wood and brick structure measured 54 ft. by 100 ft. (16 m by 30 m) and was sufficient at first for the entire population of what is now Terrasse Ontario. It was demolished in 1878 to make way for this Gothic style church which was consecrated on December 25, 1887. Joseph Venne, in his twenties at the time, was the architect. In 1908, a bell tower containing a five-bell clarion from Annecy-le-Vieux, France was added. Fire gutted the church in 1822, leaving only the outside walls. It was rebuilt by Venne and his son Émile, using fireproof reinforced concrete and incorporating the walls.

The interior is worth a look. Note, especially, the screen framing the high altar and the vaulted ceiling designed by Émile Venne. There is also a lovely communion rail in white marble with Mexican onyx columns. The pulpit is the original. It was reassembled after it had been damaged when the roof collapsed during the fire.

The presbytery at the northeast corner of Ontario and Alexandre de Sève streets was constructed in 1894 at a cost of $24,000. Noteworthy are the windows and the six-pointed stars on the dormer windows.

There are some nicely renovated houses on Plessis Street, below Ontario Avenue. The brick at 1852 Plessis was exposed recently which adds to its appearance. The little park is another recent improvement to the street. Behind it can be seen some newly constructed housing which fits in well with the area. The houses on the south side of Lafontaine, between Plessis and Panet streets, are part of the city's **Opération 20 000 logements** program designed to provide new housing in order to entice the middle-class back from the suburbs. These recent, well-constructed houses are in a style similar to the typical Terrasse Ontario house. The porte-cochère of the house at 1384-70 Lafontaine Street reveals that it is an older building. Renovated when the new houses were built, it now contains six units.

At 1477 Lafontaine is Massicote et Frères. Coal and wood were sold here at a time when these materials were the only fuels available. Now most renovated homes use electricity, while others use oil or natural gas.

On Lafontaine, between Alexandre de Sève and Champlain, are the **community gardens of Centre-sud**. This is a city-run project begun in the mid-1970s. Each spring, municipal employees prepare the earth and distribute seeds and plants, enabling city dwellers to grow their own vegetables and flowers. The plots are available on a first-come, first-served basis.

A building at the corner of Alexandre de Sève and Lafontaine displays an attractively carved wood balcony. A good insertion of new construction among old houses can be seen at 1593-95 Lafontaine Street.

As you walk down Champlain, look to the left to see factories on Papineau Street, which have closed down. Such buildings are scattered throughout Terrasse Ontario. Many were demolished recently.

At the corner of Logan is a food cooperative, the Club Coopératif de Consommation Centre-sud which is a cooperative effort to combat the high cost of food. For a few hours work per month and a $50 refundable share, one can become a member and buy food at close to wholesale prices.

At the corner of Logan and Papineau is a Richardson Romanesque church which at one time was the Irish Catholic **Taylor's Church**. It is one of the few francophone Protestant churches in Montreal. Now it houses an American-style evangelical sect. The church has rather impressive stained-glass windows and an unusual amphitheatre interior.

To the east is **Veterans Park,** originally a military cemetery (Saint Mary's Burial Ground) when British troups garrisoned in Montreal used La Fontaine Park as a parade ground. In 1944, after decades of disuse, it was officially closed and the remains and tombstones removed to the military graveyard in Pointe-Claire. During the 1964-66 work on the Jacques-Cartier Bridge, a park was established, but not before some remaining vestiges of the cemetery had to be found and given a proper burial.

Jacques-Cartier Bridge is the omnipresent backdrop to the neighborhood. Apparently, when the project was announced in

1930, the Barsalou soap factory was in the path of the bridge, and the owner hoped to sell his building at a high price. Instead, the federal government decided to build around it. This explains the dangerous sharp left curve on the inbound side. The reconstruction of the entrance ramp in 1964-66 led to the demolition of 170 homes.

On the south side of de Maisonneuve, between Papineau and Champlain, is a parking lot for Télé-Métropole, a local television station. Until recently, Télé-Métropole was the owner of about 20 flats on this land. Tenants received a notice of eviction because of demolition, in March 1976. The tenants filed a complaint with the Rental Board, which ruled that because of a technicality they were entitled to an extension of their leases until June 1977.

In April 1977 the owner of the lots obtained a demolition permit for the rear sheds. The rear balconies and stairways were demolished as well — the landlord said it was a mistake. The row took on the appearance of a slum. The Rental Board finally approved the tenants' eviction because Télé-Métropole claimed they needed the lot for a new studio — although the television network had never showed any plans or financing details to the Board.

The City Planning Department became involved ten months later by obtaining a zoning change to maintain the lot for housing. Just before the zoning by-law was to be adopted, the City Permit Service issued a demolition permit anyway. No sooner said than done, the buildings were levelled. Faced with a *fait accompli*, the Planning Department permitted another parking lot, on the condition that it be surrounded by a decorative fence.

Turn left on de Maisonneuve to come to the head office of Télé-Métropole, located at the corner of Alexandre de Sève Street which is named after the company's founder. At the corner of Ste-Catherine is the former **Théâtre Arcade**, faced with terra-cotta. The arcades which gave the theatre its name can be seen above the entrance on Álexandre de Sève Street.

During the early years of this century, classical and contemporary plays were performed before audiences of more than 800 people. Troupes were imported from France and many of the great names of Montréal theatre made their debut here. Now the building houses one of Télé-Métropole's studios.

You cannot fail to notice the Canadian Broadcasting Corporation's building, **Maison de Radio-Canada**. Local merchants began to lobby for a large construction project to revitalize the area in 1951. A decade later the project was announced. The block where the building now stands, then known as îlots des Voltigeurs, was expropriated by the municipal administration in 1963. Five thousand people were evicted, and a large number of businesses, restaurants, groceries, garages and factories disappeared.

Now a 23-storey building stands in 25 acres (10 ha) of what is mainly parking space. The Canadian Broadcasting Corporation is a governmental agency which provides radio and television

Maison de Radio-Canada seen from Panet Street.

service in both English and French across Canada. Here is the head office for the French television and radio networks (Radio-Canada), the regional and local offices of English CBC, Radio-Canada International and the Quebec northern service.

The building was completed in 1973 and Maison de Radio-Canada is one of the most modern production centres in the world. The project was completed by the corporation's architecture department under the direction of Edwin Sydney and his associate, Paul Delisle. The original concept was by Toree Bjornstad and Cornelius Ver Hagen was responsible for its execution. Offices are contained in the tower; more than two dozen radio and TV studios are located on two underground floors. Telephone 285-2690 to inquire about guided tours of the building.

To the east of the CBC building is **Molson Breweries** long a familiar name in the neighborhood. This is the oldest family enterprise in Canada, founded in 1786 by John Molson.

Sohmer Park, established in 1889, was to the west of the brewery. It contained gardens, a zoo, a circus and an amphitheatre where concerts and athletic tournaments were held. Louis Cyr, "the strongest man in the world," performed here. The Campbell Foundation purchased the site in 1923, renewed it and renamed it Campbell Park in 1930. Now the park is gone and the land is used by the brewery.

Facing Molson Breweries is the **Ste-Brigide church**, whose magnificent spire can been seen behind the buildings to the east. This church has been closed for a number of years. Next to it, at 1175 Champlain, is Saint Peter and Saint Paul, a Russian-Orthodox church.

3 Église St-Pierre-Apôtre

Just east of Beaudry Street is the St-Pierre-Apôtre church. The fact that two Catholic churches are so near one other is an indication of a once-large population in the sector. The Marie-Immaculée Oblate fathers erected a chapel here in 1848. The present Gothic Revival church was designed in 1851-53 by Victor Bourgeau and represents his first work as principal architect. The presence of flying buttresses and the semicircular apse point out how faithful Bourgeau was to the Gothic style, more so than most church designers in Quebec at that time. The pulpit has been replicated in many other Quebec churches.

St-Pierre's fine limestone walls are topped by a 235-foot (72 m) spire which contains a French carillon of 13 bells, all too rarely heard. The clock tower was designed by Joseph Venne, the architect of the Sacré-Coeur church. The 22 stained-glass windows are in fine condition. The statue over the entrance on de la Visitation Street

is of St-Peter, patron of Pierre Beaudry, who donated the land for the church. Later, Beaudry became the mayor of Montréal. The original bronze statue has been replaced with one made of bronze-plated cement.

The presbytery to the north is the Mother House of the Oblates in Canada. As was frequently the case, there was a school nearby, at 1212 de la Visitation. Now, that building houses a local recreation and training centre.

Beaudry and de la Visitation streets are undergoing gentrification as the houses which line them are renovated. No. 1208 Beaudry is the only house with wood siding in the entire neighborhood. While it has resisted fire and a harsh climate, it has deteriorated through lack of maintenance.

To the left at 1220 Ste-Catherine Street is the **Théâtre National**, now featuring Chinese movies.

The Théâtre National was founded in 1900 and furthered the careers of many Canadian writers and actors. Towards the end of the 1930s, legitimate theatre gave way to burlesque. Vaudeville was originally performed in English. Even francophone actors such as Olivier Guimond and Arthur Pétrie performed in English, because burlesque was an American import. The plays were purchased in the United States and early proprietors were anglophone (primarily Jews and Syrians). Other important burlesque theatres were the Starland and the Crystal on St-Laurent, and the Imperial on Bleury. (The latter is now a cinema). By the 1930s, burlesque in French took over and became quite popular during the Depression. Burlesque stars were adored by the public. Their dressing rooms were filled with cakes, flowers and gifts night after night. All this ended abruptly with the arrival of television in the 1950s.

The Ouimetoscope (1206 Ste-Catherine East) was the first building designed as a movie theatre in North America. Léo-Ernest Ouimet opened it in 1907, seven years before the first cinema

was built on Broadway. Ouimet gave up the thousand-seat theatre in 1921 and moved to California. The Ouimetoscope became
the Cinéma Canadien, and today it is a repertory movie house
under the original name.

Dupuis et Frères Department store celebrated its 53rd anniversary in 1920.

Looking west on Ste-Catherine, you can see a large grey building
on the right: Dupuis Frères. It was advertised as the French-
Canadian family's store and was touted as being quite different
from the department stores on Ste-Catherine Street West. As the
population of the area decreased, sales went down. The store
was modernized in a fruitless effort to revive it. The adoption of
downtown merchandising techniques coupled with poor financial management spelled disaster, and it went bankrupt in 1978.

Attempts by employees to save the enterprise were unsuccessful, and the building was sold to real estate developers. They
turned it into Les Atriums — an office building boasting direct
access to the metro, a forest of tropical plants and flowers, and
even a waterfall.

Return to Beaudry, walk to de Maisonneuve. Note the red brick
building at 1231 de Maisonneuve. Near the roof is sculpted a
cross on a maple leaf with the motto "God and Country" in
French. Here was once the headquarters of the Syndicats Catho-
liques Nationaux, originally a conservative trade union organized by the Roman Catholic church. In the 1950s, the union
dropped its religious ties and became the Confederation of
National Trade Unions, (Centrale des Syndicats Nationaux). Now
the building is used for housing.

Habitations Communautaires du Centre-sud de Montréal was
founded in 1974. This local citizens' group promotes collective
ownership through non-profit cooperative housing. As a
member of a housing cooperative, the tenant does not have to
fear that the landlord will charge a rent higher than that decreed
by the government as a condition of the subsidies received.

The committee is also concerned with parks, schools and other
socio-cultural resources. Its office is located in the first house in
Terrasse Ontario, in the first house to be renovated as part of a
cooperative managed by tenants.

Behind this house is the parc des Joyeux Vikings, named as a result of a contest held at its opening in the summer of 1980. This was an empty lot until local residents lobbied the city administration to establish this park.

As you walk along Beaudry, salute the 12 stately maple trees. This is probably the only street in the neighborhood with its original trees.

The new buildings near the park comprise a low-cost housing project put up by the city. The high-rise is reserved for old people and the handicapped, while the other buildings house families. Later, we will see newer low-cost housing units which are more attractive.

At the corner of Robin and Montcalm streets is the new **Camillien Houde Arena.** Houde was the mayor of Montreal between 1928 and 1954. He lived not far from here, at 1338 Logan. The sports complex was inaugurated on March 3, 1981 with three of **Camillien Houde's** daughters in attendance.

Camillien Houde (1889-1958) was mayor of Montreal during the following years: 1928-32, 1934-36, 1938-40, 1944-47, 1950-54. He also represented Montreal-Sainte-Marie in the provincial legislature beginning in 1922. He served as leader of the provincial conservative party from 1928-32. A persuasive and forceful speaker, he opposed conscription in 1939 and was detained in an internment camp in New Brunswick until 1944. On his return he was re-elected mayor by 100 000 votes. He also managed **L'Illustration** newspaper. He was honored as commander of the Order of the British Empire, the French Legion of Honor and the Cross of Italy.

Across the street, you can see attractive low-cost housing for families which offers spacious units with backyards. This is perhaps Montreal's most attractive public housing.

These houses were built on land cleared by the infamous fires of November 1974. Exasperated by a breakdown in negotiations with the city, the Montreal Firefighters' Association went out on strike, leaving the city vulnerable to fire. The result was a weekend of flames. Local residents took matters into their own hands and seized hoses from the fire stations. Even with the help of firemen from the suburbs, much was lost and more than 185 families were left homeless. According to the official report, fires erupted in 17 different places; at least 14 of these were criminally-caused.

Typical Terrasse Ontario row housing lined both sides of Wolfe Street until 1981. The new houses you see now faithfully mimic the architecture of the original houses.

4 Marché St-Jacques

This building was constructed circa 1920.

St-Jacques Market (1125 Ontario) was opened in 1931 to replace a structure built in 1872. This market offered fish, live chickens and rabbits inside, while fruit, flowers and vegetables were sold outside.

Upstairs was a large hall where many an election debate and patriotic rally were held. Henri Bourassa, Camillien Houde, Lionel Groulx, and John Diefenbaker spoke here at different times. The hall was the scene of a huge assembly protesting military conscription in 1942. In the limelight was a young lawyer by the name of Jean Drapeau.

The market was a meeting place for young and old alike, a colorful, animated hub of the neighborhood. It was closed in 1960 for health reasons. Now the health service of the city has its offices here. In the summer of 1982, the market was re-established on a smaller scale with outdoor stalls.

Just past the market is a fine example of building recycling. In 1967, André Perry purchased the Church of All Nations, 1135 Amherst Place, from the United Church of Canada to establish an audio recording studio. It has housed Studio de Son Québec since 1973. Québécois artists like Ginette Reno, Jean-Pierre Ferland, Louise Forestier and Gilles Vigneault have recorded here.

Centre d'accueil Ernest Routhier, at 2110 Wolfe Street, is a senior citizens' centre named for a local resident whose efforts were in large part responsible for its establishment. Across from the centre is a low-cost housing project which was built where fires destroyed a block of houses on that fiery weekend in 1974.

A sculpture above the entrance to the Bain Généreux.

The **Bain Généreux**, inaugurated in 1931, is at 2050 Amherst. During the Depression a number of public baths were built in working class neighborhoods where private bathrooms were a rarity. As is frequently the case, the Baths were named after the local alderman, Damase Généreux. J.O. Marchand designed the building which now contains a swimming pool, showers and space for 400 spectators.

Before the suburb of St-Léonard became their home, many Italians lived in this area — as the Milano Tavern on the corner of St-Timothée and Ste-Catherine attests. At one time the Feast of the Madonna was marked by couples dancing under garlands of flowers to the accompaniment of accordions.

5 Rue St-André

The houses on the west side of St-André were artisans' homes at the turn of the century. Many were later modified with an extension to the rear to provide three flats. Take time to admire the romance of these façades. The decorative touches, evident in the balconies and on the roofs, as well as the variety of colors used, make them look like a stage set. In the last few years, the prices of these houses have climbed dramatically.

Facing them is a row of houses starting at 2076 St-André and extending to Sherbrooke Street. The houses were purchased by a group of physicians who had bought up most of the block between St-André and St-Timothée. They wanted to demolish the houses, including a fine row of greystone houses on Sherbrooke Street, to put up a medical centre comprising offices, boutiques and two 20-storey high-rise apartment buildings.

Many houses were demolished. Other units on St-André were turned into rooming houses and, later, boarded up. The only protest possible for one despondent resident was to paint a sad "Farewell my street, I love you" on one of the walls to commemorate the loss of his home.

Although the city had approved the doctors' plans, protests by citizens (along with the help of some city employees) resulted in the revoking of city demolition permits.

The municipal housing authority rebuilt the block which will be sold individually on the free market because the construction cost was too high for them to be accessible to non-profit housing co-operatives.

The houses between 2079 and 2135 St-André were completed in 1982. They are well-integrated into the dimensions of the street: the colors chosen and the way they climb the slope to Sherbrooke Street is appealing.

The starting point (# 24 bus) is to the east, on Sherbrooke Street. The métro station is on Berri, north of Sherbrooke.

MAISONNEUVE

MAISONNEUVE

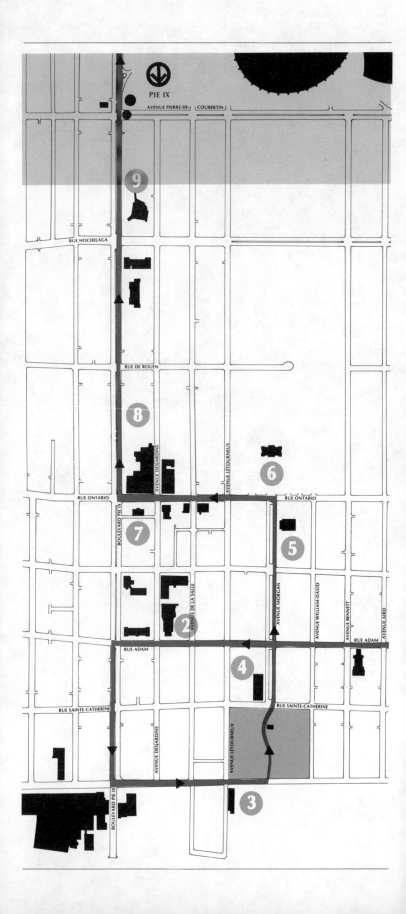

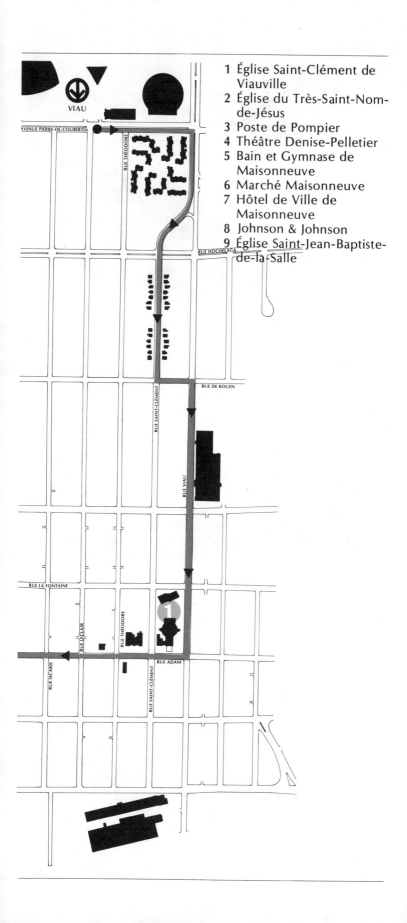

1 Église Saint-Clément de Viauville
2 Église du Très-Saint-Nom-de-Jésus
3 Poste de Pompier
4 Théâtre Denise-Pelletier
5 Bain et Gymnase de Maisonneuve
6 Marché Maisonneuve
7 Hôtel de Ville de Maisonneuve
8 Johnson & Johnson
9 Église Saint-Jean-Baptiste-de-la-Salle

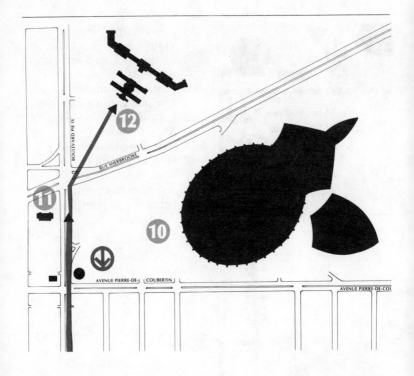

10 Parc Olympique
11 Château Dufresne
12 Jardin Botanique

History

In the days of the sailing ship, Saint Mary's Current made it difficult for small vessels to sail between Île Ste-Hélène and the island of Montreal to the city's port. To eliminate the need for a favorable wind or the use of a tugboat, a number of companies began to unload their cargos downstream of the port and move their merchandise by land for the final stretch to Montreal.

This practice led to the construction of the Dézéry Pier around which grew a settlement. The village of Hochelaga was officially incorporated in 1870. This municipality was not limited to the area around the pier but included a vast rural territory stretching from Iberville Street, in the west, to the municipality of Longue Pointe in the east, from the Saint Lawrence River, north to Côte-de-la-Visitation (where Rosemont Boulevard is now).

From then on, Hochelaga rapidly urbanized: by 1881 its population quadrupled, reaching 4,111 inhabitants. This increase, comprised primarily of workers, was due mainly to the installation of large factories such as St. Anne Knitting Mill and McDonald Tobacco. In 1883, Hochelaga became a town.

The population increase weighed heavily on the financial resources of the new municipality which was forced to borrow large sums of money to extend public services as required. The high level of indebtedness compromised the town's development. The mayor, Raymond Préfontaine, was a strong promoter of the town's annexation by the city of Montreal, saying it would improve services for the population and accelerate development of the area.

The eastern end of Hochelaga, known initially as Côte St-Martin, was unaffected by annexation. The important landowners of the rectangular area between Bourbonnière and Viau streets, the river, and St-Joseph and Rosemont boulevards, petitioned the provincial legislature to create an independent town. Consequently, the area became a distinct municipality, known as Maisonneuve. The group was led by businessman Joseph Barsalou and his son-in-law Joseph Desjardins (federal member of Parliament for the area). The municipality of Maisonneuve was created on December 27, 1883, five days after Montreal's absorption of Hochelaga.

At its inception, only about 50 families lived in Maisonneuve. Its location gave it a number of advantages: proximity to the river, railway service, vacant land suitable for industrial installations. In 1892, streetcar lines were extended from Montreal to Maisonneuve.

The municipal council was made up largely of members of the great landholding families. After ensuring the municipality had all the necessary public services, they devised an audacious plan for its industrial development. Publicity campaigns informed industrialists of the advantages of locating in the town. The council included fiscal incentives such as tax exemptions for all new factories built in Maisonneuve. The first companies to take advantage of these 20-year tax holidays were St. Lawrence Sugar 1887) and the Montreal Terra Cotta Lumber Company (1888).

This first spate of industrialization had but a limited impact on the development of the town, and it was only in 1896 that Maisonneuve really boomed. During this period of expansion in Quebec's economy, Maisonneuve's port and rail facilities were greatly appreciated.

From 1896 to 1901, a system of direct grants replaced tax exemptions as an incentive. The municipal council established the standards necessary to qualify for a grant: the type of construction and the date of completion were dictated. Ten years of use was required and the buildings and machinery were mortgaged for the value of the grant. To encourage an increase in the population, 80% of the employees had to reside in Maisonneuve. During this period, at least 10 companies (including six shoes factories) were established in the town.

From 1906 to 1915, Maisonneuve welcomed 18 more companies and became one of the largest shoe manufacturing centres in the country. In addition to footwear, shipyards as well as textile, candy and cookie factories made Maisonneuve the second largest manufacturing city in Quebec, and the fifth in Canada. The success of this industrial promotion gave Maisonneuve its nickname "Canada's Pittsburgh".

In 1910, the Michaud-Dufresne team took office at City Hall. Representing the local upper-middle class, the council started an extensive beautification program to crown the phenomenal growth of the town, now numbering 18,000 inhabitants. The construction of prestigious buildings, establishment of impressive boulevards and, especially, the creation of Maisonneuve Park modified the reputation of the town and gave it a second nickname — "The Garden of Montreal".

The emphasis on grandeur required extensive public borrowing, and soon rumors were floating of scandalous speculation on the land used for Maisonneuve Park. The park cost $6 million — a huge sum in those days. The First World War stopped industrial growth in the town, causing a grave financial crisis which made it more and more difficult for the municipality to finance its debt. Construction was at a standstill, and unemployment worsened.

Dissatisfied with the administration, the electors voted in a new slate in the 1915 election, the Maisonneuve Citizens' Association. The group proposed annexation to Montreal. While **Médéric Martin**, Montreal's mayor, considered Maisonneuve's debt unmanageable, the government of Quebec decreed the annexation in 1918.

Just as with Hochelaga 35 years earlier, Maisonneuve became another one of Montreal's wards. However it was able to maintain its distinctive character, and still displays a rich collection of institutional and industrial architecture from the turn of the century. This tour covers an area not very well known by most Montrealers, a pity since it contains some of the finest examples of city planning in Montreal.

Itinerary

The two and-a-half-hour tour of Maisonneuve begins at Viau metro station.

When Maisonneuve Park was first established in 1910, could Michaud and Dufresne have dreamed of its crowning glory, selection as the site for the 1976 Olympic Games? (The Olympic installations will be discussed at the end of the tour.) Until construction for the Olympic games reduced its size, Maisonneuve Park was Montreal's largest (600 acres).

Near the metro station are the Maurice Richard Arena, built in 1961, and Complexe Pierre Charbonneau (formerly known as the Centre Maisonneuve). Maurice Richard was a famous hockey player on the Montreal Canadiens team in the 1950s. (Cross Pierre de Coubertin Street)

Turn left and walk by **the Boyce-Viau housing complex** which was built by the city in 1971 as part of its low cost housing program. Designed by Philip Bobrow, the project received an award for best residential architectural design in Canada. Its 208 units are distributed on the site in such a manner as to insulate some of them from the noise of the city. A wide band of prestressed concrete decorates the façades and is also used for the balconies.

On both sides of St-Clément Street south of Hochelaga are examples of a completely different type of housing. They were designed just after the Second World War as inexpensive homes for veterans to purchase. Although originally identical in design, some have been modified by their occupants. (Turn left on Rouen, then right on Viau)

The Canadian National Railroad tracks lead to the industrial zone of southern Maisonneuve. The area contains many fine examples of industrial architecture of the late nineteenth and early twentieth centuries. It has been proposed to remove the now unneeded tracks and establish paths for joggers, cyclists and cross-country skiers.

In 1907, the **Biscuiterie Viau** company left Notre-Dame Street to come to the corner of Viau and Ontario. This was the site of the dairy farm purchased in 1886 by Charles-Théodore Viau, the company's founder. The factory was a typical Victorian industrial construction. The clean lines of its windows and pilasters reflected the internal structure of the building. Unfortunately a recent renovation has marred its attractiveness by covering much of the building in aluminum siding.

This neighborhood is known as **Viauville**, after C.T. Viau who established a housing development on his land. Unlike most of Montreal's residential districts, a deliberate effort was made in this then independent municipality to establish design and planning guidelines. The area south of Notre-Dame Street was to be landscaped as a park. Even more important were the servitudes placed on the property: land was sold on the condition that only two-storey brick houses with cut stone façades be erected. They had to sit 10 feet (3 m) from the sidewalk.

Following an agreement between the town of Maisonneuve and the executor's of Viau's estate, the tiny municipality was absorbed but the name Viauville persisted.

Habitations Viauville is one of two homes for the elderly, recently built in Maisonneuve. Designed by Raouf Boutros, this centre was completed in 1980. Unfortunately, École St-Paul de Viauville, a school run by the Frères des Écoles Chrétiennes and built in 1906, was demolished to make room for it.

1 Église Saint-Clément de Viauville

Saint-Clément de Viauville is Maisonneuve's second parish church. C.T. Viau had it built on land he donated in 1898. The architect was Joseph Venne. By 1913, the population of the parish had grown sufficiently to require the enlargement of the church. Construction of the new nave was directed by Venne and his partner, Labelle. Following a fire in 1926, Curé Desjardins (the parish priest) decided to install an automatic sprinkler system and St-Clément de Viauville became the first religious building in Canada with such a safety feature. Inside, an octagonal assembly of arches meeting at the intersection of the nave and transept give a Moorish effect which is as attractive as it is unusual.

Église Saint-Clément-de-Viauville shortly after its construction.

Across St-Clément Street from the church is the former Couvent Saint-Émile. Here was the first girls' boarding school in Viauville, under the direction of the nuns of the Saints-Noms-de-Marie-et-de-Jésus. This magnificent greystone building was inaugurated in 1902, with the west wing added seven years later. It has become a home for elderly nuns; modifications to the entrance sacrificed the magnificent staircase to the main floor.

Across from the convent, 4820-22 was once **the house of Dame A. Delisle Ste-Onge**. Its prominent galleries continue along the side. It and **Maison Trefflé Bleau**, across Adam Street at 4785-89, are typical examples of residential design in Viauville.

The effect of the construction restrictions on Viau's land is evident at its border between Sicard and Aird streets where grey stone gives way to brown brick.

Église Saint-Barnabé-Apôtre (4560 Adam) was designed in 1952 by Armand Dutrisac. Morgan Boulevard interrupts the series of triplexes displaying exterior staircases. It offers a magnificent view of Marché Maisonneuve which you will see later on the tour.

2 Église du Très-Saint-Nom-de-Jésus

The parish of Très-Saint-Nom-de-Jésus was created in 1888, and was the first parish in Maisonneuve. This church was built between 1903 and 1906 and was the work of Charles A. Reeves who, as municipal architect and inspector, was responsible for a number of public and school buildings in Maisonneuve. The two imposing spires were added in the late 1920s. T. Xénophon Renaud designed the richly-decorated interior in 1913. The following year the celebrated Maison Casavant of Ste-Hyacinthe, Quebec, installed Montreal's largest electric organ which unfortunately no longer works. Thirty magnificent windows were brought from Limoges, France in 1915.

A sign of the aging of the local population is the senior citizen's home, Habitations Desjardins which is situated behind the church. It replaced the **École du Très-Saint-Nom-de-Jésus**, for girls, the oldest school in the neighborhood. However, the boys' school is still used as an elementary school.

What was once the **Hospice de la Providence et du Sacré-Coeur** (1691 Pie IX) is now used for community services such as a local radio station (CIBL) and Atelier d'Histoire Hochelaga-Maisonneuve. The Atelier has a great deal of information documenting the history of this district.

(Turn left on **Pie IX Boulevard** and walk till you reach Notre-Dame Street) This boulevard was named after Pius IX, Pope during the time of the struggle to unify Italy. Many of his army, the Zouaves, were recruited in Quebec.

Affluent citizens tried to create a "garden city" in Maisonneuve through careful esthetic planning. This tree-lined boulevard, flanked by luxurious residences, was to be the central artery of the new town. The developers were influenced by the British "Garden City" concept and the American "City Beautiful" which were popular at the time. The two philosophies share a concern with improving the quality of life in the city through the creation of a more agreeable and natural environment.

Canadian Spool and Cotton factory, circa 1930.

In contrast, the area around Notre-Dame now offers a desolate view. Although the Ville-Marie Expressway extension planned in the 1970s has not been completed, the bulldozer has done its work and a major redevelopment effort would be required to heal the scars. About 1200 housing units were destroyed, contributing to the decline in population of the area.

The gigantic installation of **St. Lawrence Sugar** is a link to the very beginning of Maisonneuve's industrialization. As the first company to move into the new town in 1887, St. Lawrence was given a 20-year tax holiday and a railroad right-of-way. **Sutherland Pier**, Maisonneuve's first port installation, was built in 1889 to meet the company's needs.

Across from it, at Jeanne d'Arc Avenue, can be seen an old cooperage, where barrels were produced. It, too, was built in the late 1880s. Further west is **Canadian Spool and Cotton,** the first textile manufacturer in Maisonneuve. The factory was constructed in 1907.

3 Poste de Pompier

The distinctive building at the corner of Letourneux is the original Fire Station No. 1, built in 1914-15 under the direction of Marius Dufresne, municipal engineer. He was responsible for many of Maisonneuve's grand construction projects of the turn-of-the-century. His own house, itself a magnificent structure, will be seen at the end of the tour. This building was modelled after the Unity Temple, designed by Frank Lloyd Wright, one of the founders of modern architecture. Except for the tower used to dry firehoses, resemblance to Wright's Unity Temple (1906) in Oak Park, Illinois (near Chicago), is striking. The Fire Station building has several features in common with the Temple: square columns supporting the protruding roof, horizontal lines, and a play of angles which divided the volume of the building into a series of projections and setbacks. The Atelier d'Histoire Hochelaga-Maisonneuve is negotiating the conversion of this building into a museum of industrial and urban development.

Behind the park whose appearance has also been damaged by the highway construction, can be seen Canadian Vickers Limited, a subsidiary of the British firm of Vickers, Sons and Maxim. The building dates from 1910. Two years later, one of the largest drydocks of that time was added to their property, confirming Montreal as Canada's most important shipbuilding centre.

Passing through the gates of **Morgan Park** brings you to what was once the property of James Morgan, owner of the department store chain which used to bear his name. He lived here until 1928, in a sumptuous mansion surrounded by gardens. Two years later he gave the land to the city of Montreal on the condition that it be made into a park. The bandstand was added in 1933 and for 20 years or more, frequent concerts were given.

4 Théâtre Denise-Pelletier

Facing the park is the Théâtre Denise-Pelletier (formerly the Grenada Cinema). Behind its Rococo façade are glorious decorations by Emmanuel Briffa who designed many of Montreal's most opulent theatres and cinemas in the 1920s and 1930s. A repertory group, la Nouvelle Compagnie Théâtrale, acquired the building in 1977. While improvements were made to the stage, the exquisite Italianate decorations were preserved. Denise Pelletier was one of Quebec's greatest actresses whose untimely death in 1976 occurred just before she was to bring her impressive portrayal of Sarah Bernhardt to Broadway.

Morgan Boulevard was planned to highlight Maisonneuve's two most impressive public buildings — the Market and the Public Baths. Public Baths were common at the time, since few working class flats had bathtubs. Maisonneuve's leaders also wanted to promote the idea of it as a model city — clean and healthful.

5 Bain et Gymnase de Maisonneuve

Marius Dufresne designed the de Maisonneuve baths and gymnasium in 1915. Its classical style façade was modelled on New York City's Grand Central Station. The horses and rider on the pediment were sculpted by M.R. Dubert, as were the nymph and gymnast reclining at either end of the balustrade. Alfred Laliberté designed the fountain with young bathers.

The interior of the building has been modified more than once. It was used as a training centre for the Montreal police force from 1920 to 1960 and now is a recreation centre for the elderly, under the name Centre Morgan.

6 Marché Maisonneuve

Maisonneuve's market opened in September 1914. In those days, a market was an important place in the life of a city, as can be seen in the care which Marius Dufresne took in designing the building. Note its symmetry and how it was positioned so as to dominate the view. In the Beaux-Arts style, the building has a massive portal topped by a pediment. Four turrets frame a central dome. One of Alfred Laliberté's most important works stands in front of

Morgan Boulevard with the market and public baths, circa 1916.

the market building. Designed initially as a fountain, *La Fermière* was cast in bronze at the then exhorbitant cost of $20,000.

The market building was completed in 1932 with the construction of exterior shelters (later demolished). It was used mainly for cattle, unlike Montreal's other markets which concentrated mostly on fruits and vegetables. The market closed in 1962, a victim of changing shopping patterns. Since then, it has been used by various city of Montreal departments, but now has returned to its initial use in a small way: in 1980, following pressure and lobbying from local groups, the city established a small exterior market, a shadow of the buisiness which used to be transacted in this hall of commerce.

(Take Ontario back to Pie IX) This part of Ontario Avenue became the administrative and business main street of Maisonneuve during its intensive industrialization. **Molson's Bank** (4250 Ontario) was designed by Howard C. Stone in 1911. This sober greystone building now houses a branch of the Bank of Montreal. Across the street, a branch of the **Bank of Toronto** was also built in 1911. Hogle and Davis designed this terra-cotta-faced building in an 18th-century French style. Marius Dufresne had his office upstairs. The building is now occupied by Carrefour Jeunesse, a group which tries to prevent juvenile delinquency.

The construction of a second fire station in 1909 testifies to the concerns of the municipal council. Insurance for a commercial building was less expensive if it was near a fire station; this plain, utilitarian building designed by Charles Reeves was another way the municipal council encouraged business.

Facing the station is Le Rond Point, a collection of shops installed in 1977 in the old **Dufresne & Locke shoe factory**. Thomas Dufresne, father of Marius and Oscar, founded this company in 1891 and moved it here in 1900. Unfortunately, the conversion of this building has masked the original style of the façade.

7 Hôtel de Ville de Maisonneuve

Magnificent and austere, Maisonneuve's City Hall stands at the corner of Pie IX Boulevard. Erection of this building in 1912 began Maisonneuve's program of constructing impressive — and expensive — public buildings. Cajeten Dufort designed this classical edifice. Its façade is composed of an imposing Corinthian colonnade with a wide entablature made up of a sculptured frieze and balustrade. An elegant sculpted pediment crowns the main entrance. The heavy bronze doors open into a large lobby bathed in light. Inside is a superb marble staircase with a landing, lit by impressive stained glass. A fascinating sketch mounted upstairs shows Maisonneuve as it looked before the First World War.

The Institut du Radium moved into the building in 1926, after Maisonneuve's absorption by Montreal. The organization had a worldwide reputation for its pioneering research in cancer treatment. Following its closure in 1967, the city of Montreal installed some of its offices here. The building is now the site of the local public library and of the Maison de la culture.

8 Johnson & Johnson

Architects Cayouette et Saïa received awards from Save Montreal and Canadian Architect magazine for their recycling of two pre-Second World War factory buildings into the new headquarters of Johnson & Johnson (2155 Pie IX). They convinced the company to maintain its facilities in Maisonneuve instead of moving downtown. Two buildings, one built in 1926 (on the right) and one in 1912 (with an addition of 1936) were recycled and new buildings faced in brick and concrete added.

This is a good example of the Post-Modern style in its use of multiple materials, and the linking together of varying rhythms and volumes. The form of the street was maintained with the placement of the smaller of the new buildings, framing a courtyard which focusses the two main axes of the complex. The other new building houses a cafeteria and exercise room lit through an atrium by natural light.

Pie IX Boulevard at Ste-Catherine St, circa 1915.

As you walk up Pie IX toward Sherbrooke, you come to the former **Académie de Saint-Nom-de-Marie** and the **École Saint-Jean-Baptiste-de-la-Salle** at Hochelaga Street. Charles Reeves designed both these buildings in 1917 and 1918, respectively. Although they are of different sizes, the architect has succeeded in creating a harmonious grouping by making use of the same vocabulary for two façades. Reeves' school designs are noteworthy for imposing volumes and majestic entrances. The extensive substructure, which he favored symbolically, links the local stone used in the façades to the ground whence it came.

9 Église Saint-Jean-Baptiste-de-la-Salle

The early 1960s marked a new style in Quebec church architecture. During the Quiet Revolution when Quebec society became more secular and more modern, church architecture became more symbolic, as much sculpture as construction. Saint-Jean-Baptiste-de-la-Salle (1964), was designed by Lemay, Leclerc & Trahan and is one of the best examples of this expressionist style.

10 Parc Olympique

What can be said of the Olympic installation built for the 1976 summer Olympics? The original cost estimate in 1972 for the entire complex — covered stadium, swimming centre, velodrome, housing for athletes, parking and other service facilities — was $310 million. Mayor Jean Drapeau had told the international Olympic Committee that the city would stage modest games. Then it was decided that something more prestigious should be attempted. The construction cost reached $1.02 billion. A provincial study, the Malouf report, revealed a tangled web of mismanagement and profiteering.

Guided visits to the stadium, swimming centre and velodrome are offered by the Régie des Installations Olympiques.

The Olympic Park is one of the largest sports complexes in the world. Conceived by Roger Tallibert, the construction of these buildings required ingenious techniques to adapt European prefabricated concrete technology to the Montreal site and climate. Instead of inviting local architects to enter a competition for the structure (the usual procedure for Olympic installations), which would have boosted Quebec architecture, Mayor Jean Drapeau imported a foreign architect.

In addition to technical problems,

delays in the preparation of the plans and, later, modifications were so serious that it was thought for a time the site would not be ready for the Olympics. To catch up, work went on 24 hours a day, seven days a week. Costs soared.

Still, the Olympic stadium, swimming pools and velodrome are arguably an important stage in modern architecture, due to the plasticity of their design.

The stadium is in the form of a giant mollusk. The western end is 180 feet (55 m) high, the eastern, 140 feet (43 m). It covers an area of 725,000 square feet (67 400 m²). At present, the stadium has 53,858 seats on three main levels with six floors.

The building is composed of 12,000 prefabricated elements. The basic structural element is the self-stabilizing tubular console. The frame of the stadium is composed of 34 full consoles and four consoles truncated at the base of the tower. The consoles form the eliptical shape of the stadium and support the roof, the spectator stands, the stairways and the huge technical ring which is a stabilizer element and contains the lighting and audio system.

According to the original plan, the mast was to be 552 feet (168 m) in height with a 226-foot (84 m) overhang. From it was to be suspended a retractable, flexible roof which would cover the entire playing field and allow the stadium to be used all year round. Tallibert's original plans were judged too costly and unrealistic. For a decade, the specially crafted roof lay in storage while debate ranged over what to do. Construction of the tower was completed in 1986, and Tallibert's roof installed the next year.

The Olympic swimming pools are located under the tripod base of the tower. The guided tours of the Olympic site offered by the Régie des Installations Olympiques begin there.

The Olympic Velodrome is an elegantly designed multifunctional building. Tallibert was successful in integrating its form with that of the stadium. The building is composed of prestressed and post-stressed prefabricated concrete which has made it possible to enclose the entire area of the building — some 174,000 square feet (16 200 m²) — without any interior supports. The roof is a scalloped, perforated dome built on the arc of a sphere with a radius of 525 feet (160 m). It rests on four supports positioned around the circumference of a circle 565 feet

(172 m) in diameter. Three of the supports are located on the southwest side of the building, each supporting two of the six principal depressed arches (or ribs) of the roof, which converge at the fourth support on the northeast end of the structure. The ribs are made up of 144 concrete voussoirs assembled in an arch. Each weighs between 50 and 100 tonnes. Giant cranes were used to install the voussoirs which were temporarily supported by 144 steel towers. Once attached and stabilized, the ribs from six immense arches connected by a trellis of transverse membranes. Skylights on these double Y-shaped trellises permit a great deal of light to enter.

Parking facilities for spectators along Pierre-de-Coubertin Avenue were constructed — at an excessive cost — with gardens and training grounds on the roof.

An Expos game in 1980.

11 Château Dufresne

Oscar and Marius Dufresne reproduced the grandeur of Maisonneuve public architecture (of which they were the principal proponents) in their own residence. Château Dufresne, as their double house was known, was built between 1916 and 1918, one of the first reinforced concrete buildings in Montreal. Its designer, Lebon, was inspired by Versaille's Petit Trianon. Marius Dufresne supervised the work.

The building is composed of two identical wings which housed the brothers and their families in 44 rooms. Italian marble, Japanese wood and stone from Indiana were some of the exotic materials used for the structure. Inside are furniture and artwork from various eras and countries — bedrooms are furnished in the Louis XV and Louis XVI styles, there is a Tudor and a Gothic study, Classical and Renaissance dining rooms, Second Empire salons and even a Turkish room. The ceiling frescoes are by the Italian painter Guido Nincheri. Surprisingly, many of the moldings, ceiling decorations, fireplaces and floor panelling were prefabricated, chosen from American catalogues.

After the death of the Dufresne brothers, the building was used by the École Ste-Croix, a private classical college run by a Catholic order. The building was taken over by the city of Montreal in 1957 and remained vacant for eight years until the Musée d'Art Contemporain was installed. It remained there until 1968.

In 1976, the Château was officially recognized by the provincial ministry of Cultural Affairs as a historic monument and restored through a grant from the McDonald Stewart Foundation. Now it houses the Musée des Arts Décoratifs. Five rooms have been restored and are open to the public.

Before crossing the street to the Jardin Botanique, you can see in the distance two pyramid-shaped highrise buildings. Housing for the athletes was provided in the **Olympic Village**. Architects Durand and D'Astous were responsible for the buildings which strikingly resemble a condominium project in Baie des Anges on the Côte d'Azur. This lack of orginality was recognized through the awarding the 1976 *Prix Citron* ("Lemon" Prize) by the Montreal Society of Architecture. Entrance to each unit is outside, from the balconies which stretch along the entire length of building. This set-up is much more suited to the climate of Mediterranean France than it is to Montreal's winters.

12 Jardin Botanique

The Botanical Garden is located on the north side of Sherbrooke Street. This lush expanse of land is quite pleasant to stroll in. Established in 1931 by Brother Marie-Victorin, the garden is said to be the third largest in the world and contains some 20,000 different botanical species planted outdoors and in acres of greenhouses. Plants are identified by their scientific and common names, and special displays are changed throughout the year.

Some of the collections, including that of 1200 varieties of orchids, are unique. The pleasant grounds decorated by flowers and other plants and trees is well worth a visit, as are the greenhouses which include a section for tropical plants and one for desert plants.

The greenhouses include the largest collection of dwarf trees (*bonsai* and *penjing*) outside of Asia. The Université de Montréal's botanical institute has been located in the main building since 1939, helping to create a direct link between horticulture and fundamental botany.

The Pie-IX metro station is one block south, at the corner of Pierre-de-Coubertin and Pie-IX boulevards.

LITTLE
BURGUNDY

LITTLE BURGUNDY

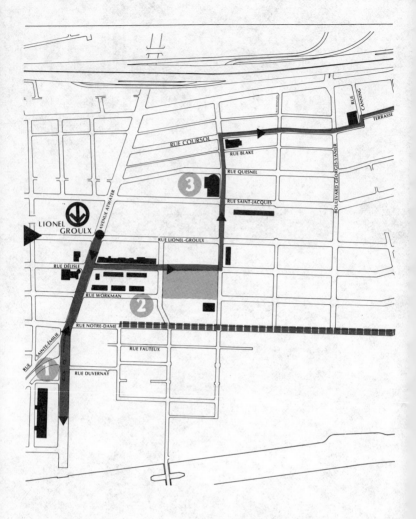

1 Atwater Market
2 Îlots Workman/Delisle
3 Église Ste-Cunégonde
4 Îlots St-Martin
5 The Lachine Canal

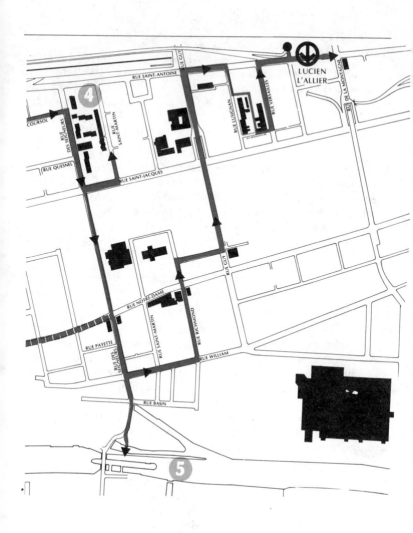

History

The name "Little Burgundy" was first applied to the extensive plain which begins near present-day McGill Street and extends west to the middle of St-Henri. This plain was criss-crossed by brooks and streams such as the Saint Peter River. It was given its name because of its similarity to the geography of the Burgundy region of France.

Today, Little Burgundy is defined as that part of Montreal which is bounded on the north by the Canadian Pacific Railway land (between Notre-Dame and St-Jacques streets) and the Ville-Marie autoroute, on the west by Atwater Street, on the south by the Lachine Canal, and on the east by Guy Street.

The history of the area begins with the completion of the Lachine Canal in 1825. It is here, along the banks of the canal, that Canada's industrial revolution began. Companies such as Montreal Rolling Mills, Canada Marine Works, as well as flour mills, saw mills, a shipyard and a tinwork were established here.

After the installation of industry along the canal, the Guy family farm in the eastern half of Little Burgundy was subdivided, and row houses were built on the land. The Montreal and Lachine Railway was built across the area in 1847, while two years later the western part of Little Burgundy was developed by Auguste Quesnel. He sold part of this area to two developers, Alexandre Delisle and William Workman, and bequeathed the rest to Charles Coursol, his nephew. The land became the town of Ste-Cunégonde, incorporated in 1876.

Ste-Cunégonde's growth from a rural town to an industrial city brought with it urban problems. Jobs were plentiful, yet wages were low. Prices rose without a corresponding increase in the wages of workers, and most people rented their homes. The result was that a family could not afford to pay much for rent, setting a limit to the amount landlords could charge. Landlords, feeling that they were not obtaining enough profit, neglected repairs, allowed property to deteriorate. More industries crowded along the canal, others moved onto residential streets. Additional tracks of the Grand Trunk Railway (later Canadian National Railway) further divided the community. Soon the streets of Little Burgundy were dirty, noisy and congested. It was an unpleasant place for people to live. An 1897 study entitled *The City Below the Hill* described the poor social, sanitary and housing conditions of this area. It remained that way until the 1960s.

In 1965, the City of Montreal began a massive redevelopment program on the scale of the huge American urban renewal projects of the 1950s and early 1960s. During the ensuing decade and-a-half, Little Burgundy was *en chantier* — a vast construction site. The destruction and reconstruction of Little Burgundy is not quite finished and the final effects are not yet known.

There are a number of municipal low-cost housing projects in Little Burgundy, including Les îlots St-Martin. The project was scheduled to cost well over $80 million and called for 14 subsections. Work on the program was begun in 1968. The basic plan was to: Eliminate all existing structures from the north side of St-

Antoine Street to the C.P.R. tracks, in order to make room for the Bonaventure Autoroute; Strengthen the industrial area between Notre-Dame Street and the canal; Create a residential area between St-Antoine and St-Jacques streets; Create two commercial areas within the residential zone with Vinet Street and des Seigneurs Street as the two commercial axes.

The plan has had both supporters and critics since its inception. Arguments about the elimination of rundown housing and grimy factories are countered by humanist concerns supporting the maintenance of neighborhood life which provides community pride. Statistics show that the transformation of the area has concentrated in one section those who are on welfare, separating them from other people with higher incomes. Since the beginning of redevelopment, two-thirds of the original population has left Little Burgundy.

It is important to note that Little Burgundy, so well known as an area of unemployed, unskilled workers, was once a very proud community of craftsmen, tradesmen and professionals. This community pride needs renewal as much as anything else.

Itinerary

This tour will show the cultural mix of the area — English, Irish, French and Black — and point out some changes to lament and some changes to laud.

The tour is rather long: lasting about three hours. If you wish to split the walk in two, you can take the # 35 bus west on Notre-Dame to Lionel Groulx metro station halfway through the tour.

Actually, the tour is perfect for bicycling. You can buy a picnic lunch at Atwater Market, carry it with you until the Lachine Canal Bicycle Path which is about two-thirds of the way through the itinerary. There your tour of streets can be interrupted to cycle along a tree-lined path, stopping at a picnic table to eat.

1 Atwater Market

Our tour begins at Atwater Market, the low building with a clock tower a few blocks to the south of the Lionel Groulx metro station. It was constructed in 1933 by entrepreneur Charles Dansereau to replace a smaller structure at the corner of Mountain and St-Jacques streets. The space was sorely needed, and there were always more vendors than places available.

In the early days, Atwater Market was filled with bustling homemakers from Ste-Cunégonde, St-Henri, Pointe-St. Charles, St-Joseph and many other surrounding communities. Fresh fruit and vegetables were available at reasonable prices. There were also flowers for the drawing room, shrubs for the yard and seeds for the do-it-yourselfers.

Life in the market goes on today much as it has in the past. Although the number of shoppers dwindled during the 1960s and 1970s as supermarkets sprung up, Atwater and Jean-Talon markets managed to survive. Fourtunately, in the last few years there has been a resurgence of the old-fashioned market and the city has reopened a number of them. It looks as if Atwater Market will always be here.

The city of Montreal, in accordance with its redevelopment plan for Little Burgundy, planned to create a 22-acre (5-hectare) recreational centre to the east of the market. The park was to serve the communities of Pointe-St-Charles, St-Henri and Little Burgundy — about 30,000 people in all. As you can see, no park was created and the area is still used by Canadian Pacific and other companies.

This sign hung in front of the Union Church for many years.

Just to the south of the metro station is Union Church and the Église Ste-Irenée. **Union Church** was established in 1863 by the Côte-des-Neiges Presbyterian congregation to serve the black community of Montreal. The present building was constructed in 1899 to house both an Anglican and a Presbyterian congregation. Until recently there was a sign at the front of the church asking parishioners to be tolerant of the neighboring Catholics, explaining that all are Christians under God. Original plans for the construction of the metro station called for the demolition of the Union Church. Fortunately it was preserved.

The parish of Ste-Irenée was created for the influx of workers into Little Burgundy and St-Henri during the late 1800s. In 1908 this greystone church was erected, but the attached presbytery was added much later.

Union Church and **Église Ste-Irenée** portray a clear contrast in religious architecture: The buildings themselves reflect the organizations that they represent — the monolithic structure of Catholicism next to the smaller fortress of the Protestants.

2 Ilôts Workman/Delisle

Ilôts Workman/Delisle is a public housing project, the first of many to be seen in Little Burgundy which are part of the city of Montreal's redevelopment program. This particular group was constructed between 1967 and 1971 and consists of three buildings providing 42 units.

In his study entitled *Prospectives 80*, Marcel Simard has compiled interesting data concerning the incomes of the residents of the buildings. In 1965, before the redevelopment program, 78 out of 98 families in this area were salaried, i.e., someone in each of these households was earning money. In 1973 however, only eight out of 29 families studied were actually employed; the rest received their income from the state. In other words, an area that was 80% self-supporting became 72% state-financed after redevelopment. Urban renewal of this sort tends to create a welfare ghetto as public housing is only available to those on very low incomes.

Delisle Street provides a striking contrast between the old and the new. On one side we see the Workman/Delisle housing project and on the other, a row of tenement houses built in the 1800s. The north side is one of the few blocks with no demolished houses. These houses are a reminder of the fact that the streets of Little Burgundy were not always littered with cars. Horses used to be the popular means of transportation, and these buildings were constructed with that fact in mind, they had entrances for horses and carriages as well as for people. Horses were kept in stables behind the house; a laneway separated the stables of one street from those of the next.

The lanes served as places of commerce and community. On any given day you could find a number of people moving slowly down the lanes, each having a particular service to offer the inhabitants of the houses. You might see an iceman leading his horse and wagon and stopping off at each icebox to replenish his customers' stock. The rag man might come through, pulling a cart containing the clothes he had to sell, calling out that they were just the right size for your youngest son or your middle daughter. He would call them by their names, too. A couple of hours later the knife sharpener would come by, ringing his bell, ready to sharpen your scissors or knives and to chat about the news from dozens of other neighborhoods.

The laneways were the scene of another activity, less picturesque but more essential. Here were the little sheds, with doors that creaked each time they were opened, informing the whole neighborhood that once more nature had called. The term outdoor privy was a misnomer: out of doors it might have been, but private it was not. On a hot summer night the air was thick and heavy. Not only was the smell unpleasant but the waste material, along with the garbage that was strewn about, made the laneways perfect breeding grounds for rats and disease.

(Go along Delisle Street, past the baseball field, and into the park) **Vinet Park** was established in the late 1970s and is a positive result of the city's urban renewal program.

Vinet and Delisle streets form the heart of historic Little Burgundy. This is the centre of what was once the city of Ste-Cunégonde, founded by a few men in the 1860s: Frédéric Auguste Quesnel, landowner and politician; William Workman, first president of the City and District Savings Bank and a former mayor of Montreal; and Alexandre-Maurice Delisle, landowner, businessman and representative for the riding of Montreal in the first Parliament after the 1841 Act of Union. The fourth man involved in the affairs of Ste-Cunégonde was a judge and former mayor of Montreal, Charles Joseph Coursol, nephew and adopted son of Quesnel. They controlled all the land from Dorchester to Notre-Dame, from Atwater to Guy. According to one of their brochures, they intended "to provide a gardentown for the English metalworkers of the Montreal Rolling Mills."

The hamlet received an influx of workers and the city of Ste-Cunégonde grew. In 1891 the population was equally divided between French- and English-speaking people. Listed among the residents were doctors, lawyers, machinists, tailors, masons and roofers. Although professionals were numbered among the residents, Ste-Cunégonde was primarily a town of laborers and tradesmen.

The Anglican **Church of St. Jude** (southwest corner of Vinet and Workman) was purchased by the municipality in 1877 and remodelled to serve as a combination city hall, post office, fire station and police station. You can see it across the street, to the right of the park chalet.

One member of the police force was **Louis Cyr**, Quebec's famous strongman. At age 19 he was famous for his weightlifting feats and the newspapers called him "Today's Samson".

G. Lambert, Canadian heavyweight boxing and wrestling champion and director of a gymnasium in St-Henri, invited **Louis Cyr** to demonstrate his strength in Montreal. He appeared at his hotel carrying a 200-lb (90 kg) barbell in each hand and his broad shoulders just made it through the doorway. He performed at the Mechanic's Hall before a full house. The mayor of Ste-Cunégonde was in the audience and he asked Cyr to join the police force.

Cyr agreed and soon lived up to his reputation, imposing a majesty of force to the law that was never equalled. He was capable of subduing five or six men at once and would then pick them up and literally carry them off to jail. On September 23, 1885, Cyr and three other policemen went to the aid of some pedestrians who had been waylaid by a band of troublemakers and, in no time, he subdued the delinquents. As Cyr returned to the police station with two criminals under each arm, he was ambushed by five men who had already killed one of his colleagues with a hatchet. Cyr knocked down two of his assailants, but received a heavy blow on his neck. He would have been killed if three other constables had not arrived to help him. A very short time later, Cyr left the streets of Ste-Cunégonde to retire to his farm. There is a statue in his honor at St-Jacques and Coursol streets, about a mile west of here (not on the itinerary).

The houses at 541-561 Vinet Street are an example of urban renewal of the 1980s. These modest suburban-style "town houses" were built in the early 1980s on land which was cleared 20 years before when the original buildings were demolished. In the 1960s, urban renewal meant the elimination of substandard housing through demolition. These owner-occupied homes house somewhat more affluent people than the traditional population of the area.

3 Église Ste-Cunégonde

The magnificent Ste-Cunégonde Church (at the corner of St-Jacques and Vinet streets) was built in 1906 by Omer Marchand, the first Quebec architect to receive a diploma from the École des Beaux-Arts in Paris. Marchand's training is apparent in the styling of this church — a Romano-Baroque cathedral. It is 98 feet (30 m) high, 160 feet (49 m) long and 60 feet (18 m) wide. The gigantic dome which covers the church was — and is — an engineering marvel: amazingly enough, it has no internal support columns. The church seats 1200 worshippers. It is illuminated by huge stained-glass windows.

Since the congregation has grown smaller, heavy operating expenses of the church forced its closure in January 1971. Although numerous feasibility studies of alternate uses for the building were made, none have been attempted. In France, many deconsecrated churches have been converted into concert halls or are used for other secular purposes. Another idea would be to rent it to a Protestant congregation, one of which recently built a new church not far from here at a time when Ste-Cunégonde stood empty.

Traditional Roman Catholics may be interested in knowing that Ste-Cunégonde celebrates the Tridentine mass each Sunday.

Across from the church, on St-Jacques Street is Iberville Square. It was refurbished a few years ago, after the city had allowed it to deteriorate since urban renewal days. The statue of Pierre Le Moyne replaces one which disappeared in the 1960s.

East of Vinet, on the south side of St-Jacques is a very pleasing example of infill housing. Once trees grow, the pronounced rhythm of the balconies and rooflines of these houses will look very attractive.

The Church of Saint Jude, at Coursol Street, was built in 1878, after its Anglican congregation vacated what became the Ste-Cunégonde City Hall at Workman. Note the similarity in appearance of this church to the Catholic churches of the area. Apparently, Anglicans appreciated the same design for churches as did the Roman Catholics. It later became the Bible Way Pentecostal Church.

As you walk east along **Coursol Street**, note the rhythm of the dormer windows in the roofs. This street is one of the few left in Little Burgundy that appears very much now as it did when it was established in the 1880s. The houses have been preserved and renovated. They are divided into two types: the greystone row houses between Vinet and Dominion, and the brick cottages between Dominion and Canning. Both blocks enjoy the shade of many trees that have lined the street for decades. These trees were probably a factor in the decision to maintain the street's original appearance.

Before subdivision, Quesnel's land was shaped like an inverted pie wedge with the smallest end near the corner of Atwater and Dorchester (where the **Montreal Children's Hospital** now stands) and the wide end near Notre-Dame. Canning and Atwater streets formed the sides of Quesnel's property. He built his mansion on Dorchester, at the top of the hill, commanding an excellent view of the property.

Below the house was a large pond and further south, in the area where you now are, was the village of Delisle, surrounded by peaceful meadows of green grass and tall trees. Small brooks and streams of cool spring water bubbled through the fields. Animals and birds completed the tranquil pastoral scene.

Then came the completion of the Lachine Canal and, soon after, railroads such as the Montreal-Lachine, the Grand Trunk and the Great Northern came thundering in. Industries arrived and Notre-Dame became a commercial avenue.

Quesnel saw the changes and knew what they would mean: The days of peaceful village life and summer grazing were over. With the arrival of Montreal Rolling Mills, the town of Ste-Cunégonde was born.

The Negro Community Centre, at 2035 Coursol, is a medieval-looking structure which was erected in 1890 to replace a building on the corner of Notre-Dame and des Seigneurs. It was then known as the West End Methodist Church. The top floor, which stands out because of the use of a different type of stone, is a recent addition which houses a gymnasium.

The original members of Montreal's black community probably came from the United States to work on the railroads, in an area bounded by St-Antoine, Mountain, St-Jacques and Atwater.

The building became the Negro Community Centre in 1926. It now serves the black communities of N.D.G., Little Burgundy, LaSalle, and Côte-des-Neiges. Activities include French, music and dance classes; basketball, volleyball and floor hockey. The centre also offers counselling and a library with 1300 volumes on black culture and history. (Continue east to St-Martin Street)

4 Îlots St-Martin

The houses along the west side of St-Martin Street have been renovated and restored by the City of Montreal. They are a classic display of good urban renewal in that they blend equally well with the old as with new construction. Note the old red brick and the new metal roofs. Compare these houses with the ones in the housing project on the other side. St-Martin Street retains the feeling of community and pride that is not readily apparent in larger housing projects. Îlots St-Martin is another low-cost housing project on the east side of the street.

The community garden at des Seigneurs and St-Jacques was first established in 1975. Behind it is a greystone tenement dating back to the 1890s and renovated by the city.

It was on this part of des Seigneurs, between St-Antoine and St-Jacques, that **Georges Vanier**, the first French-Canadian Governor General, grew up. A druggist, quoted in the booklet *Les Gens de la Petite Bourgogne* remembers the family well; Georges would often come into the pharmacy, dressed in the uniform of the Collège Militaire Royal in St-Jean.

Georges Vanier (1888-1967), soldier and diplomat, born in Montreal, was admitted to the Bar in 1911. He was decorated during the First World War and became a colonel in the Royal 22e Régiment in 1938. He represented Canada at the League of Nations in 1930. Minister of Canada (1939) and later Canadian ambassador to the Free French in Algiers in 1944, and in Paris after the Allied liberation of that city. He was Canada's delegate at the International Peace Conference of 1946 and served as Governor General from 1959 until his death. He wrote **Paroles de Guerre** (1944) and **Un Canadien Parle aux Français** (1944).

On the next part of the tour, we will take a look at the parish of St-Joseph, which is the old commercial and industrial section of Little Burgundy. The new red brick building that you see on the left, as we walk down to Notre-Dame, is St-Joseph's School.

Notre-Dame Street is one of the oldest streets in Montreal, established by Dollier de Casson in the 1660s and extended as a highway to Lachine, a day's journey away. At first this highway was known as the Chemin du Roi, but, gradually, different sections were given different names. The section that passes through here and was extended into St-Henri in 1840 was named after the parish — St-Joseph. The greystones built on the south side in the 1880s are some of the last remaining signs of the 19th century settlement, most of which has been obliterated.

The Bank of Montreal at the turn of the century.

The Bank of Montreal building (1850 Notre-Dame) was erected in 1894 and is noteworthy for its shaped-gable roof. Of interest is the type of material used in its construction: red sandstone imported from Great Britain. This stone was easily shaped and allowed sculptors to create the ornamental fantasies, characteristic of the turn of the century. The prestigious banks were veritable temples of finance.

Across the street, at 1870 Notre-Dame, is a building which was originally a branch of the Merchant's Bank of Halifax. It was constructed in 1895 by the well-known architect Edward Maxwell. It later became a branch of the **Royal Bank**.

(If you wish, you can take the #35 bus west to the Lionel Groulx metro station, and finish the other half of the tour at another time) (Go south on des Seigneurs and walk to the canal)

It is quite a walk to the Lachine Canal. In the past, many Little Burgundy residents made the walk daily to get to work. As you go past William Street, look to the west to see a **grain elevator**. Most of the grain from the Prairie provinces is shipped to Europe through Montreal. Before the opening of the St. Lawrence Seaway in 1959, ocean-going ships picked up the grain at the end of the Lachine Canal. While the area south of des Seigneurs is still zoned for industrial use, it is under-utilized. On the northwest corner of William and des Seigneurs is a Quebec government-financed meat processing plant, one small example of revitalization of local industry. (Follow the curve of the street and walk to Lock number 3, just to the left of the bridge)

5 The Lachine Canal

The Lachine Canal was once a waterway important not only for Little Burgundy and Montreal, but also for the rest of Canada. For over a century it served as the gateway to the Great Lakes and was part of a system of locks, canals and waterways extending from the Gulf of Saint Lawrence into the heart of North America. The canal made it possible for oceangoing ships to bypass the treacherous Lachine rapids and continue on downstream, carrying goods back and forth.

The idea of a canal extending from Montreal to Lachine, linking up existing rivers and streams to eliminate the dangers of the rapids, was an idea as old as Montreal itself. Talk had already begun in the 1660s when fur traders and explorers alike had to leave their ships at Montreal and continue by canoe. Serious work began in 1821. It was completed in 1825, and the canal remained in operation until the opening of the St. Lawrence Seaway 134 years later.

The canal was an important factor in the economic growth of the area for two reasons. It not only enabled companies to maintain direct contact with Europe and the interior of North America, it also meant inexpensive power. Water from the canal was used in the production of steam, the driving force of industry during the 19th-century.

It is not suprising that after the canal was completed in 1825, industry moved to its banks. Companies such as Montreal Rolling Mills, the Cantin shipyard and the Montreal Lachine Railroad were eager to take advantage of the canal's potential. These companies later became Stelco, Canada Marine Works and Canadian National Railroad, respectively. Near where we are now standing was once Ogilvy Flour Mills. To the east was the James McDougal Foundry and Machine Shop, while across the canal was John

Redpath's sugar refinery, now Redpath Sugar. Part of the refinery building was demolished in 1982, the remainder may be converted for use as housing. Other companies in the area were Forsythe Mills and J.A. Craig Furniture Manufacturing.

Industry attracted workers: Shipyards required carpenters, joiners and painters, while steel mills needed metalurgists and other metal craftsmen. Later, as the companies expanded, a larger, less-skilled labor-force was required. A community grew up next to the factories around Notre-Dame Street and in the area between Notre-Dame and St-Jacques. The population of Ste-Cunégonde increased.

During the last few years, Parks Canada established a bicycle path along the Lachine Canal. To the east, it is a bit more than a mile (2 km) to Old Montreal. Westward, the path leads all the way to Ste-Anne-de-Bellevue at the tip of the island. Return to William Street, turn right and walk to Richmond Street (Cyclists take St. Martin Street, one block back).

The large light-blue building is part of Canada Post's centralized mailing procedure. It is a gateway plant and handles much of Montreal's bulk mail.

Along the south side of Notre-Dame are some greystone buildings built around 1870. They serve as an indicator of the class of people that once lived here, since greystone buildings usually mean that the street was once prestigious. Now the street has a number of antique stores; much of their stock comes from the old houses of Little Burgundy.

Shops abounded in this area. There were dry goods stores, dressmakers, grocers, saddle makers, barbers, cabinetmakers and doctor's offices. Notre-Dame Street was the direct link between the parish and the business district in Old Montreal. It was so important that the first (horse-drawn) streetcar went into service here.

All that remains of St-Joseph's Parish is **St-Joseph's Church**, constructed of greystone in 1860. The church's design is like that of a country church, seemingly out of place in its urban setting. At its maximum size in 1891, the congregation numbered 10,000. Six priest and two laymen were required to administer to the spiritual needs of the faithful.

St-Joseph's Church played an unusual role in the history of Montreal. At the Christmas Eve mass of 1879, the interior of the church was lit with electric lights and this is believed to be the first indoor use of electricity on the island of Montreal.

At 1620 Notre-Dame (corner of Guy Street) is the headquarters of the Montreal branch of the **Salvation Army**, housed in what used to be a factory. This office, opened in the late 1960s, distributed second-hand furniture and clothes that are contributed by the general public. Another Salvation Army service in the area is the Men's Hostel on the corner of Guy and St-Antoine streets.

(Cross the CPR overpass) This bridge, crossing the site of what was once the Montreal-Lachine Railroad, offers a view of the Montreal skyline. To the east is downtown: a phalanx of skyscrapers; to the north is Mount Royal.

The railroad tracks were removed in 1978. Over the next decade a series of single-family homes were built as part of the city's 20,000 logements program. The area was subdivided into suburban-style lots. Unfortunately, no land was set aside for public green space — always rare in Montreal — and the design of some of the houses leaves much to be desired.

The tracks started as a single line, with but one train going from Montreal to Lachine and, then, returning. As industrialization increased, the track became busier and a second set was soon added. When the Grand-Trunk Railroad bought out the Montreal-Lachine, freight yards were opened here. Grand Trunk was later absorbed by Canadian National Railway and the freight yards were expanded. The yards and numerous sets of subsequent tracks split the area of Little Burgundy in half.

On the other side of the bridge, beside a housing project, is a Hydro-Quebec installation. Part of it is a building of the Montreal Light Heat and Power Company, constructed in the 1930s when private companies controlled the utilities. Hydro-Quebec was formed by the 1962 nationalization and merging of these companies organized by the then-Minister of Natural Resources, **René Lévesque.**

René Lévesque, premier of Quebec beginning in 1976, was born in New Carlisle in 1922. He served as a war correspondent during the Second World War and continued after the war as a radio and television journalist. He was elected to the provincial legislature in 1960 as a Liberal and became minister of public works and hydraulic resources (1960-61), then minister of natural resources (1961-65), a position in which he supervised the nationalization of electricity companies into Hydro Québec. He was one of the co-founders of the Mouvement Souveraineté-Association and, in 1968, the Parti Québécois. He became premier of Quebec in 1976 following an election in which his party gained more than two-thirds of the seats. Although he was unsuccessful in his referendum for Quebec independence in 1980, he was re-elected a year later.

At 750 Guy Street is a five-storey building which once housed Toilet Laundry, a company which was established in the 1890s. One former employee has recounted her experience here in the 1930s. Her salary was $3.50 for a week consisting of six days, each beginning at seven in the morning and ending at six or seven at night. She was also required to work overtime without any additional compensation.

Although abandoned, the building is a fine example of industrial architecture — notice how gracefully it seems to climb the hill. Despite the fire which gutted the interior, the structure of the building is still sound and it could be recycled.

(Walk north to Wrexham Street) Just before that tiny street —
which seems more like a back lane than a real street — was once
Belmont School, built in 1877 by the Catholic School Commission
as a commercial school for boys. It was later taken over by the
Protestant School Board which, subsequently, closed it because
of an insufficient number of pupils in the area. Abandoned for
years, the school building burnt down in 1979. It has been replaced
by new condominium construction.

Diminutive **Wrexham Street** is interesting because of the semi-
circular shapes of the entrances which look almost like carriage
entrances.

[Turn right on St-Antoine (Cyclists should remain on St-Jacques
to avoid one-way St-Antoine Street)] The next two cross streets,
Lusignan and Versailles, are prime examples of some of the
streets left untouched by the city's urban-renewal-through-
demolition program of the 1960s and 1970s. Their upgrading was
delayed until the end of the 1970s when young professionals
bought the houses and renovated them. It is a phenomenon
common in San Francisco, Toronto and elsewhere.

These houses were built around 1880 and the streets named after
former landowners.Camilien Houde, that charismatic Montreal
mayor of the 1940s, once lived on Lusignan.

As recently as 1980, the asphalt of these two streets were in poor
shape and the general appearance was one of neglect. It is very
encouraging to see the improvements that have been made.

Part way down the block is a mini-park, the result of a 1981
municipal program, Place au Soleil, which beautified back lanes.
This is probably the most successful example in the city.

Rockhead's Paradise was once at the corner of St-Antoine and
Mountain. Montreal's biggest black nightclub first opened it
doors as a tavern in 1928. Later, a lounge and a two-storey nightclub were added. Rockhead's was celebrated throughout the
northeastern United States until a few years ago. It had always
been one of the best jazz, rhythm & blues and soul clubs any-
where. The biggest names have played here — people like Pearl
Bailey, Sammy Davis, Cab Calloway and Louis Armstrong.

Rockhead's was known not only for its performers, but also for
the audience. The club's patronage by Stephen Leacock, Walter
Gordon, Joe Louis, Morley Callaghan, and the Harlem Globe-
trotters indicates that this sort of music entertains all kinds of
people.

Rufus Rockhead was the proprietor until 1980. He was the first
Black in the province to receive a liquor license. After his death,
the magic was gone and Rockhead's is now closed.

*The tour ends at l'Aqueduc Street and the Lucien Allier metro
station, which opened in 1979. Cyclists are permitted in the Montreal metro system only on weekends.*

LINCOLN-
TUPPER

LINCOLN-TUPPER

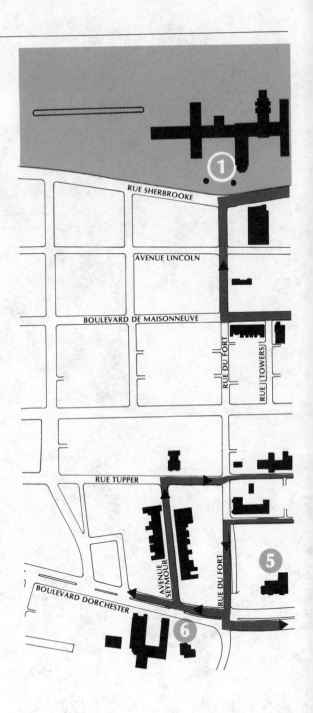

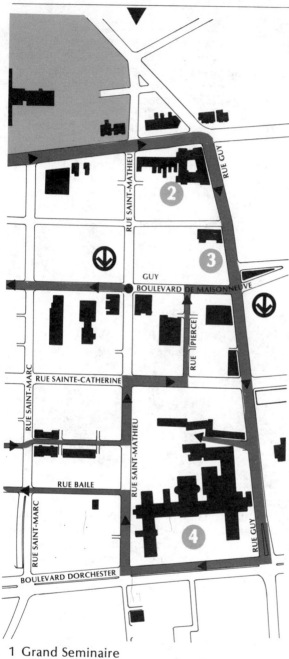

1 Grand Seminaire
2 The Grosvenor
3 Village Lincoln
4 Maison Mère des Soeurs Grises
5 Shaughnessy House
6 Monastère des Franciscains

History

Lincoln-Tupper is a residential area located to the west of the central business district of Montreal. It has always been a pleasant place to live, providing services and plenty of moderately-priced apartments. Only recently have the people living in the area begun to consider it a neighborhood; in the late 1970s some of them organized the Shaugnessy Village Association which takes its name from one of the loveliest houses in the area.

This 1.5-hour tour is a blend of old and new, for Lincoln-Tupper contains the second oldest construction in Montreal and the newest buildings of the 1980s. In this small part of Montreal are 19th-century town houses like Boston's, and highrises like Manhattan's.

The Martello towers.

The first European settlement in Lincoln-Tupper was a small mission to the Amerindians, located at the foot of Mount Royal. It was founded by the Sulpician priests in 1676. They retained ownership of the adjacent lands after the British conquest of 1763. Lincoln-Tupper was the first community outside the old walls of Montreal and remained rural in appearance until 1861. At that time, the entire area formed part of the Domaine des Prêtres de Saint-Sulpice. While a portion of these lands were cultivated by the priests, the rest remained unsettled for varying lengths of time. The later character of the neighborhood was determined by the types of people and institutions to whom the Sulpicians chose to sell the property.

By 1854, when the Sulpicians built their seminary and chapel on the site of the fort, little of their land had been settled; in fact, only Sherbrooke, Ste-Catherine, Dorchester and Guy streets had been laid out. On this tour you will see one of the three oldest houses in Lincoln-Tupper, built during the 1850s.

In 1861, the Sulpicians sold a large plot of land to the Soeurs Grises. After that date, Lincoln-Tupper began to develop in a systematic fashion. Dorchester and Sherbrooke streets became residential avenues lined with trees behind which stood the homes of Montreal's upper middle class. The area was then a part of the affluent Golden Square Mile (see that tour). Lincoln-Tupper's interior streets were set out in an east-to-west progression with rows of stone and brick town houses built on them. Here lived the professional and business class of the steadily growing city. It was only after 1890 that commercial enterprises came to Lincoln-Tupper and for many years they were restricted to Ste-Catherine. While many of the buildings in the western portion of the neighborhood were demolished during the 1920s, the apartment buildings which replaced them retained Lincoln-Tupper's scale and character.

Drastic changes affected the area during the 1960s as developers erected scores of shoddily-built apartment towers, greatly increasing the density of the neighborhood. As the number of older buildings began to decrease and the population to rise, Lincoln-Tupper seemed destined to become just another high-rise desert.

As redevelopment accelerated, residents of the area became aware that the loss of their neighborhood (and in many cases, their homes) was imminent. By the late 1960s, they began to value the diversity, charm and human scale provided by the pre-1960 Lincoln-Tupper.

In 1975, a by-law was instituted which prevented the construction of more highrise apartment buildings. Since there were already many in the area, further construction would probably have destroyed the remaining sense of neighborhood. Since then, many private renovations of old houses have blossomed, some of which you will see during the walk.

Itinerary

Access: St-Mathieu exit of the Guy metro station

Across the street is the local police and fire station built in 1931 in the Art Deco style. It was designed by Shorey and Ritchie. Note the volumes and the fire hose tower. The design of the door frames was repeated in order to emphasize the windows. Houses on St-Mathieu Street are remnants of an earlier era.

Victoria School (1822 de Maisonneuve) was built as an elementary school in 1888 and enlarged circa 1911. It is now used by Concordia University. At 1850 de Maisonneuve is the **Royal Montreal Curling Club** which was founded in 1807 and is the oldest curling club in Canada. It is housed in a simple 1929 brick building with pleasant stone details.

At the corner of St-Marc Street (2005 St-Marc) is a magnificent mansion designed by Hutchison and Steele in 1889. Note the well-executed treatment of the limestone, the rounded corner, dormer windows and the carved band and frieze.

The Wray-Walton-Wray Funeral Home (1459 Towers) was initially a private residence. Although the building was constructed in various stages, the additions complement the original design. In general terms, this structure is in the English medieval style, with pointed gothic windows and crenellations. The anachronism of a building on this boulevard displaying crenellations indenting the tops of its walls makes the house a charming and unique structure.

The greystone houses on de Maisonneuve between Tower and Fort streets have changed little since they were built around 1900. This handsome group of buildings is one of the few remaining greystone ensembles on de Maisonneuve Boulevard.

At 2055 Fort Street is an Art Deco house by Henri S. Labelle. It was one of his first works, completed in 1925. Note the two loggias and the decorative band across the façade.

1 Grand Séminaire

The reflecting pool in the Sulpician grounds.

The Sulpician seminary is north of Fort Street and faces Sherbrooke Street. The Messieurs de St-Sulpice was the first religious order of Montreal, and the entire island was once their domain. Behind the massive fieldstone wall are the two towers which, along with the Séminaire de St-Sulpice at Place d'Armes, are the oldest existing structures on the island of Montreal.

The Martello towers were built no later than 1695, and possibly as early as 1683, just 41 years after Paul de Chomedey, Sieur de Maisonneuve, first colonized the island. Originally, the towers were part of a fort used to protect converted Amerindians. The walls of the fort and two towers to the north were demolished when the

Grand Séminaire was begun in 1854. The latter construction housed a college for the sons of the Quebec's élite. As *L'Opinion Publique* noted on October 19, 1826: "... instead of a few savages learning the first points of the dogma, there are five or six hundred students, part of the new inhabitants of North America, receiving religious instruction and higher education..." To the left (west) of the seminary is a reflecting pool. It is flanked by tall trees and had no practical use, but was apparently designed as a place for contemplation and meditation.

John Ostell designed the main part of the Grand Séminaire. It is in the form of a long rectangle, parallel to the street, which is interrupted at five places by projections of different sizes. It is built of greystone in the Classical revival style. A triangular pediment with an oeil-de-boeuf opening is above each end and each entrance. The openings are symmetrical, both horizontally and vertically. While the western part of the building, the Grand Séminaire itself, has five floors, the remainder of the building is four storeys high.

The exterior was unified by the classical treatment of the openings, masonry and the roof. Cut and polished limestone was used; the quoins at the corners and the joints on the gently projecting parts below the pediments were designed to be prominent. This served to underline the articulation of each portion, and accentuate the classical lines of the façade and the ends. A stone entablature line between each floor accentuates the horizontal effect in the edifice. The entrance doors are framed by portals with Doric pilasters and display a well-proportioned entablature. Some of the original decoration elements have disappeared.

The height of the windows diminish progressively to create the impression of an attic storey with square windows below the roof. While the windows are varied, their treatment and their proportions lend an impression of unity. Those of the main chapel are arched, while the College chapel has bi-lobed windows and rosettes.

Both John Ostell and Maurice Perrault, the two architects responsible for most of the design, had extensive academic training and had already collaborated on large buildings such as the original Court House in Old Montreal. Ostell's original plans were respected and used by Perrault. The chapel, with projecting apse, was designed by Omer Marchand. His respect for the original design is expressed in his successfully integrated addition.

However, two more recent additions break the continuity: the north wing constructed in 1940 by Paul Lemieux and the annex of Duplessis, Labelle and Derome, completed in 1960, which was constructed in a modern style with a beige-colored stone.

In 1971 plans were announced to build residential units on the Sulpician land. This would have meant the disappearance of historic parkland in the heart of the city. A preservation group, "Green Spaces", was formed and successfully lobbied the minister of cultural affairs to classify the Martello towers as historical monuments. With classification came a directive protecting an area within a 500-foot (150 m) radius of the towers from demolition or modification, without the permission of the minister.

Unfortunately, this zone did not include the woods along the northern part of the property, and 10 years later the Sulpicians sold a portion of the land (located near Atwater Avenue) to an apartment developer. Save Montreal and other organizations were unsuccessful in preventing the destruction of the woods.

The Somerset Apartment Building (2054-2090 Sherbrooke Street) was saved from demolition because it is within 500 feet of the towers.

The office building at 1980 Sherbrooke was designed in 1954 by L. Gravel and H. Pony. Just as the Baroque style of the 17th century introduced the use of curves and elaborate ornamentation as a reaction to the restrained classical style, the use of a concave shape in this building was a response to the verticality of the International Style, which was then in vogue.

The impressive **Masonic Temple** at 1850 Sherbrooke was designed by Saxe and Archibald in 1929. The building houses the

Freemasons, a charitable fraternal organization with secret rites. On the pediment is carved a list of virtues. For those whose Latin is rusty, the words mean: faith, charity, truth, liberty and hope. The playset on the right belongs to the Concordia University Daycare Centre, which uses part of the building.

Edward Maxwell designed the house at 1840 Sherbrooke for J.R. Gorden. The former Crichton School, at 1832 Sherbrooke, was built in a subdued English medieval style at the turn of the century.

Château Versailles at 1669-57 is a hotel in the tradition of the small, well-appointed continental guest house. Its owner, André Villeneuve, bought four town houses between 1958 and 1972 and filled them with period furniture.

The stone and brick façade of the two town houses at 1625 and 1629 Sherbrooke have been cleaned, shaming their sisters. A row of greystone residences on the south side of Sherbrooke house stylish boutiques.

2 The Grosvenor

The Grosvenor apartment building (1610 Sherbrooke) was built in 1905 and designed by architects Finley and Spence in the English Renaissance style. Walk through the lobby to the inner courtyard. Can you believe you are near a busy thoroughfare? Here is an enclosed garden providing a welcome respite from the noise and dirt of the city. The courtyard is especially pleasing on a mid-summer evening.

At its prime at the turn of the century, Sherbrooke was not merely an elegant street, but one with texture and variety developed through the complementary use of different architectural styles and building materials. Notice how the curve of Côte-des-Neiges adds grace to this intersection. On the northeast corner is the only remaining group of red sandstone houses on Sherbrooke Street; indeed, it is one of the few left in Montreal. Built as single-family houses around 1900, the red stone was imported from Great Britain. A fire in late 1982 heavily damaged the corner building, destroying a wonderful tower on the side.

On the northwest corner of Sherbrooke and Côte-des-Neiges is the **Bank of Montreal**. While bank buildings are often located on corners, it is rare that one complements its surroundings as successfully as this bank does. Built in 1928, it is a replica of the J.P. Morgan Bank in New York City, also situated on a corner. This restrained classical building is serene and refined, both inside and out.

3 Village Lincoln

Proceed down Guy to Lincoln Street. Village Lincoln displays a post-modernist hybrid of new and old. Unfortunately, the architect's use of traditional details coupled with new designs does not suit these Victorian buildings.

Place Norman-Bethune, at de Maisonneuve Boulevard, is a recent addition to Montreal's public squares. It was established in 1978 as a place to install the statue, a gift from the People's Republic of China. **Norman Bethune** lived not far from here.

For both esthetic and historical reasons, Bethune's **statue** should be facing east, along de Maisonneuve. Instead, he faces an office building, which houses Multimags, a store with an extremely wide-range of domestic and foreign magazines and books of all political, social, artistic and other persuasions.

Mansions Garage, across from the metro exit on Guy Street, once housed the limousines of the affluent residents of the Golden Square Mile. Completed just prior to the Great Depression, this multi-storey garage is still in use. Note the sculpted coat-of-arms and other details inset near the roof.

Toronto-Dominion Bank, on the northwest corner of Guy and Ste-Catherine, is a splendid example of Classical design and was built in 1908. Such impressive buildings were designed as a symbol of the wealth which the bank controlled. The sand-blasting of the façade, completed in 1976, has revived its former elegance. While a great many of Montreal's buildings do need a good scrubbing, sand-blasting is not to be recommended. The dust which is raised adds to air pollution; in addition, sand-blasting actually damages brick and stone façades by removing the protective coating. A water-based solution is much less harmful.

The **Faubourg Ste-Catherine** complex is to the west of Ste-Catherine Street. The developers recycled an 1920s automotive show room building into a 'festival marketplace' offering a wide variety of foodstuffs and 'soft merchandise'. Greenhouse windows and an atrium roof provide a great deal of natural light.

The Church Home, at 1221 Guy, was built in 1859 by Edward James Major, an inspector for the city of Montreal. Apparently, this was a prestigious post, for Major could afford to buy a large piece of property and maintain a very comfortable residence. His land once stretched from Ste-Catherine to Dorchester. His house, known then as Erin Cottage, was purchased in 1890 by the Anglican diocese of Montreal to house the Church Home for

Elderly Ladies. The two wings added in 1919 and in 1957 do little
to change the original appearance. The roof resembles that of
Viger Station (St-Denis tour) and other train stations of the late
19th century. The rooms have not been subdivided and are enormous by present-day housing standards; the dining room can
seat about 60 people. The house and its yard remain a spot of
tranquility in the city.

The Habitant-style cottages behind the Soeurs Grises couvent.

Walk across Guy Street to the Grey Nuns property, and through
the gateway at 1200 Guy to the **Habitant-style cottages** located
behind the convent. These are the only examples of traditional
Quebec architecture in the western part of Montreal. With their
pitched roofs, dormer windows and small doorways, they recall
the Breton villages in which their design originated. There is
some controversy over the date of their construction. Some
experts think that they were built at the same time as the convent
(1871). Others consider this a very late date and suggest that the
year 1830 is more accurate, pointing out that the treatment of the
masonry is very different from that of the convent and chapel. In
any case, the cottages are an additional delight.

4 Maison Mère des Soeurs Grises

Maison Mère before construction of the chapel spire.

Walk down Guy and turn right on Dorchester Boulevard to best appreciate the religious complex. From its creation, the Soeurs Grises order owned a great deal of land in the Pointe-à-Callière section of Old Montreal. With the rapid development of the port in the mid-1800s, their work was impeded by increased commercial activity near their hospital. The nuns decided to acquire land which would be more suitable for their hospital, and selected this area in the Saint-Antoine district. They purchased the property in March 1861 from the Sulpicians and a Mr. James Mullins, and they still own 450,000 square feet (40 500 m²) in the Lincoln-Tupper area.

The Soeur Grises complex forms an "H", made up of a main building with façade on Dorchester Boulevard and two lateral wings perpendicular to it. The walls are in hammered stone from the base to the cornice with accentuated corner quoins. The gable roof is pierced at regular intervals by dormer windows.

Lack of funds delayed construction for eight years. Victor Bourgeau and E.A. Leprohon were commissioned to draw plans for a hospital, asylum, convent and chapel. Construction began in 1869, and the nuns moved into the east wing of the hospital in October 1871. The original wing measured 700 by 50 feet (208 m by 15 m).

The rest of the buildings was constructed in stages. In the spring of 1874, the nuns decided to construct a chapel topped by a tower and to build a new wing which would extend to St-Mathieu. This extension was to house old people and orphans, while the nuns would live in the original building. The entire building was supposed to be 524 feet (157 m) wide. The chapel in the centre extended 174 feet (52 m) to the rear. It was to be constructed in what was then termed Romanesque. It was actually a copy of a plan executed by the American, Samuel Sloan.

Construction was interrupted in 1887 and the western wing was completed only in 1898. When it was built, the new hospital housed 700 people: nuns, servants, old people and orphans. The work was completed by Joseph Venne who followed Bourgeau's design but the new part was not as large as planned, making the building assymetrical. The western wing extends only 173 feet (52 m). Except for the chapel façade, borrowed from Sloan, the Grey Nuns' convent is quite similar to the Hôtel-Dieu (St-Louis tour) which was designed by the same architects.

In 1975 the Grey Nuns wanted to sell this property to raise funds for the restoration of their original hospital and convent in Old Montreal. The minister of Cultural Affairs classified the chapel as a cultural property, meaning that any redevelopment of the Grey Nuns' land would have to receive his written approval. Later that year, a redevelopment plan for the site, which would have entailed demolition of all parts of the building except for the chapel, was announced. Due to public pressure (not the least of which was from Save Montreal) the minister rejected the project and classified the entire site as a historic monument, early in the following year.

The future use of the site is uncertain. In 1978 the Ministry of Cultural Affairs spent $500,000 to replace the copper roof. Little else has happened and the buildings remain under-utilized with only a few nuns living there.

The Bell-Dandurand house, at 1740 Dorchester, was demolished in December 1981 despite efforts of local residents to have it preserved. It was built by Adam Bell in 1871 and lived in by Ucal-Henri Dandurand, a real estate developer, at the turn of the century. Although it had been subdivided and used for many years as a rooming house, its stairs, wood trim and plaster decorations were treasures of 19th-century craftsmanship.

The lot remained vacant for a few years until a rather unattractive hotel was constructed. Once Dorchester was a fine street, lined with the large homes of Montreal's merchant princes. One by one these mansions have disappeared, due to changing lifestyles and tastes. The widening of Dorchester in the 1950s to permit more vehicular traffic chased the remaining owners from their homes.

Prime Minister Pierre Elliot Trudeau lived for a time in a row house at the corner of St-Mathieu and Dorchester.

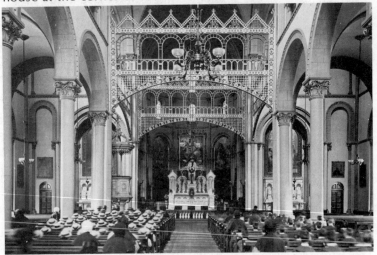

The Soeurs Grises chapel. Note the elegant wroughtiron tie rods.

At 1185 St-Mathieu is the entrance to the **Grey Nuns museum and chapel**. The museum is well worth a visit, for it covers an important portion of Montreal history. The nuns are very happy to have visitors; *the doors are open from 9 a.m. to 5 p.m. Monday to Friday.*

Before turning left on Baile, note the row of greystone houses on St-Mathieu, which complement the Grey Nuns buildings and reflect late 19th-century Montreal.

Baile Street was first established between 1876 and 1877. It was named after the Reverend Baile who had been Father Superior of the Sulpicians during the mid-19th century. The row of houses on the north side of the street were built first and were most likely the work of the Montreal Building and Investment Association, an important group of developers in the late 19th century.

Reverend Gould's house, at 1812 Baile, was built in 1880 as a stately nine-room mansion. It was later subdivided for use as a rooming house, and most of the rooms were converted into three or four small alcoves which contained little more than a bed and a hot plate. Its present owners are, themselves, restoring it to its days of grandeur. The stained-glass windows with birds and flowers are very attractive.

At 1830-40 Baile is an apartment building constructed by the Patenaude family in 1928. The open courtyard has an impressive staircase. The building is similar in design to Roxy Court (St-Louis tour). Note the way the street name is written above the transoms: apparently this was the accepted spelling at one time.

The row of houses at 1947-67 Baile was constructed in 1889-1890 by Hutchison and Steele. They share with the house at 2095 St-Marc (seen at the beginning of this tour) Tudor details and a fine use of stone. Norman Bethune lived at 1955 Baile when he was a student at McGill University.

5 Shaughnessy House

Shaughnessy House, at 1923 Dorchester Boulevard, is one of Montreal's finest examples of Victorian residential architecture. It was built in 1874 as two semi-detached houses and converted into one dwelling three years later. Sir William Van Horne, general manager of the Canadian Pacific Railway, lived here between 1882 and 1890, at which time it was taken over by Lord Shaughnessy, the third president of the CPR. The Sisters of service of Canada, an anglophone Catholic order, owned the property during the 1960s and early 1970s. In 1974 the sisters put the property up for sale, and Phyllis Lambert (one of a handful of people responsible for the safeguarding of much of Montreal's architectural heritage) purchased the house to prevent its demolition.

It is now part of the **Centre for Canadian Architecture,** an extensive repository of information about the art of building design and construction. It reflects all facets of architectural practice. Books, writings, designs and models are included in the centre's resources as well as photographic archives — one of the largest in Canada, and the only one dedicated to buildings.

Peter Rose designed the contemporary structure which surrounds the old house. It is clad in traditional greystone, the first use of that material in decades.

From here you can see **Judah House** (1980 Dorchester), a fine example of eclectic Victorian architecture. It is one of the oldest mansions along Dorchester. You cannot fail to recognize it: the small tower with peaked roof is reminiscent of Victorian homes throughout the eastern coast of North America. The volumes and the contrasting colors are particulary impressive from this distance.

6 Monastère des Franciscains

Continue walking west until Seymour Street. On the south side of Dorchester, at 2010, is The Franciscan Monastery. The Franciscans were one of the last Roman Catholic orders to come to Montreal, for their first members arrived only in 1890. They were originally housed in the St-Joseph parish church, but by 1892 the premises were too small. Construction of the church and monastery began in 1893 but was not completed until 1900.

In 1892, two benefactors gave Judah House to the Franciscan Fathers. The various monastery buildings were built at different times on the land to the west of this mansion. In its final form, the monastery complex is in a "U"-shape. The heterogeneous buildings include the church and the monastery, the original Judah House, the priests' residence and the library. The buildings are of a restrained design with mansard roofs used throughout.

The Gothic-style church is in the form of a rectangle with a polygonal apse extension. The façade is divided laterally into three bays and has four buttresses crowned by pinnacles. The gable roof and the pointed windows accentuate the vertical style of the building.

Beyond the Franciscan complex is the **Maison Masson**. Its 1850 construction date makes this splendid mansion one of Lincoln Tupper's oldest houses. The Honorable Joseph Masson was an alderman, a director of the City Gaslight Company and a vice-president of the Bank of Montreal in addition to possessing substantial real estate. After his death in 1855, his children formed Masson Estates Limited. It is difficult to determine which one of them lived in the house then, since the city directory of the time identifies the resident simply as J.W.A.R. Masson.

The steep mansard roof and corner pavilions are in the Second Empire style. What is particularly lovely about this house is the simplicity of its detail in comparison with other Second Empire buildings. The surfaces are smooth and unadorned except for the entrance; the windows are arched but without any decorative treatment. The property is still enclosed by its original stone and wrought iron fence — one of the most magnificent in Montreal.

Proceed up Seymour Street which possesses a remarkable unity of scale. Although not architecturally unique nor very historic, Seymour is a pleasant residential street which, for some reason, has escaped the hand of progress during the past 100 years. It is one of the few streets in Montreal which are lined on both sides with greystone houses.

The house at 1173 Seymour displays a traditional tin roof parapet while next door, at 1169, is a recent metal replacement. Take a look at the loggia above the door at 1189.

The two buildings at the head of Seymour Street (2085-2105 Tupper) are not very good examples of renovation. The columns seem too thin for the original greystone, and the semi-circular balconies and overhanging roof have no link with the original architectural vocabulary.

Turn right on **Tupper Street** which was named Quiblier when laid out in 1873. It was renamed in 1876 to honor Sir Charles Tupper, one of Canada's Fathers of Confederation. He was later prime minister for the grand total of 68 days before being defeated. The rest of Tupper Street was built up by such groups as the Montreal Building and Investment Association from 1877 to 1890. The row of one-storey brick houses on the south side are in the tradition of English country cottages which create a village-like atmosphere, certainly rare in Montreal.

At the northwest corner of Tupper and Fort stands a 20-storey apartment house occupying its entire lot. With no setback on Tupper, the building comes right up to the sidewalk, encroaching on the public space.

The house at 1271 Fort is noteworthy for two reasons: its attractive wood trim, and because it was the first house to be renovated in the Lincoln-Tupper area.

The house at 1958 Tupper exhibits a recent, well-executed reconstruction of the roof, using sheet metal. Its bright color complements the wood trim that was also added.

The row of houses from 1947 to 1941 were designed with unusual keyhole-shaped stained-glass windows. Only the one furthest to the right has retained all this glass, for the windows of the others were replaced circa 1960.

The fraternal twin buildings on the east side of St-Marc are very attractive. The Claridge, at 1251, is a storey shorter and somewhat narrower than The Marbridge at 1245, but they share buff brick and the pleasant color of verdigris (copper patina) on the cornices and oriel windows. The Marbridge was built in 1913. Across the street, a similar building has been renovated recently.

The row of eight brick houses on the south side of Tupper (1844-1817 Tupper) are in excellent condition. Like houses on streets already seen, they look like an English village of the 1870s. Note the artistry of the carved bargeboard and other wood. While the houses on the north side of Tupper are somewhat taller and do not blend in with one another quite as well, the total effect of the street is charming.

Walk up St-Mathieu to Ste-Catherine, turn right on Ste-Catherine and walk to Pierce Street. In 1981, a delapidated four-storey walk-up was demolished to be replaced by the apartment building at 1440 Pierce — a stylish complex in concrete brick. While some of the houses which make up the terrace on the eastern side of the street have undergone private renovation, on the whole the terrace needs some serious attention.

The tour ends at the entrance to the Guy metro station which is just one block to the right along de Maisonneuve Boulevard.

WESTMOUNT

WESTMOUNT

To Montrealers, it would be unthinkable to not include Westmount in a guidebook of their city. This independent municipality, surrounded by Montreal, contains an exceptional variety of 19th-century buildings. The summit of "La petite montagne" — as the smaller mountain to the west of Mount Royal was once called — is the home of many of Montreal's wealthiest families. Lower Westmount also has a particular charm and snobbery. Unlike other areas of Montréal, covered in this book, most houses in Westmount were rarely subdivided nor did they deteriorate in value, so that people with low incomes could afford to live in them.

To say to an anglophone Montrealer in the 1960s and 1970s that you lived in Westmount was to say that you were part of the establishment. By this you were not just speaking of money, but also a sense of style, a way of life. The stereotypical Westmounter had that polite, "British" sense of restraint which at its best puts the other person at ease — and at its worst, seems terribly cold.

To tell a francophone you lived in Westmount in the time of the greatest tension between English and French Montreal meant something else. The two solitudes rarely interacted and the Québécois generally saw Westmount as the last bastion of the British Empire.

Times have changed, and Westmount is no longer as homogeneous as it once was. More of its residents now are francophones, consequently the municipality's ethnic make-up approaches the Montreal norm somewhat more closely.

Actually, Westmount is on the tour because it contains so many fine buildings of the 19th century and some from earlier eras. Ironically, the Save Montreal tours which were a basis for this book never included Westmount because its architectural heritage was comparatively better protected than buildings in the city of Montreal. About 15 years ago, the Westmount Historical Society compiled a list of buildings of historical importance: most of them still stand today. Residents are generally concerned with the appearance of their streets; new development is often stopped by quiet pressure on the municipal government.

History

In the 1670s, the Sulpicians established an outpost of which two martello towers still stand on Sherbrooke Street east of here (see Lincoln-Tupper tour). Land on the slopes of the Petite Montagne was granted for farms a few years later.

The area became known as Côte-St-Antoine by the early 19th century. A former Indian trail which served as the link from the farms to the Sulpician's property and thence to the market became known as Côte-St-Antoine Road.

To the west of this area was "Monklands", built in 1799 and later a residence of the Canadian Governor General. The stone mansion is now known as Villa Maria, (located near its namesake metro station) and is used as a convent and girls' school.

Sherbrooke Street was extended as far west as Côte-St-Antoine in 1842. The land was ceded by the Sulpicians on the condition that the city would erect a fence along the entire length of the new street west of Guy. Ste-Catherine Street was extended west to Greene Avenue in 1854.

Population growth in the new area was slow: by 1859 there were only about two dozen houses in the area. After Confederation (1867) the village began to enlarge. Horse car lines were laid down in the early 1870s, and several generations of children rode this transportation system to its western end to picnic in the orchards of what is now urban Westmount. The village of Notre-Dame-de-Grâce, including the territory which is now Westmount, was incorporated in 1874. Five years later, its name was changed to Côte-St-Antoine and its western boundary established as it is today, at Claremont Boulevard. The name was changed to Westmount in 1895, in acknowledgement of the anglophone majority, who then made up 95% of the town's population.

Streetcar service and use of the automobile by affluent Montrealers in the 1920s had a stimulative effect on Westmount's development. Many of Montreal's wealthiest families began to leave the "Golden Square Mile" to live in the new town. Still, it took a while for Westmount to acquire its high status: It was only after the Second World War that a Golden Square Mile mother would approve of her daughter marrying and moving to Westmount.

CENTRAL WESTMOUNT

1 Maison Hurtubise
2 Westmount City Hall

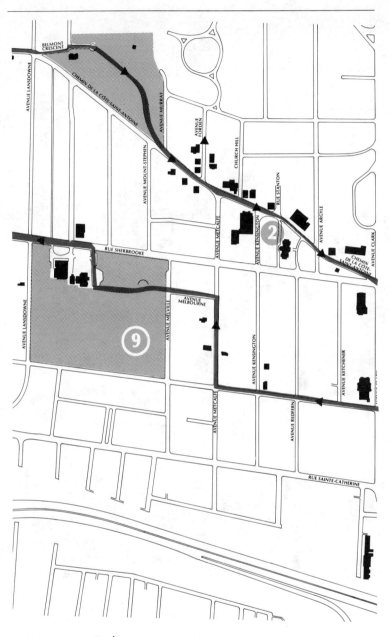

9 Westmount Park

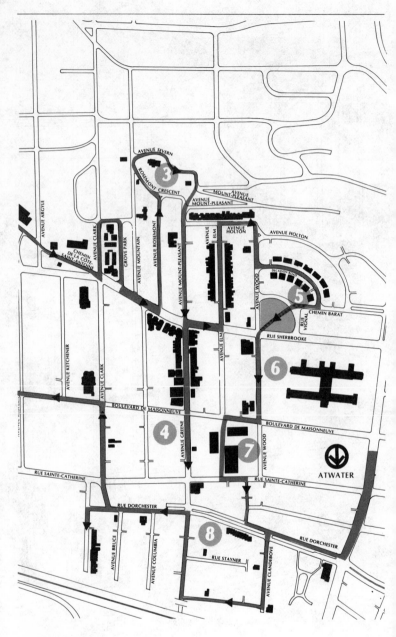

3 Rosemount
4 Greene Avenue
5 Priests' Farm
6 Maison Mère des Soeurs de
  la congrégation de
  Notre-Dame
7 Westmount Square
8 The Towers

Itinerary

The tour begins on Côte-St-Antoine Road. Since it would be an uphill hike from the # 24 bus on Sherbrooke Street it is easier to take the # 124 bus from Vendôme metro station to Côte-St-Antoine (The first traffic light after Sherbrooke). The tour should take about two hours. Its midpoint is the Atwater metro station.

The house at 649 Côte-St-Antoine is in a style which is considered typically Victorian. Actually, the label Victorian is misleading since many architectural styles were combined during the reign of Queen Victoria. This is a Second Empire mansion, as its mansard roof and the Ionic pillars framing its porch and bay windows testify. The colors used on the wood trim today may not have been the ones its first owner used when it was built in 1869, but they are certainly the shades favored by Victorians of those years.

The gambrelled-roofed house at 605 Côte-St-Antoine stood on land farmed by the nuns who lived in Villa Maria. Until the mid-1955s, their order still owned this house in which lived a priest who went each morning to celebrate mass at the convent chapel. Built in the mid-1800s, it is now a private home.

1 Maison Hurtubise

The Hurtubise House at 563 Côte-St-Antoine is the only remaining 17th-century farmhouse in Westmount. It was built by Pierre Hurtubise in 1688 on land granted to his father by de Maisonneuve.

The farmhouse remained in the possession of the Hurtubise family for almost three centuries until it was purchased by the Canadian Heritage of Quebec. An appointment can be made to see the inside of the house by contacting that group.

The house has changed little since its construction. The main floor was raised above ground level so that the entrance would not be buried by heavy snowdrifts, and to provide openings in the basement walls from which rifles could be fired during Amerindian attack. This area seemed quite far from the settlement of Ville-Marie when the Hurtubise family moved here. As a result, people dubbed the house "la haute folie" to show their disapproval of such a foolish plan.

The house is typical of 17th - and 18th-century vernacular construction, with distinctive steeply-gabled roof, fieldstone walls, and tiny panes of glass in dormer windows. Much of the interior panelling is fastened with hand-forged nails, while the roof beams in the attic are handcut and fastened together with dowels. In the basement are three cedar beams with the bark still on them, supporting the main floor. The barn to the left of the house was built in the mid-19th century.

The red brick dome of the Byzantine-style **Stanley Presbyterian Church** (now the Seventh-Day Adventist) can be seen at the summit of Victoria Avenue. The Presyterian congregation moved here in 1913 from its location on Stanley Street, to be near its members.

The little house at 555 Victoria Avenue was built in 1954, but seems much older since old brick and bargeboard decorations were used in order to integrate it with the older houses around it.

Details of the roof.

At 513-15 Côte-St-Antoine Road is **Riverview,** built in 1876. It is an adaptation of the American "stick" style of Tudor Gothic architecture. Attached to the back wall is an 18th-century house which was built by the Hurtubise family.

The dull-colored house with the Dutch gable roof (466 Côte-St-Antoine) was built not long before the First World War. An interesting point about this house is that its bricks had to be completely replaced in the early 1960s.

Charles Saxe was the architect of the Italianate villa at 517 Roslyn Avenue, built in 1913. 420 Côte-St-Antoine is a well designed house with an impressive carved Gorgon above the entrance. It was probably built in the 1930s.

An English Tudor manor house was built in 1926 at 72 Belmont Crescent. It is a well-done homage to that 16th-century style.

Walk through **King George Park**, also known as Murray Park. William Murray built his house, West Mount, here in 1850. A row of trees line what used to be the approach to the house. Robert and Frank Findlay designed the pavilion crowned by a clock tower which was built in 1932 on the site of the house.

Westmount seen from King George Park.

Return to Côte-St-Antoine by the street which bears Murray's name. Edward Maxwell designed a house for his father and a smaller one for himself at 188 and 184 Côte-St-Antoine. Following William Morris' **Arts and Crafts movement**, of which Maxwell was an admirer, the houses combine in a pleasing manner a number of different decorative materials — ceramic tiles, wood shingles, plaster carvings.

The Arts and Crafts movement emphasized comfort, simplicity of concept and rational structure. Vernacular vocabulary was adopted and local materials and handicrafts were emphasized as was careful finishing. Other protagonists of the movement were Percy Nobbs and Robert Findlay.

The two houses at 168 and 178 Côte-St-Antoine are quite old and were part of a group of four named **Metcalfe Terrace** to honor the governor general whose aides lived in at least one of the buildings. They were built circa 1840 by Moses Judah Hayes, one of the first Jews to hold public office in Quebec. He was a judge and later the chief of police of Montreal. It is said that Westmount's first town meetings were held in one of these houses.

Opinions vary as to whether the walls of the houses were originally stuccoed, as at No. 168, or exposed fieldstone like No. 178. A mansard storey has been added to 168 Côte-St-Antoine. The other house retains the original central chimney and heavy wooden window frames. The criss-cross fence in front of it is almost a century old itself.

At 8 Forden is a mansion designed by Edward Maxwell, who was also the architect of a number of houses in the Golden Square Mile. While the cartouche over the portico is rather ornate, the rest of the façade on this 1904 house is more restrained. The house was built for D. McNicoll, a vice-president of the Canadian Pacific Railway. The house faces what was originally its front lawn, now the site of functional houses. The latter would, at least, have been unobtrusive if they were faced in the same color of brick.

On the other side, at 9 Forden is a house which has Prairie School features. This style, developed by the American Frank Lloyd Wright, features horizontal lines and an overhanging roof.

Shaar Hashomayim Synagogue (450 Kensington) was built in 1921. Appropriately, its domes allude to the Middle East. Additions in the mid-1960s have added a new entrance, a colonnade on the west side and a museum and library along Metcalfe Avenue.

St. Matthias' Church (131 Côte-St-Antoine) was completed in 1912. It was designed by George Ross and David McFarlane in a medieval style. Displayed in front is the bell of the original church, dating from 1875.

The houses at 111-105 Côte-St-Antoine have Gothic decorations in the stone around the openings.

Further along Côte-St-Antoine is a symbol of traditional Westmount: the **Westmount Bowling Club**. The clubhouse dates from the turn-of-the-century. A sunny summer afternoon still finds middle-aged and elderly Westmounters playing lawn bowling.

St Andrew's Church, the modern brick church across from the bowling green, is the third on the site. It was built in the mid-1960s and its shape is similar to the new cathedral in Coventry, England. The original wood frame church that was established in 1886 by the first Presbyterian congregation of Westmount burned down in 1904.

Selwyn House School (95 Côte-St-Antoine) now a boys' private elementary and high school, was built in 1934 as Argyle School and is in the **Collegiate Gothic style**. It is the latest addition to the town centre which was established where Côte-St-Antoine meets Sherbrooke Street. From its doorway can be seen what is perhaps Montreal's best example of well-integrated buildings constructed over several decades.

The Collegiate Gothic style was inspired by the mansions of Tudor nobility which resembled abbeys. It was used by many large anglophone institutions in the second half of the 19th century.

2 Westmount City Hall

Westmount City Hall (4333 Côte-St-Antoine) was built in 1928 by Robert and Frank Findlay. The baronial Tudor style suits its triangular site.

At the apex of the triangle is Garden Point where Westmount's **War Memorial** was built at the same time as the city hall. George Hill, its sculptor, also designed the statue to Sir Georges-Étienne Cartier (St-Louis tour) and the monument to the Boer War in Dominion Square (Downtown tour).

It is believed that the house at 39 Côte-St-Antoine dates from the mid-18th century. Under the stucco façade are thick fieldstone walls. In the walls of the basement can be seen the remains of huge round logs on which the house used to rest.

Académie St-Paul (11 Côte-St-Antoine) was built in the early 1920s, as its shallow, Art Deco entrance attests. J. Omer Marchand was its architect. **The Church of the Ascension of our Lord** (375 Kitchener) was built in 1927-28, a late example of Gothic Revival.

Continue along Sherbrooke till Clarke, up Clarke and then right on Anwoth and down Grove Park. The houses which are on Clarke Avenue and Grove Park Street were designed by Percy Erskine Nobbs (see McGill tour) in the late 1920s.

Unlike suburbs of the 1960s, the houses were designed not to be identical but to resemble one another. Beginning with a Scottish farm house, Nobbs employed his usual painstaking attention to brickwork. The steeply sloping roof fitting snugly on the walls is similar to early Quebec construction.

Note the gargoyles on The Stonehenge at 4250 and 4200 Sherbrooke Street, built in 1929. These apartment buildings are well-suited to their oddly-shaped lots.

Rosemount Avenue has some interesting homes of the late 1800s. At 33 Rosemount is a fine brick house with Queen Anne tower and gable. Next door are semi-detached houses in the Romanesque style designed by Edward Maxwell (1896).

Nearby, at 52 Rosemount, is a house of the 1860s, faced with smooth stone. Despite its austere appearance, it displays a quiet elegance behind the trees.

The next part of the tour entails some uphill walking. Turn left and walk up Rosemount Crescent. Rosemount Cottage, at the intersection of Mountain Avenue and Rosemount Crescent, was probably the house of the coachman or gardener for the Rosemount estate. The use of stone, brick and clapboard and the interesting windows make this small house quite lovely.

The house at 490 Mountain is in the religious Gothic style which was popular for houses and other buildings in the late 19th century. Stone label stops around the windows and a lynch-gate entrance are similar to those used in English churches. This house is made of a combination of rough cut and smooth dressed greystone.

3 Rosemount

Rosemount in 1881.

Opposite it, Severn Avenue leads to the former estate of Asa Goodenough, manager of the Exchange Coffee House on St-Sacrement Street (Old Montreal tour A). In 1846 he offered to sell his property, including the house at 16 Severn Avenue (built before 1840), a coach house, stables and land for a total cost of £2500. John Young, Montreal harbor commissioner (Old Montreal tour A), purchased the estate and added another three-storey dwelling in the mid-1850s (18 Severn Avenue). Both houses are of local greystone, the older handcut, the newer, machine cut.

Walk along the curve to the house at 474 Mount Pleasant Avenue which was built in 1891. Its generous use of shingles and clapboard displays a style of construction popular in the United States at the time, especially for cottages on the seashore.

Take the stairs which lead to lower Mount Pleasant Street, go down past Sherbrooke Street.

4 Greene Avenue

The City of Westmount made Greene Avenue more attractive for strolling shoppers in the late 1970s. The sidewalks were widened and paved with bricks — a decoration later adopted by the city of Montreal for its commercial streets. Cars were slowed down to make the street more pleasant to walk along, and benches and flowerpots were installed. Unlike streets such as Prince-Arthur (St-Louis tour) and Duluth (Plateau Mont-Royal) which were also refurbished to attract the public, Greene Avenue has managed to retain a good mix of expensive and utilitarian stores. It is like the main street of a small town which traditionally offers a diverse mix of services.

There is also a good variety of building styles on Greene Avenue.

The Royal Bank building at 4192 Ste-Catherine was designed by Edward and William S. Maxwell in 1904. It is a Classical building made of very large sandstone blocks.

The Post Office, (1304 Greene Avenue) now occupied by boutiques, was built in 1914 in the Baroque style. Its impressive corner entrance is flanked by walls with engaged columns.

The Double Hook bookstore at 1235A Greene sells only Canadian books. No. 1216 Greene has attractive details around its bow window.

(Return to Sherbrooke Street) Edward and William Maxwell designed the house at 4103 Sherbrooke. It is a townhouse which stands close to the sidewalk. The immense bay window defines the *piano nobile* or main floor. Unlike most houses of this type, the entrance is not on the main floor but at street level. When this house was built, in 1907, few affluent Montrealers chose to build their home on a city street. They were fortunate to have Mount Royal which was large enough to allow the wealthy to build spacious mansions on its slopes.

Elm Avenue north of Sherbrooke Street is a small street lined with row houses built about 1895, most of which show an impressive variety of castellated rooflines. Take a look at the imposing turrets which crown 423-25 Elm Avenue. In the late 19th century, greystone façades were abandoned in favor of a mixture of colors — here the red sandstone contrasts with bands of buff stone. The house at 434 Elm also has a castle motif, with battlements at the roofline. No. 437-39 Elm has crenellations and stained-glass windows, while 488 Elm has a stained-glass panel. Another form of turret is displayed on 492 Elm which reverses the usual pattern and displays smooth red stone for the main areas, and rough blocks for contrast. The top of the houses at 493-95 also have a medieval motif.

Houses on **Holton Street** are more modestly designed, yet the street as a whole has a pleasant rhythm. The terrace of houses at 47-41 Holton is a repeating pattern of alternating units. Built in 1903, they are a late example of eclectic cut stone decoration, similar to buildings along Sherbrooke East (St-Denis tour).

At 486 Wood Avenue is J. Omer Marchand's house, built in 1912. He designed the Mother House — you can see the statue of the Virgin Mary which crowns its green dome to the southeast. Although the house is on a small site, it manages to look quite impressive. Behind the tall window is a three-sided balcony enclosing a large open volume.

5 Priests' Farm

In the 1920s, the former orchard owned by the Sulpicians was sold and converted into a housing development, known as The Priests' Farm. Decasson Street is flanked by two different styles of houses, both designed by the architectural firm of Shorey & Ritchie. They followed the "garden suburb" concept developed in England by Richard Norman Shaw. Single-family homes, either separate or semi-detached, are surrounded by yards and other green space. Streets are curved or grouped into short blocks to provide a sense of community and to conform with the slope of the land. The lanes behind the streets give access to the garages and utilities of the area and provide play areas for children.

Although **Queen Elizabeth Park** between Elm and Vignal is not very large, it is pleasantly landscaped.

6 Maison Mère des Soeurs de la congrégation de Notre-Dame

The north façade of the Maison Mère at the beginning of this century.

The Mother House of the Sisters of Notre-Dame (2040 Sherbrooke Street) is an imposing building, set in spacious grounds. It was designed by J. Omer Marchand in 1904 and combined a number of facilities — headquarters for the order, hospital, retirement home, school of higher education.

Before deciding on the plans for this building, the order's administration visited a number of institutions in Ottawa, New York City and Boston to judge what design would best combine a reasonable cost, attractive appearance, security and longevity. When Marchand was chosen as architect it was his first major commission in Montreal after having completed his studies at the École des Beaux-Arts in Paris.

The Mother House was one of the first of Montreal's first religious buildings to use a pale-colored construction material for its façade, a characteristic of the Beaux-Arts style. As a result, it was nicknamed the white monastery.

The main sections of the building front on Sherbrooke and de Maisonneuve with a central chapel joining them to form an "H". The Sherbrooke Street façade is the most opulent part. Four perpendicular wings are attached, two of which seem to guard the main entrance. This portion of the façade is of Romanesque and Renaissance influence. Note how the façade leads the eye to the statue of the Virgin Mary which crowns the dome. The rose window of the portal, the arched windows, the capitals and attached columns are Romanesque, while the pediment and cupolas are reminiscent of Byzantine design, even if they were also used in Renaissance architecture. Dawson College, Quebec's largest anglophone cegep (junior college), will soon acquire the building.

Temple Emanu-El (4134 Sherbrooke Street) was built in 1959 to replace the 1911 byzantine-style building which was constructed on the same site for Montreal's first Reform Jewish congregation.

The Church of the Advent (4119 de Maisonneuve) was built in 1892. It is a miniature Gothic Revival building. This congregation has used its building for longer than any other Westmount church.

7 Westmount Square

Westmount Square is the work of a master architect. German-American modernist Mies van der Rohe designed the complex which was completed in 1966. Although four towers were planned originally, the three that were built still form one of the world's most striking examples of the International Style. Approaching from de Maisonneuve gives the best view of the subtle change of patterns they form with one another. Underneath the towers is a collection of Montreal's most exclusive stores, as well as a connection to the Atwater metro station, should you wish to end the tour here.

If you are continuing on the tour, go through Westmount Square and out the Ste-Catherine Street exit. Walk down Gladstone to Dorchester Boulevard.

If you begin this tour on another day, leave the Atwater metro through Alexis-Nihon Plaza, a multi-functional building with stores, offices and apartments. Walk along Atwater Avenue to Dorchester, turn right, past Saint Stephen's Church (1903) and Weredale Lane, a hidden oasis worth a peek. A toll-gate was erected near this spot when Dorchester Boulevard was extended into Westmount in the middle of the 19th century.

8 The Towers

A terrace is a row of houses, designed as a unit and built by one developer. Westmount's first terrace, 4130-40 Dorchester, was built circa 1880 when this area was considered to be far from Montreal's centre. Originally three-storey homes, the buildings were later converted into duplexes. The six houses have narrow façades, with numerous windows designed to provide the maximum amount of daylight to enter the interior.

(Going along Dorchester, the first street is Clandeboye Avenue) The carpenter gothic trim of the house at 130 Clandeboye Avenue has been highlighted nicely.

Established in 1970, Stayner Park was the result of the efforts of local residents. At the end of Clandeboye is a lovely castellated house, Pierrefonds, built in 1897 as a medieval fantasy. Legend has it that one of the founders of the Canadian Pacific Railway built it for his mistress.

Prospect is a fine street, although the view is a disappointment. The owners of the house at 65 Prospect were influenced by the San Francisco style of painting Victorian houses.

As you walk up Greene Avenue, take a peek at Stayner Street, another attractive little block. Note the beaver and maple leaf decoration above the balcony at 71 Stayner. It was rare in 1889 to use a wholly-Canadian motif such as that.

The row of houses at 4258-70 Dorchester Boulevard is a wonderful example of Victorian whimsy. Built in 1900, the roofs boast tin turrets and battlements, like a transplanted Camelot.

John Archibald designed his own home at 4278 Dorchester. Although built only 15 years after the Victorian fantasy just seen, its sharp lines and subdued ornamentation show that by 1915 the era of Victorian excess had ended.

The houses on Hallowell Street display an attractive mix of stone, wood and metal. The wooden balconies at 61-75 are distinctive since they rise three storeys. "Group of Seven" painter A.Y. Jackson lived at 69 Hallowell in 1912.

The houses at 237-41 Clarke Avenue have Gothic-shaped windows with a Moorish touch to the cornice. They were built in 1899.

For much of its history, Westmount had few French-language Catholics. **St-Léon de Westmount** (4311 de Maisonneuve) was designed by G.A. Monette, a Montreal architect. In 1903 the church was made up of an apse and transepts with a temporary façade which was only one-third the height of the present nave. Only in 1920 was the church modified to its present appearance. The Florentine style façade includes a vestibule topped by a balustrade which is similar to the *narthex* of latin basilicas and is flanked by a detached bell tower.

Oscar Gauthier, the parish priest, and Guido Nincheri, an architect, painter and sculptor refurbished the interior from 1928 to 1944. The Romanesque interior is made up of a large nave with side aisles, which lead past a transept with rounded arms made up of apsidioles to the circular choir which forms the apse.

The stone of the exterior is lined with pierre de savonnières, from France. Frescos decorate much of the interior: Saints are portrayed above the nave, paradise after the Apocalypse is illustrated above the transepts. Saint Léon and important figures in his life stand with Saint Peter at the gates of heaven, which are painted over the choir.

The Florentine mosaic on the panelling is a unique collection of different marbles. The pulpit, altars and confession booths are also of marble. The bronze doors to the confession booths were designed by Nincheri and poured in Florence. Equally attractive is the bronze gate to the communion balustrade. The wood sculptures are by Alviero Marchi. He selected Honduran walnut wood because of its color and uniform texture.

Kensington Avenue was once terminated by **The Quinlan**, one of the first apartment buildings in Montreal. A gracious double building, it was designed by Edward and William Maxwell, and is believed to be the only small apartment building they ever designed. John Quinlan and Company (the last major stone mason company in Montreal) constructed the building as its head office, using stone which came from the quarry just behind the apartment building. Although the porticos with Tuscan columns and sculpted arches were classified as historic monuments by the Ministry of Cultural Affairs, the building was demolished in 1976.

The large house at 321 Kensington Avenue is worth a detour. It was built for a prosperous hotel owner in 1880. George Maybank's hotel was in Montreal, not in Westmount. The smaller municipality saw itself as a residential community and did not allow restaurants or other commercial establishments. It was only a few years ago that Westmount began to allow liquor to be served in its restaurants; there are still no bars or taverns.

Just before de Maisonneuve is 311 Kensington, a distinguished 1914 Italianate villa of well-cut stone.

Walk along de Maisonneuve to Metcalfe Avenue which has many examples of wood decorations. The half-wheel decoration on the gable end of 333 Metcalfe (1890) was turned on a lathe powered by treadles or steam. The ridges and hollows of the design were cut with chisels, with gouges and scrapers held against the rotating piece of wood. The houses at 338-40 have another common wood decoration: rods turned into a line of balls which were placed together to form brackets over the windows. The sunburst decoration and other carvings at 344 Metcalfe (1888) are fine examples of the carpenter's craft.

While Lord Mount Stephen, later president of the Canadian Pacific Railway, once owned **Hazlehead** (364 Metcalfe), he never lived there. He preferred something a bit roomier such as his house on Drummond Street (see Golden Square Mile tour). Although the brick has been stuccoed over and the bargeboard detail of this mid-19th century house removed, you can still see traces of the typical Victorian country cottage in the large front porch and varying rooflines.

9 Westmount Park

Melbourne Avenue, a small street lined with Queen Anne style houses, leads to Westmount Park, perhaps the loveliest park in all of Montreal. Although not as large as Mount-Royal, Lafontaine or Angrignon parks, it contains within its boundaries a variety of pathways, streams and hidden nooks which make it a delight to explore.

The flagpole surrounded by upright stone blocks is the Centennial Monument constructed in 1967 by the Royal Canadian Engineers. On the inner side are the coats-of-arms of all the provinces.

Westmount Jubilee Park, as it was initialy named to honor Queen Victoria's 1897 diamond jubilee, was the first public park in Westmount. Originally assembled from a number of farms, its natural condition was maintained for the first few years and it included a heavily wooded ravine and two ponds complete with ducks.

In about 1912, the park was extended on the south side, towards the school. During the next 50 years, flower beds and a bandstand were added, and in 1964 a new landscaping was carried out which added hillocks and other modifications.

Westmounters being conservative by nature, a great many letters were sent to the editor of the local newspaper protesting these changes. Still, the present effect is quite charming.

The park is extensively used, especially during the summer. Yet it is so well designed that everyone — the children playing on the swings, the sunbathers lying around the pond, the office workers eating their lunch and the schoolboys playing football — can coexist, yet be totally unaware of one another.

Within two square blocks of this area are an arena, swimming pools, meeting hall, senior citizen's residence, greenhouse, elementary school and a library. This is Westmount's community centre.

Westmount Library before construction of the children's annex.

The Westmount Public Library opened in 1899. Designed by Robert Findlay, this Richardsonian Romanesque brick building has delightful stone carvings, leaded glass and plaster work decorating the exterior and the interior. Over the entrance are bas-reliefs glorifying knowledge. Attached to the library is the Westmount Conservatory, a fine example of a 19th-century greenhouse, well worth a visit.

Victoria Jubilee Hall, a companion building to the library, was also designed by Findlay. It was destroyed by fire in 1924. The present Victoria Hall was built the following year. Sandstone was used to imitate a medieval English building, and in the wintertime it looks much like a 19th-century ice castle.

During the summer months, a floral clock lies near the bus stop in front of the new senior citizens home. **Arlington Lane**, on the north side of Sherbrooke Street, was once an Amerindian trail which led from a settlement north of Côte-St-Antoine to the river.

The Westmount YMCA, at 4585 Sherbrooke, was built in 1911. Its brick façade is distinguished by a stone portico and trim.

The tiny house at 370 Lansdowne is a remnant of the rural settlement of Côte-St-Antoine. Built circa 1865, it is the only house in the area with clapboard walls. Adding to its country character are the vertical pine board walls of the kitchen.

The light-colored stone and windows of **Westmount Baptist Church** (1923) contrast pleasantly with its dark brick. The entasis of the pillars — the slight bulge added midway up the column to correct an optical illusion — is more apparent here than in the columns of other buildings.

Victoria Avenue is a commercial street, like Greene Avenue. The Visual Arts Centre at 350 Victoria Avenue is housed in what was built as Bitcliffe's department store in 1910. It was a very modern building at the time, with ample windows and a steel superstructure.

A cluster of interesting shops line Victoria, including Bouquet de ballon (344A Victoria) which sends clowns to deliver bunches of balloons on special occasions.

In Victorian times, stores were often built with a residence above, so that the shopkeeper's long hours would not keep him too far from his family. One such house is 351 Prince Albert which is noteworthy because it retains its original entrance, complete with carved balcony above.

The terrace at 4870-96 Sherbrooke, just to the right of Prince Albert, was also designed with the ground floor for shops and housing above — typical arrangement of that era. Note the checkerboard pattern in stone below the openings.

The # 124 bus goes to the Vendôme metro station, a few blocks away.

UPPER WESTMOUNT

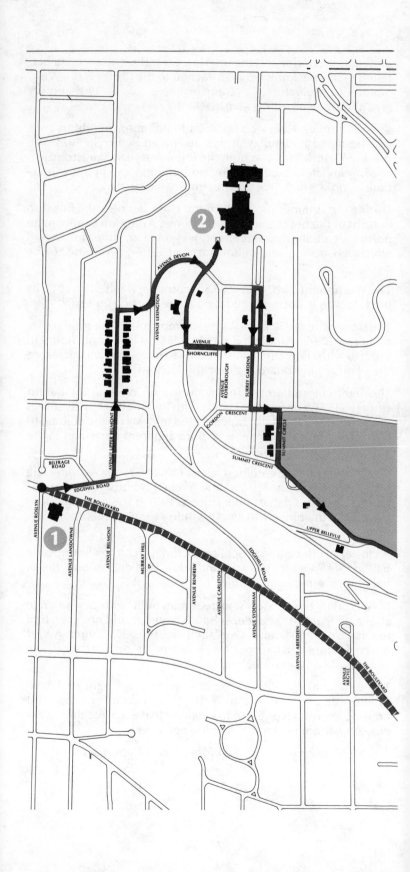

1 Dominion-Douglas United
   Church
2 Oratoire St-Joseph du
   Mont-Royal
3 Summit Park
4 14 Sunnyside Avenue

The second part of the tour of Westmount covers its most exclusive residential area. After the First World War, the summit of Westmount mountain replaced the Golden Square Mile as English Montreal's most affluent area. Consequently, it is usually this part of Westmount that both tourists and Montrealers like to explore.

One of Montreal's least-known green spaces, Summit Park, crowns the Petite Montagne. Around it spiral streets lined with the substantial houses of the wealthy.

The tour begins on The Boulevard, whose name epitomizes Westmount's sense of self-importance. The #66 bus leaves from the Guy Street exit of the Guy metro station.

There are two imposing apartment buildings in the Château style at 3940 and 3980 Côte-des-Neiges Road. **The Gleneagles** and **The Trafalgar** were built in 1929. Architects Ross and Macdonald designed the former, while the latter was designed by Hutchison and Wood. These buildings contain spacious, elegant apartments, some occupying two floors. They were recently converted into condominiums.

Since there are a number of magnificent homes on The Boulevard you may be tempted to get off the bus, if you wish to spend more than an hour on this walk.

As you travel along The Boulevard, look carefully behind three row houses on the north (right) side of the street. **Braemar** (3219 The Boulevard, just past Mount Pleasant Avenue) was built in the 1830s in a style not frequently used in Montreal. A deep two-storey verandah encircles this splendid mansion. It is believed to have been first occupied by a British army commander. In the 1850s it was owned by a wine merchant and grocer who gave it its Scottish name. In the 1880s, one of Queen Victoria's ladies-in-waiting lived in it. It is now reputed to have a friendly ghost, a sea captain.

The Study, at 3233 The Boulevard, was designed as a private residence in 1914 by Robert Findlay and is now a small school.

Another noteworthy house stands at the intersection of The Boulevard and Clarke Avenue, a block further. Joseph Baker designed the house at 603 Clarke Avenue, which was completed in 1966. Some people have compared its austere appearance and forceful design with that of Japanese architecture.

1 Dominion-Douglas United Church

(Get off the bus at Edgehill Road) Dominion-Douglas United Church was completed in 1927. It is a massive, Gothic building. Its magnificent setting and the large openings in its stone exterior make it very graceful. It was built for a Presbyterian and a Methodist congregation which left the Golden Square Mile and relocated in Westmount to accommodate their members.

Turn up Edgehill Road and walk along Upper Belmont Street, typical of the most affluent part of Westmount. Beyond Sunnyside, the houses on Upper Belmont reflect the style known as stockbroker's Tudor when used in the wealthy areas of the northeastern United States.

The house at 815 Upper Belmont is an Italianate villa built in 1930 of light, fine-grained stone. The sculptured panels on the upper floors are especially well done. The house has been converted into a private school.

(Return to Devon, walk up it past Lexington Avenue. A smooth stone house whose unusual curves you see in the distance will come up later on the itinerary).

2 Oratoire St-Joseph du Mont-Royal

Although St-Joseph's Oratory is located in the city of Montreal, it is accessible from Summit Crescent in Westmount. The enormous basilica — its dome is one of the largest in the world — was begun in 1924 and completed in 1955. Dalbé Viau and Alphonse Venne created the original design for this Italian Renaissance style basilica in 1924. Work was interrupted for a number of years and started again in 1937. The work was entrusted to Lucien Parent who followed the plans of the French Benedictine, Dom Paul Bellot. While the design was simplified, they respected the original dimensions and proportions. The oratory has been compared with Montmartre in Paris and the Duomo in Florence.

The oratory's interior was decorated by Henri Charlier who designed the alter, crucifix and the sculptures of the 12 Apostles. Marius Plamondon created the large windows, Roger de Villiers sculpted the Stations of the Cross and the bronze statues are by Robert Prévost.

The original chapel suffered a fire in 1951 but has been faithfully restored. The present nave and bell tower date from 1910 while the altar is original. In 1955, in honor of the 50th anniversary of the oratory, Paccard et Frères of Annecy-le-Vieux, France lent the carillon of bells which had been designed for the Eiffel Tower but never installed because of technical problems. Donations later permitted the permanent acquisition of the carillon. The exterior stations of the cross were completed by Ercolo Barbieri in 1962 following models designed by the local artist Loius Parent.

Carillon concerts are given during the afternoon on Tuesday through Saturday at noon, 1:30, and 2:30 p.m. During the summer, an additional concert is held at 7:30 p.m. On Sunday, the schedule is 9:45, 10:45 a.m. and 2:30, 4:00 p.m.

Organ recitals are held every Sunday throughout the year at 3:30 p.m. In the summer, an additional concert is held on weekdays at 11:30 a.m. During July and August, full organ concerts are scheduled for Wednesday evenings at 8:30 p.m.

Dwarfed by the basilica is the little shrine constructed in 1904 by Brother André, a simple, devout man who was responsible for making this a shrine for pilgrims. Revered for his healing powers, he has been beatified and is only one step below Roman Catholic sainthood.

In 1957, Victor Prus designed the house at 95 Summit Crescent, on the other side of Devon from the oratory. Its distinctive roof is reminiscent of Le Corbusier's early work.

A bit further along, at **78 Summit Crescent**, is a spectacular house, built in 1968, reportedly at a cost of $3 million. Its cool, polished granite walls and the unusual curves of its roof make it stand out against its more conventional neighbors.

Walk along Shorncliffe until Surrey Gardens, which offers an impressive view of the oratory.

The house at 37 Surrey Gardens was built in the 1950s in a French provincial style: note the vents jutting up from the copper roof. At 31 Surrey Gardens is a somewhat earlier house displaying a similar style.

Across the street, at 36 Surrey Gardens, is a house built in the same period but in the modernist style. The clean horizontal lines of the roof make a pleasant contrast with the vertical windows.

Continue on Surrey Gardens, away from the oratory. Turn left on Gordon Crescent. The next right turn leads past 100 **Summit Circle**, designed by Fred Lebensold whose work was mentioned on the Golden Square Mile tour. This is one of his finest houses. It was built in the late 1950s. The entrance is distinguished and the low slung look (more noticeable from the back) does not seem out-of-date, a sign of fine architecture.

Instead of making a modernist statement, the designer of the house at 90 Summit Circle created a faithful replica of a 18th century Quebec house, two hundred years older in appearance than its 1938 construction date. In the 1700s, houses had steep roofs to prevent snow from collecting, and relatively small windows with tiny panes of glass because glass was expensive and windows would allow heat to escape.

3 Summit Park

This area, owned by McGill University until 1928, was sold to the city of Westmount on the proviso that it always be maintained in its natural condition. A group of hillocks and marshy woods, Summit Park is now a wildlife and flower sanctuary. Many different birds nest and feed here because it is kept in a natural state. During the spring, more than a hundred different species can be observed. The best entry to the park is further along this street, near the lookout.

It is probable that the house at 72 Summit Circle was originally a barn built around 1885. Note the opening to the hayloft above the door.

The second house down Upper Belvedere, at 114, was the first modernist house in Westmount, built just after the Second World War.

Westmount Lookout, although not as spectacular as the one on Mount Royal, is a good location from which to view the city and its river. Residents of Summit Circle are lucky enough to enjoy this view through their living room windows. Bronze arrows embedded in the concrete wall point out important landmarks (some of which are obscured by leaves during the summer).

No. 22 Summit Circle was probably built as a summer house in the early 20th century for a family whose permanent residence was in Montreal. Its location on the top of the mountain meant that access was originally via a steep staircase from Sunnyside Avenue below.

Continuing along Summit Circle, we can see some of the houses on the street below. Two stone houses whose roofs are similar (at 55 and 65 Belvedere Place) were built originally as one house. This Elizabethan manor was built in 1929, at a time when such enormous homes were going out of style. Consequently, the central section of the house was removed in 1961, to create two dwellings — both large by today's standards.

As Summit Circle winds downward, it affords a view of the Université de Montréal (Outremont tour) on the top of one hill and Mount Royal. These two little mountains, plus the one you have just ascended, are the three dominant features of Montréal's topography.

Another example of stockbroker's Tudor is at **61 Belvedere**. The house at 68 Belvedere is believed to have been designed by Percy Nobbs, or a disciple of his: its cosy appearance and fine detail evokes his style.

The Fisher family, involved with the Southam publishing firm, once lived at 57 Belvedere. While it is still surrounded by spacious grounds, increased property values may soon result in subdivision of the property and construction of small houses.

The façade of the separated "Siamese twins" (55 and 65 Belvedere Place) can be seen on the left.

Near the junction of Belvedere Road and Sunnyside Avenue is a rock garden which appears to spring out of an outcrop of the mountain. Above it were once the quarries from which builders extracted stone for the construction of Upper Westmount's homes.

4 14 Sunnyside Avenue

Perhaps the most impressive mansion in all of Westmount is at 14 Sunnyside Avenue, constructed in 1911 for a member of the Quebec legislature, Charles A. Smart. Ross & Macfarlane were the original architects. Later extensions and alterations were designed by Percy Nobbs who was also responsible for the design of the ironwork fence and gates in 1921. An interesting feature of the gates, at the far end, is a lily which is shown unfolding from bud to bloom. This sort of frozen naturalism was common in the work of Nobbs, an avid angler and sportsman.

Retrace your steps and continue the descent down Belvedere. Percy Nobbs built his own house at 38 Sunnyside Avenue. It displays over the entrance a delightful sculpted cherub holding an "N" and the date of the house's construction (1914). The bay window on the east side is a recent addition by the architect who now lives in the house.

Continuing to descend, you pass the house at 15 Belvedere which was designed in 1906 by Robert Findlay in the Scottish baronial style. This house was named Oaklands when it was inhabited by a dry goods importer.

From across the street can be seen Braemar, mentioned at the beginning of the tour. From this vantage point, no new construction hides it, only trees.

Unlike most Upper Westmount houses, those at 4-6 Belvedere are semi-detached.

Turn left on The Boulevard, go up Trafalgar, following the curve right. The Gothic villa at 3025-21 was built in 1848. In the yard to its right are pediment and pillars. They are one of the portico entrances which were removed from the Quinlan apartment building that once stood on Ste-Catherine Street at the foot of Kensington Avenue, in lower Westmount. They were placed here by a descendent of John Quinlan.

Straight across from Trafalgar is **Parkside Place** (4047 Côte-des-Neiges) — a series of townhouses grouped around a central court. Built in the 1920s, they retain a pleasant sense of privacy on a busy thoroughfare.

From 4040 to 4000 McDougall, between Trafalgar and The Boulevard, are fine examples of successful in-fill housing completed in 1982. Note the interesting rhythm of the fenestration and the round arches over the upper floor windows.

This ends the tour of Upper Westmount, both the #165 bus on McDougall and the # 66 on The Boulevard return to the Guy metro station.

MOUNT ROYAL PARK

You can reach the park on foot from the head of Peel Street or by Park Avenue near Pine Avenue. Bus # 165 (Guy metro station) leads to bus # 11 which goes east to the Beaver Lake portion of the park. Going west, the # 11 bus leaves the Mont-Royal metro station. Cars can take Côte-Ste-Catherine Road to Camillien Houde Road.

The park spreads out across a wooded hill which is familiarly known as "The Mountain". It juts out of a relatively flat plain. Geologically it is an igneous intrusion through sedimentary rock. The Mountain is part of the Monteregian chain of eight mountains.

The park was designed by Frederick Law Olmsted, considered the father of North American landscape architecture. He also designed New York City's Central Park. Olmsted was a firm believer in the curative powers of nature for both body and soul. He felt that spiritual and physical rejuvenation was only possible through frequent communion with nature. That is why he conceived a network of roads and paths interspersed with panoramic views allowed for the observation of the contrasts of a universe in miniature.

For Olmsted, designing a park meant adopting the form of the terrain and accentuating its diversity. He was successful in creating a work of art which conformed to the natural topography.

Mount Royal Cemetery

Access to the protestant cemetery is from Camillien Houde Road (from the park) or by Mont-Royal Avenue and Forest Road.

This cemetery is remarkably attractive. Its varied and luxuriant vegetation, grandiose monuments and winding trails are reminiscent of the grand London cemeteries, such as Highgate and Brompton.

Buried in this cemetery are those who literally created Montreal during the last century. It is interesting to note that the cemetery was established 20 years before Mount Royal Park.

Cimetière de Notre-Dame-des-Neiges

The catholic cemetery is located beside Mount-Royal Cemetery. Access is by Souvenir Road or Côte-des-Neiges Road (# 165 bus from Guy metro station).

Although less impressive than the protestant burial ground, the monuments of Notre-Dame-des-Neiges are fascinating. Irish names, Cyrillic letters and Chinese characters testify to successive waves of immigration. Some gravestones are decorated with images of the deceased person at the prime of life.

An area is set aside for veterans of the two world wars; the Union des Artistes has a plot which is reserved for artists of the stage, screen, radio and television.

MOUNT ROYAL CEMETERY

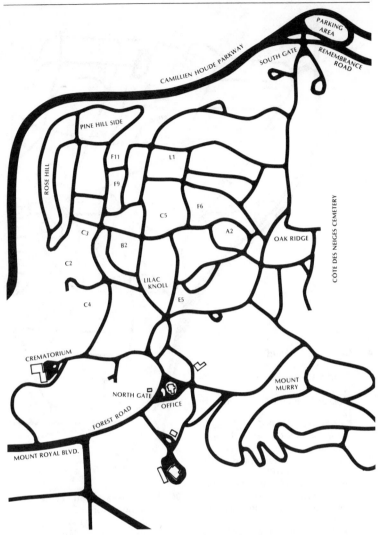

A2 **Révérend William Squire**, died in 1852 (A 234-S).
Révérend Francis Fulford, died in 1868 (A 248-A).

C2 **J.W. McConnell**, philanthropist, died in 1963 (Rose Hill 67).

C3 **Sir John J.C. Abbott**, Prime Minister, died in 1893 (C 395).

C4 **John Molson, Jr.,** financier, died in 1860 (C 62).

C5 **David Thompson**, explorer, died in 1857 (C 507).

E5 **Sir Hugh Allan**, shipping magnate, died in 1882 (E 198).
Sir Arthur William Currie, soldier, died in 1933 (E 169).

F6 **Sir George Simpson**, fur trader, died in 1860 (F 101).
Sir William Christopher Macdonald, philanthropist, died in 1917 (F 440).

F9 **Mrs. Anna Leonowens**, governess to the King of Siam, died in 1915 (F 738).

F11 **Sir Alexander Tilloch Galt**, statesman, died in 1893.

G1 **Sarah Maxwell**, héroine, died in 1907 (G 200-M).
Firemen's burial ground (G 125-126).

L1 **John Redpath**, manufacturer, died in 1869 (L-1).

LK **Ernest Henry Wilson**, botanist, died in 1930 (Lilac Knoll 40).

M2 **Sir J. William Dawson**, professor, died in 1899 (C 100).

PH **Sir Herbert Samuel Holt**, businessman, died in 1941 (Pine Hill Side 245).

PH **Charles Melville Hays**, railway president, died in 1912 (Pine Hill Side 246).

NOTRE-DAME-DES-NEIGES CEMETERY

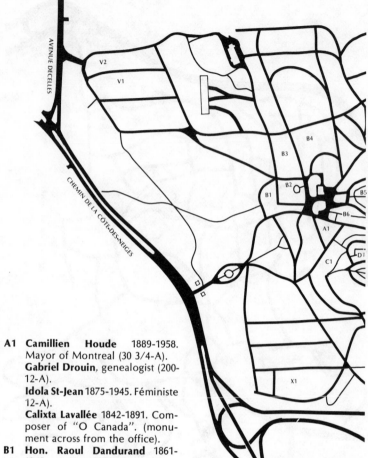

A1 **Camillien Houde** 1889-1958. Mayor of Montreal (30 3/4-A).
Gabriel Drouin, genealogist (200-12-A).
Idola St-Jean 1875-1945. Féministe 12-A).
Calixta Lavallée 1842-1891. Composer of "O Canada". (monument across from the office).
B1 **Hon. Raoul Dandurand** 1861-1942, senator (61B).
Sir Lomer Gouin 1861-1929. Premier of Quebec (66-B)
Monument for the Patriotes 1837-1838.
Treffle Berthiaume 1848-1915. Founder of La Presse (262-B).
Justine Lacoste Beaubien 1877-1967. Founder of Hôpital Ste-Justine for children (272 1/2 B)
Louis de Gaspé Beaubien 1867-1939. Financier (272 1/2-B)
Pamphile-Réal du Tremblay 1879-1955. Chairman of La Presse newspaper (276-B).
B2 **Louis Fréchette** 1839-1908 writer (213-B).
B3 **Lord Thomas-Georges Shaughnessy** 1853-1923. President of the Canadian Pacific Railway Company (379-B).
Pamphile Le May 1837-1918. Writer. (380-B).
Fernand Rinfret 1883-1939. Journalist and politician (301-B).
B4 **Théodore Viau** 1879-1938. Owner of the cookie factory (1013-B).
B5 **Louis Archambault** 1829-1906. Founder of "Société des Artisans" (29-B).

B6 **Édouard-Raymond Fabre** 1799-1854. Bookstore owner (1-B).
C1 **Ludger Duvernay** 1799-1852. Founder of la Société Saint-Jean-Baptiste (58-C).
Sir Auguste-Réal Angers 1839-1919. Lieutenant-Governor of Quebec (42-C).
Sir Adolphe Chapleau 1840-1898. Premier of Quebec (64-C).
D1 **Jean-Louis Beaudry** 1809-1886. Mayor of Montreal (59-D).
F1 **Jane Gilroy** 1830-1855. First burial in the cemetery (56-F).
Pierre-Thomas Lévesque 1824-1906. Seigneur de d'Ailleboust et de Ramsay (58-F).
Pierre-Louis Panet 1761-1812. Judge (58-F).
Jules Fournier 1884-1918. Journalist (112-F).
G1 **Olivier Guimond** 1893-1954. Actor (1341-GA).
K1 **Robert Nelson** 1794-1873. Active in the Rebellion (18-K).
Wolfred Nelson 1793-1863. Leader of the 1837 Rebellion (18-K).

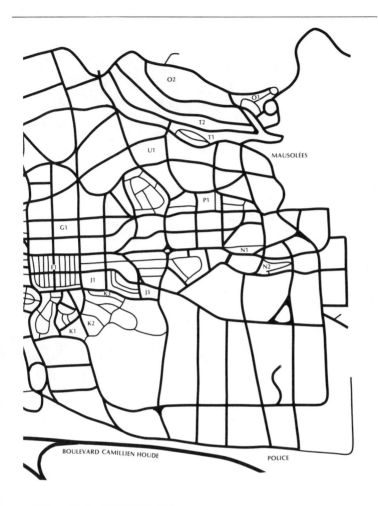

BIBLIOGRAPHY

Atelier d'Histoire Hochelaga-Maisonneuve: *L'Histoire du logement ouvrier à Hochelaga-Maisonneuve*. Presses Solidaires, Montreal (1980).

Atelier d'Histoire Hochelaga-Maisonneuve: *L'Industrialisation à Hochelaga-Maisonneuve 1900-1930*. Presses Solidaires, Montreal (1980).

Atelier d'Histoire Hochelaga-Maisonneuve: *Passeport pour Hochelaga-Maisonneuve*, Presses Solidaires Inc., Montreal (1981.

Atelier d'Histoire Hochelaga-Maisonneuve: *Évolution de l'architecture industrielle. Un quartier type: Hochelaga-Maisonneuve*, Presses Solidaires, Montreal (1982).

Belisle, Louis-Alexandre: *Référence biographique Canada-Québec*, Les Éditions de la Famille Canadienne Ltée, Montreal (1978).

Communauté urbaine de Montréal: Répertoire d'architecture traditionnelle sur le territoire de la communauté urbaine de Montréal. *Les Banques* (1980); *Les Édifices scolaires* (1980); *Les Édifices publics* (1981); *Les Églises* (1981).

Courcy-Legros, Louiselle and Verret, Jocelyne: *Petite histoire du Plateau*. Montreal (1979).

Couture, Pierre: À ville internationale et cosmopolite, communauté universitaire diversifiée, *Forces* No. 54-55 (1981).

Dictionary of Canadian biography, University of Toronto Press, Toronto (1966+).

Gabeline, Donna; Lanken, Dane and Pape, Gordon: *Montreal at the Crossroads*, Harvest House, Montreal (1975).

Gendron, Viateur: *Le Port de Montréal, renseignements généraux*, Port of Montreal, Montreal (1982).

Gubbay, Aline and Hooff, Sally: *Montréal's little mountain. A portrait of Westmount*, Trillium Books, Westmount (1979).

Hatton, Warwick and Beth: *A feast of gingerbread from our Victorian Past/Pâtisserie maison de notre charmant passé*, Tundra Books, Montréal (1976).

Larue-Langlois, Jacques: Montréal, métropole des spectacles, *Forces* N° 54-55 (1981).

Linteau, Paul-André: *Maisonneuve — comment des promoteurs fabriquent une ville*, Boréal Express, Montreal (1981).

Marsan, Jean-Claude: *Montreal in evolution*, McGill-Queen's University Press, Montreal (1981).

MacLennan, Hugh: *McGill; The story of a university*, George Allen and Unwin Ltd, London (1960).

Mather, Edith (phoographer) *Les rues de Montréal, façade et fantaisie/ Touches of fantasy on Montreal Streets*, Text: René Chicoine. Tundra Books, Montreal (1977).

Montreal Society of Architecture: *Exploring Montreal*, Greey de Pencier Publications, Toronto (1974).

Montreal Urban Community: *Annual Report* (1981).

Morin, Michel: Montréal, un des vingt complexes industriels, commerciaux et financiers les plus importants du monde. *Forces* N° 54-55 (1981).

National Harbors Board: *Montréal et son port* (1982).

Noppen, Luc: *Les Églises du Québec (1600-1850)*, Éditeur Officiel du Québec/Fides (1977).

Rumilly, Robert: *Histoire d'Outremont (1875-1975)* Leméac (1975).

Tourisme Québec/CIDEM-Tourisme: *Montréal, prenez l'tour du Québec*. Montréal (1982).

Trépanier, Léon. *Les Rues du Vieux Montréal au fil du temps*, Fides, Montréal (1968).

Wagg, Susan: *Percy Erskine Nobbs, architecte, artiste, artisan — architect, artist, craftsman*. Published for the McCord Museum by McGill-Queen's University Press, Montreal (1982).

INDEX

Photographs:

Acknowledgements

This book would never have been written if it were not for the pioneer work of a few volunteers, including Dominique Hoepffner, Adèle Isaacs, Norman Spatz and Richard Vincent. They were the ones who, in 1975, first developed the Save Montreal walking tours which are the basis for this guidebook.

We would also like to acknowledge the support of Phyllis Lambert who allowed us the use of the archival material compiled by the Groupe de Recherche en Bâtiments de Pierre Grise. We would like to single out Robert Lemire and Jean-Claude Marsan for their unwavering support and the generous sharing of their knowledge and the fruits of their research.

The personnel of the Notman Photographic Archives actively helped in our research for illustrative documentation. Our research was also facilitated by the inventory of Montreal buildings, placed at our disposal by the ministère des Affaires culturelles. It was compiled by Madeleine Forget and Jacqueline Allée. Invaluable aid was offered by the staff of the archives of the Royal Bank of Canada, Holt Renfrew & Co Limited, the Canadian Broadcasting Corporation and the Atelier d'Histoire Hochelaga-Maisonneuve, as well as the Museum of Fine Arts and the McCord Museum.

Amongst the many people who helped our work, we would like to especially thank Jocelyn Croteau, Raymonde Gauthier, Aline Gubbay, Sally Hooff, Gérald McNichols-Tétrault; Jennifer Harper and Brian Merrett for their contemporary photographs. The support and work of the following people also helped our project: Claire Adamson, Paul Dubuc, Nick Farkas, Joseph Greco, Jacques Lachapelle, Jocelyne Marquis, Edward Pitula, Michael Price, Steve Raulerson, François Rémillard, Patricia Scouten, Susan Stevenson, Suzie Toutant, Claude Watters.

Thanks are also due to the graduate architects who worked on the maps — Dinu Bumbaru, Yves Tremblay and Jean-Pierre Landry.

Without the financial aid of the Heritage Montreal Foundation, the Samuel and Saidye Bronfman Foundation, the ministère des Affaires culturelles, the ministère de l'Environnement, Imperial Oil Limited and Alcan Aluminium Limited, our preliminary research would have been made more difficult.

We would also like to thank Jean Basile who gave us the necessary encouragement to start the project. Finally, we would like to thank André Bastien, our publisher, and the members of his staff, in addition to all the other people who helped us in so many ways.

Graphic Design by France Lafond
Maps by Yves Tremblay and Dinu Bumbaru
Typesetting by l'Enmieux

Legal Deposit second quarter 1983
© Éditions Libre Expression, 1983
Second Edition, 1987
ISBN 2-89111-155-9

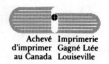

Achevé   Imprimerie
d'imprimer Gagné Ltée
au Canada Louiseville